UPANISHADS
For The Modern World

UPANISHADS
For The Modern World

Dr. G.K. PILLAI

JAICO PUBLISHING HOUSE
Mumbai Delhi Bangalore Kolkata
Hyderabad Chennai Ahmedabad Bhopal

Published by Jaico Publishing House
121 Mahatma Gandhi Road
Mumbai - 400 001
jaicopub@vsnl.com
www.jaicobooks.com

UPANISHADS FOR THE MODERN WORLD
ISBN 81-7992-347-9

First Jaico Impression: 2004
Third Jaico Impression: 2007

Printed by
Sanman & Co.
113, Shivshakti Ind. Estate, Marol Naka
Andheri (E), Mumbai - 400 059.

This book is dedicated to the intelligent and interactive primal energy that motivates my spiritual quest and lets me enjoy the blissful experience of existence. I am deeply obliged to its grace that enables my awareness to understand the true meaning and purpose of life and gives me the capacity to communicate the holistic vision of existence to the modern world.

Other Books By the Same Author

1. An In-depth Study of Central Excise Duties in India.
2. Value Added Tax - A Model for Indian Tax Reform.
3. Mystic Awareness for the Modern Mind.
4. VAT - A Way Out of the Indian Tax Muddle.

CONTENTS

CONTENTS

E-MAIL pillaigk@hotmail.com
  pillaigkin@yahoo.com

Foreword to
"Mystic Awareness for the Modern Mind"

The new interest in spirituality that has assumed significance in the west reflects the yearning of modern man to the ultimate reality behind the universe. It is gratifying to note that with all the modern scientific instruments and discoveries, the west is reaching the same conclusions which the seers and sages of our country had reached thousands of years ago simply by their intuition. Their mysticism is still an enigma to the western thinkers. The more the scientists delve into the mysteries of the matter and mind, the more they admire the wisdom of the Upanishads. One simply wonders how the Vedic Rishis could proclaim that space (Aakash) is all pervasive. Researchers in the atomic field proved this fact only in the 20th Century.

This is the reason why Mahatma Gandhi told us that India might be lacking in the material field, but it has an immense treasure of spiritual knowledge, which will guide humanity towards a life of contentment and happiness. This spiritual knowledge is the real strength of our country, which has sustained us during many trials and tribulations.

In his book "MYSTIC AWARENESS FOR THE MODERN MIND", Dr. Pillai gives all the spiritual knowledge that a rational man needs for peace of mind. He examines all the scientific explanations to the origin and evolution of the universe, life and mind. He finds several inconsistencies and inexplicable coincidences in scientific knowledge. After examining the origin of the universe and matter, Dr. Pillai evaluates the evolutionary explanation of the diversity of life and the neural basis of the mind.

Dr. Pillai's work is a great effort to link science and spirituality. He does not give any new explanation but a rational perspective is evolved from the existing collective wisdom of humanity. His sincere effort to make "Compassionate Wisdom" the basis for new age spirituality is definitely laudable. I recommend this book to all persons interested in spirituality.

This well-written book is based on a vast wealth of scientific information. The author deserves high acclaim for a noble effort to give a positive contribution to social upliftment.

Chandrasekhar
Former Prime Minister of India

P.C. ALEXANDER, M.P.
CHAIRMAN
PARLIAMENTARY STANDING
COMMITTEE ON INDUSTRY

Off.120, Parliament House Annex,
New Delhi - 110 001
Tel.: 23017779, 23034120
Fax: 23014948
E-Mail: pcalex@sansad.nic.in

PREFACE

I came to know Dr. G.K. Pillai and about his philosophical and intellectual pursuits when I had the privilege of releasing his book MYSTIC AWARENESS FOR THE MODERN MIND at a largely attended function in Mumbai in July 2001. The present book, which is the result of several years of intensive studies by Dr. G.K. Pillai of the Upanishads in the context of the latest scientific discoveries of the mind, is a welcome addition to his MYSTIC AWARENESS FOR THE MODERN MIND. In his new book he presents a worldview of the Upanishads which is not only rational but aimed at meeting the spiritual needs of the modern century.

It is universally accepted that the Upanishads embody the essence of the wisdom on existence. The Upanishads, rightly described as the greatest Indian heritage, give the answers to many puzzles that science has failed to resolve. An interesting feature of the Book is that the author uses the dialogue route to unfold the vision of Upanishads to the modern reader. Through the interface with a young student from the west, Dr. Pillai tries to unravel the mysteries of the mind and evaluates the contemporary relevance of the Upanishads.

In the first part of the book the author explains how the Upanishads help remove the common misconceptions about the meaning of life. He explains how the wisdom of the Upanishads transcends the conventional boundaries of human thought set by time and space and presents it in an ambience intelligible to the modern mind.

The latter part of the book beginning with chapter six, gives glimpses of the latest scientific knowledge of the brain, consciousness and the mind. Presented in an intelligible conversational style of explanation, these chapters expose the reader to the recent scientific discoveries, which have unraveled some of the mysteries attributed to the mind.

A very valuable part of the book is the concluding chapter that takes us to the ultimate question about existence. The author cogently explains the process of evolution, supplementing it with the insights of the Upanishads. The book answers several existential questions with convincing explanations. I must draw the special attention of the reader to the two interesting epilogues, which considerably enrich the value of the book - the vision of Ashtavakra and Patanjali's pathfinder. Dr. Pillai's penetrating analysis of these works makes them intelligible to the common man.

This book is not meant for light reading. It is an absorbing analysis of the wisdom of humanity accumulated over time through scientific and speculative means and the reader should have the patience and mental make up to comprehend it. I compliment Dr. Pillai for presenting a masterly study of a highly complex theme and commend it to the inquisitive explorers interested in knowing more about the meaning and purpose of life.

(P.C. Alexander)

20 November 2003
New Delhi

INTRODUCTION

"The Supreme Self is the essence of existence that shines as pure awareness in all minds. It is beyond our thoughts and actions and is free from evils, desires and death."

"Brahman is the eternal reality of the universe that underlies all visible and invisible beings. It is both the cause and the effect and consciousness dwelling in the core of all existence."

[Brihadaranyaka Upanishad]

"The Supreme Lord is pure consciousness embedded in every heart. We experience our thoughts, actions, and emotions only in the presence of that primal cause of creation."

[Shvetashvatara Upanishad]

"Isn't it a silly idea?" asked Mike. "Do you think an ancient piece of oriental thought can change the mindset of hardened hate mongers of the modern world? When they are busy collecting nuclear warheads and biological weapons of mass destruction, how can you preach the message of unity and peace?"

"Our first priority is to beef up global security against such misguided monsters. Then we must catch the criminals wherever they hide and bring them to justice," he concluded with lot of indignation.

Before we proceed further, let me introduce Mike, the agitated anti-terrorist. He is an American student who came to India for a personal experience on the impact of Eastern spirituality. We spent considerable time discussing the relevance of Vedic thoughts to the modern world. This book is the outcome of our combined efforts, to unravel the wisdom of the Upanishads. While exploring ancient and modern thoughts of the West and the East, we tried to find parallels and points of convergence, for creating a rational worldview on existence.

"Yes," I nodded for a breather, to put across my point.

"It is true that these miscreants immensely hate all the great assets of civilization like democracy, freedom of thought and choice. They exhort millions of gullible youth to sacrifice life for the cause of religion, region or language. Unfortunately, advanced technology puts the entire world at their mercy."

"But can you solve the problem of global terror by killing a few fanatics and their misguided followers? The infection has spread far and wide. Cutting some limbs here and there cannot contain or cure the disease."

I found my sober counsel on the current reign of terror, had somewhat mellowed his uncompromising attitude. It was evident that deep in his psyche, utter helplessness and confusion prevailed. Behind the brave facade, I knew he had no effective solution, to eradicate the menace of modern terrorism.

Similar impotence prevails all over the civilized world, which could be demolished at will by a few trigger-happy tyrants. The immense capacity to create holocaust anywhere at any time has made them extremely arrogant and unconcerned about the loss of life and the rule of law. The exclusive attention of the global media enhances their sense of pride and invincibility. It inspires the lower cadre to create more devastating catastrophes. Eventually, thousands of innocent lives are lost at the altar of terror. The killers are promised very attractive heavenly rewards for defending the domains of their faith on earth! For them, death is the prelude to an eternal pleasure cruise in heaven.

"It is difficult to find rational solutions when impulsive and emotional responses dictate the course of global events. I am not trying to reform anyone with new ideas or to improve the level of tolerance. All I wish is, to hold a mirror of wisdom before impressionable youth to make them understand what existence is all about. It is a secular attempt to create a worldview that would enable malleable minds to resist the influence of bigotry and indoctrination."

"Can you achieve this almost impossible goal by simply spreading the message of the Upanishads?" he asked.

"There is no harm in trying. The existential wisdom of the Upanishads can be presented in a contemporaneous format to convince even diehard terrorists that non-violence is a divine attitude."

I added, "The Upanishads give us a unique perception of life that conforms to the latest scientific discoveries. They contain a convincing message of unity that can be easily understood by the modern mind. In fact, the Upanishads support the basic tenets of all religions that repose faith in a supreme entity. It can also give effective spiritual solace even to the victims of AIDS and other fatal diseases, who live in constant fear of death. I agree it is extremely difficult to convey its ancient wisdom across barriers of inherited and imbibed ignorance."

Having aroused his curiosity, I gave a brief account on the relevance of the Upanishads in the present times.

"They give rational solutions to existential enigmas that still confound humanity. The insights of the Upanishads are not attributable to the thoughts of a single individual or to any particular period. Actually, they represent the collective wisdom of many generations of thinkers belonging to one of the earliest known civilizations. The Hindus assume that the Upanishads are the philosophical bulwark of their holy scriptures known as "The Vedas". But the Upanishads do not support religious practices to propitiate a variety of gods or the division of society on the basis of caste. They present a truly secular worldview that promotes compassionate wisdom to care for the poor and deprived."

Briefly stated, the Upanishads reflect the highest level of awareness reached by selfless seekers of knowledge in ancient times. They logically remove the misconceptions of the meaning and purpose of life to achieve the correct perception of reality. The mystics who conceived them never claimed any intellectual property rights for their path-breaking inferences nor did they set up institutions to propagate any patented wisdom. They were simple, enlightened teachers willing to instruct the inquisitive disciples on the true meaning of existence. With overwhelming realization on the transient nature of the material world, they probably understood the futility of preserving personal identities and achievements. By living up to the ideals of compassion, austerity and humility, they became excellent role models for exuberant disciples.

It is a fact that the insights of the Upanishads transcend conventional boundaries of human thoughts beset by severe conceptual constraints. Since scientific knowledge is solely based on material features of the world confirming to definite space-time dimensions, our natural inclination is to readily accept the ideas explained in a modern manner rather than in an archaic context. The Upanishads frequently refer to the life style of an ancient civilization that would appear mythological to the contemporary world. But if they are consistent with the current level of knowledge, we cannot simply brush them aside as outlandish perceptions.

That is why I am presenting a different version of the Upanishads.

"The objective is to present a rational worldview based on latest scientific knowledge about matter, life, and the mind supplemented by mystic wisdom of existence. It can hopefully, rewire the modern mindset that constantly seeks more material comforts and power than peace and contentment. Ample proof is also presented to show that the Upanishads give truly workable solutions for existential enigmas that defy scientific solutions."

"Yes, you may be right," said Mike.

He added, "The vision of the Upanishads may not require any support of scientific explanations. They may correspond to all scientific knowledge we have on the origin of the Universe and evolution of life. The recent philosophical thoughts in the West, particularly after John Locke, ignored altogether the spiritual dimension of human existence. The holistic approach of Plato and Platinus that integrated spiritual and material worldviews was later abandoned in favour of an uncompromising materialistic interpretation of life propounded by reductionism."

The modern paradigm of existence is a crude mixture

of Newtonian, Cartesian and mechanistic interpretations that do not admit any metaphysical approach to life. They try to draw up a realistic map of the visible world giving no room for the mapmaker. In short, our technology driven civilization has created only an incomplete worldview, which does not admit the wisdom of spiritual speculations. They simply skirt basic issues on the excuse. that scientific enquiries cannot delve into the domains of spirituality. As aptly put by Einstein "they drill a great number of holes in a board of wood where drilling is easy."

"We badly need a harmonious paradigm of existence that can explain the relevance of our short sojourn on an insignificant planet. In fact, the West is now showing active interest in reviving the spiritual values to resolve moral and ecological crises of modern times. Maybe, the exquisite experience of understanding the Upanishads can remove some of the misconceptions of materialistic worldview. We can begin our voyage now with a brief discussion on the meaning of the word Upanishads."

"It literally means, sitting closely in rapt attention. The broader implication is an intimate and interactive situation in which a teacher renders spiritual advice to ardent disciples. A great sage of India called "Adi Sankara", compiled commentaries for the more important Upanishads, which he considered as the foundation of all knowledge. We have no clear idea about the actual number of Upanishads that existed as unwritten Holy verses."

Some of them might have been lost in transmission by word of mouth from generation to generation. Hundreds of them were probably in circulation in verse or prose form and in different styles of narration. They use many humorous anecdotes and interesting allegories to drive home the complex subject of spiritual wisdom. But in one form or the other, all of them convey the same basic concept of a universal Spirit called "Brahman".

"Many Vedic scholars mention about one hundred and eight major Upanishads. Adi Sankara considered ten of them as the important ones. We can accept two more in that major category. In this book, we confine our discussions to twelve of them namely, Katha, Kena, Prasna, Isha, Mundaka, Mandukya, Taitheriya, Aitareya, Chandogya, Brihadaranyaka, Kaivalya, and Shvetasvatara. Each one gives us a clear idea on a select topic. We may find some overlapping of thoughts as the central theme of "Brahman" recurs regularly in all stories. They try to interpret the same subject from different perspectives and contexts. We may find a few inconsistencies and distortions, probably due to additions and alterations made by innumerable instructors.

"Another striking feature of the Upanishads is that they do not claim to give us the exact details on various natural phenomena nor any specific solutions to personal problems. They help us to construct a harmonious perspective that blends well with scientific knowledge of the material world. We get a unique experience of eternal existence in the ocean of 'universal consciousness', which enriches the mundane life with a compassionate vision of unity. Our ignorance is dispelled with the supreme knowledge that the same kind of awareness subsists in all beings. Once the basic unity of life is understood, the root cause of conflicts and worries simply disappears."

"The learning of the Upanishads is not like the downloading of disembodied information from the Internet or memorizing lessons in comfortable classrooms. The knowledge that we gain from such deep insights stays with us for a lifetime. In olden days, students used to search out for enlightened masters who could impart knowledge through the narration of stories set in a social or mythological context. They gave convincing answers that enabled disciples to meet the challenges of life with the courage of true convictions."

"The learning process culminated in the creation of a compassionate mindset that cared for the less blessed brethren. The disciples emulated the frugal life style of the teacher, who did not accumulate any material possessions or aspired for positions or power. The master practiced ultimate spiritual wisdom, as an enjoyable way of life. It created an indelible impression in the developing psyche of the youth."

Mike said, "Where do you get such competent teachers without selfish motives? You know, the modern gurus are the worst role models. They are more interested in marketing individual brands of spirituality and writing best sellers, containing cocktails for instant salvation. They conduct expensive interactive sessions with yoga and meditation in star hotels for achieving "Nirvana". The teachers want money, not sainthood for selfless service. Not that I am finding fault with their attitude to spirituality; they also render some service to humanity. But surely, they cannot be equated with enlightened masters of the Vedic tradition."

I agreed. "That is why I am suggesting some unorthodox learning methods without the help of a teacher. We first evaluate the wisdom of the Upanishads using scientific explanations about the material world. The converging perspectives of science and the Upanishads, can then unfold a new worldview, to guide us towards real spiritual wisdom. Such shortcuts are the only effective means to acquire knowledge in times of competitive commercialism."

"Of course, it is not easy to take the reader on a guided tour to the highest level of spiritual wisdom. Initially, I delved deep into them with a genuine interest to learn the ancient speculative wisdom of existence. Having received the gift of a unique spiritual experience, I wanted to convey it to the common man. The updated version of Upanishads could easily overcome the prejudice against ideas belonging to the distant past."

In addition to the stories of the major Upanishads, I present in epilogue I, the gist of Ashtavakra Gita, which converts the concept of consciousness into a practical philosophy of life. It shows the powerful influence of the Upanishads on subsequent spiritual thoughts that focused on creating a more equitable social order. It is evident that Buddhism and Jainism adopted many of the explanations of existence from the major Upanishads.

In epilogue II, a summary of Patanjali's 'Yogasutras' is presented for the benefit of more inquisitive minds. It indicates a different path for achieving self-realization. In Western thoughts, the unified approach to existence and spiritual wisdom are rarities, except in the philosophical works of Schelling and Hegel. They are completely ignored, in the avalanche of knowledge derived from successful scientific enquiries proposed by Cartesian concepts. Patanjali gives a practical guide to reach the yogic state of mind without renouncing the responsibilities of worldly life.

"At the very outset, we encounter the god of Death. The dialogues reveal logically, even to the uninitiated, the eternal wisdom of the Upanishads. In suitable contexts, I indicate very briefly the latest scientific ideas on the topic under discussion to enable the reader to evaluate the scientific basis of Vedic inferences."

"More than anything else, I hope the Upanishads,

would help us to exorcize the ghost of hatred and distrust from the modern mind. Undoubtedly, the need of the hour is to wean away impressionable youth from the deadly influence of zealots. The Upanishads can remove hatred and conflicts by highlighting the basic unity that defines all forms of life. The message of non-violence and compassion can make our planet, a better place to live.

Mike, who is an eager student of philosophy, agreed to come along for a tentative dip into the ocean of ancient wisdom. He said, "Before we plunge into Vedic thoughts, I would like to know more about what you mean by the modern mindset? How is it different from the ancient one? Don't you think the mind, after all, is the same stuff at all times?"

I agreed. "After the main stories of the Upanishads, we will take a quick detour to the latest scientific discoveries on the mind. As you know, in the last four decades, we have acquired plenty of correct information on the brain, consciousness, and the mind. They are now better understood with the help of scan technologies and computer simulations. Although we have not yet fully unraveled the non-physical features of the mind, science has, in the recent past successfully removed many misconceptions. After understanding the mind, we can upgrade our conscious capacities with the answers in the Upanishads that creates a universal outlook."

So we set out on an exciting voyage to evaluate the relevance of the Upanishads for the modern world. We present only verifiable facts and steer clear of expressing views on the assumptions of various faiths. In the dialogues that follow, for convenience the letters "M" and "P" are used to represent Mike and Pillai. The questions are in italics for easy recognition.

Before I take you to the main stories of the Upanishads

and their current relevance, let me explain the terminology of the core concept of "Brahman". We use many equivalent words like the Supreme Self, consciousness, universal consciousness and the Supreme Being or Spirit to signify the same all pervading intelligent energy. As far as possible, I try confine to the word Brahman, but in some contexts its equivalents are used for elegance. The word "self" signifies the localised presence of Brahman or the Supreme Self in a human body. The reader may feel confused with such terminological variations, but they do not convey any different connotations. All of them lead to the same concept of indefinable and intelligent energy that the Upanishads consider as the cause of all existence.

CHAPTER ONE
DEADLY COUNSEL

"When consciousness leaves the body, mortal life comes to an end. But existence continues eternally in new conscious forms of life bestowed with the intelligence to explore the unknown."

[Brihadaranyaka Upanishad]

"Beyond all senses, mind, intellect and ego, is the essence of existence, the ultimate cause. One who realizes that endless entity is relieved from the cycle of birth and death."

"The unborn Supreme Self is beyond all descriptions. Scriptures and speculations give us no clue. The right path alone can take us to the wisdom that reveals its undeniable presence in all mortal beings."

[Katha Upanishad]

"The most beautiful things cannot be seen; can only be felt with the heart."

[Helen Keller]

P: Let us begin our spiritual pursuit from the cessation of mortal existence. Assume that just a few hours ago you succumbed to a massive heart attack. Your mortal remains have become the focal point of a confused domestic scenario of shock and sorrow. The mourners pay obeisance to your body, which would not have received such endearing attention earlier. You may not like the undignified posture of the body, but who would now care for your preferences?

Eventually, after a few hours of waiting and wailing, you are packed off, for the ultimate disposal. You become the last entry in a list of ancestors in the family chronicle. And the curtains fall forever on an exclusive episode of existence. But the serial continues with transmitted genes carrying on the affairs of life, presumably, in more competent bodies of the progeny.

With unfailing regularity, from time immemorial, humanity has been witnessing such situations of great anguish. We spend a lot of our waking life speculating about death and its consequences. Many people try to avert its untimely occurrence, but the real event of termination does not hurt, as consciousness leaves the body simultaneously.

Death is undeniably the cruel culmination of our extremely short span of life on earth. The process of ageing and death in all biological forms of matter seems to follow an inbuilt genetic instruction. In fact, every cell has a program for self-destruction to inhibit its infinite capacity for division. If there is any certainty in life, it is the inevitability of death!

M: *Some scientists say that DNA contains the blueprint for growth as well as termination of life. After passing through different stages of development within a given timeframe, the cell reaches a pre-determined exit stage. Had the process of growth continued indefinitely, it would have been disastrous to the species. Possibly, the acquired genetic errors of copying culminate in a massive malfunctioning of cells leading to death.*

P: Yes, according to evolutionary explanations, death is essential for preserving precious resources of the earth for fitter ones to continue successful reproduction. It is true, that without such a marvelous exit mechanism, the survival of life on the planet would have perished very early. The unchecked aggregation of the spent ones would have put an unbearable burden on meagre resources of the planet.

About two billion years ago, ageing and death became an integral part of life. They got implanted in life with the introduction of sexual mode of reproduction in some microbes called "protoclists". Of course, that does not establish any link between sex and death. Death is not a sexually transmitted affliction, but the outcome of a decline in the orderly flow of metabolic processes. Experiments using "death genes" on cells having infinite capacity for growth showed evidence of an instant breakdown of metabolic processes.

Death genes are active in all forms of embryo-based life. But some microscopic organisms, like bacteria, are beyond its deadly reach. They remain eternally alive, reproducing without enjoying sexual union. Maybe, inheriting a death gene is the price for sexual indulgence. Sex is, undoubtedly, the most important invention of nature that ensured better chances of survival. The embryo creates more competent progeny with improved physical and mental capabilities to meet the multitude of challenges from the environment. Without sex, the accumulated errors in genetic instructions would have wiped out human species long, long ago. Sex is not only an exquisite personal experience; it is also necessary for continuation of life.

Refraining from sex, scientifically speaking, is an unpardonable crime against humanity.

M: Tell me, what actually happens when we die?

P: As I told you, normal death is brought about by the deterioration of the metabolic processes that energize the organs. The intriguing question is, can we accept that existence ends with the cessation of basic functions of the biological form of matter. The physical and mental boundaries that separate us from the external world disappear on death, leaving mortal remains to merge with nature.

The ingredients of matter like atoms and molecules that create cellular bricks of the body, may acquire fresh lease of life in different combinations and contexts. Or they may get recycled and eventually return to the great cosmic drama of existence.

The mere death of an organism does not destroy the essence of life in it. In fact, ultimately when earth evaporates in about five billion years or even earlier, all building blocks of life would go back to the original galactic warehouse, for yet another cycle of nuclear fusion. The important fact to note is that consciousness that leaves a body at the time of death continues to keep the light of life burning elsewhere. The off springs do not perish with the parents. They carry forward the torch of consciousness that enables them to survive in the struggle of life. The capacity to become conscious which is an essential sign of life is affected by the termination of a particular organism. Death may put out some lamps, but the light of life is kept burning eternally.

M: You mean death is a sexually transmitted certainty but it cannot break the continuity of life. Okay, that gives us the latest scientific knowledge on death. What is the vision of the Upanishads on death?

P: Well, they give lot of correct surmises on death. Let us start with Katha Upanishad, which explains the mystery of death in a simple narrative style. The story begins with an old man seeking divine favour by performing religious rites. Giving away alms to learned persons from the upper caste was an integral part of the ceremony. The miserly man did not want to gift away his productive wealth even for the sake of procuring heaven. He gave away old cattle and barren lands to please the gods. On seeing the flagrant sacrilege of the sacred rites, his young son Nachiketa was terribly distressed. He believed in following scriptures strictly, both in letter and in spirit.

Unable to bear the old man's unholy aberrations any longer, his son dared to ask, "Father, whom will you gift me for heavenly rewards?" The old man lost his cool at the persistent taunting of the impudent brat. He finally shouted a curse: "I give you to the god of death!"

In Hindu mythology, various elements of nature are generally designated as gods. Death is conceived as a god strolling on a buffalo with a noose to rope in ripe souls destined to hell. He keeps a competent chartered accountant, to track the span of life allotted to all human souls. Not only that, he also maintains a history sheet of all the good and the evil deeds of each and every person. The quality of performance on earth, leads one to either heavenly pleasures or hellish tortures. Nachiketa accepted the curse literally and proceeded to hell.

He said, "Father, please do not repent on your curse to consign me to death. Many people who had lived here are already dead and gone. Those who live now would have to take the same path."

He added, "Just as ripened corn falls to the ground and springs up as a sapling in the next season, a man has to learn when his time comes. If God wills, he would be reborn."

Normally, no sane person would accept hell willingly. It is the dreaded abode of the god of death, fully equipped with torture chambers that give guilty their due rewards. The boy was determined to enter hell to fulfill the vicious curse of his dear dad. As usual, Yama, the terminator, was on his dreaded tour to pluck souls, which were ripe for receiving punishments. When he returned to hell, after three days of deadly work, servants told him that a Brahmin boy was waiting to meet him. Since the time allotted for his earthly existence was not over, he was not allowed to enter as a resident. He was an uninvited visitor or at best a passing guest. A guest, according to custom, should be received with generous hospitality and high obeisance. As the boy had to wait on arrival, Yama offered him three boons to make amends for the irreverence shown to the esteemed visitor.

The first boon was taken for securing forgiveness from his enraged father. He wanted to get back home without incurring displeasure. It was readily granted.

The second boon was taken to learn the secrets of conducting the "fire sacrifice". It was a Vedic ritual for achieving heaven, the world of eternal happiness that belongs to the gods and other celestial beings. In heaven, one has no fear of death or any other calamity that visits ordinary mortals. No hunger or thirst is ever felt in the abode of gods. Yama, the god of death granted the second wish by teaching Nachiketa all the correct steps involved in performing the fire sacrifice. The boy learnt the ritual exactly as he was taught. Immensely pleased with the intelligence and dedication of his disciple, Yama decided to name it as "Nachiketa sacrifice".

He was then asked to choose the third and final boon. Nachiketa said, "Please tell me, Lord, what happens when a man dies? I want to know what existence is and what its extinction means."

He added, "When one dies, some people think he is gone for ever. Some others assume that existence continues in other forms."

Nachiketa wanted to learn the true facts about existence from none other than the god of death. Who else could be more competent to solve the puzzle of death?

Yama was extremely reluctant to grant the third boon. He told the boy, "Even gods cannot understand the mystery of death." He offered Nachiketa many kingdoms, immense wealth, beautiful wives, many children, and so on, but the boy was not tempted by the long list of alluring gifts. Other inducements like celestial entertainment by enchanting maidens, divine music, decorated chariots, powerful warriors, and even longevity failed to evoke interest in his determined mind.

Nachiketa stood his ground and insisted on gaining the true knowledge of death and existence.

Finally, his wish was granted. Even the god of death, who is not moved by prayers and pleas of mortals on their deathbed, could not resist the earnest quest for knowledge. He could see that Nachiketa was well informed on the perishable nature of material possessions that would not give him enduring peace and happiness. The boy knew that the wisdom of existence learnt from the very destroyer of life, would give him true solutions to all existential puzzles. And he wanted to get it at any cost.

In Katha Upanishad, a suitable context is created to impart the essence of existential wisdom. The legend of Nachiketa, daring to face death and rejecting all worldly inducements for knowledge, heightens the sense of curiosity in eager disciples. While admiring his persistence, they spontaneously focus attention on the instructions from the god of death. The story gives the disciples an abiding conviction that knowledge is the only priceless possession.

M: No wonder they coined the strange name "Upanishad". One has to sit really close to the teacher and listen carefully to learn all about the mystery of death. It is indeed a frightening path of enquiry particularly for young aspirants of knowledge.

P: The Terminator began a lengthy discourse, albeit with great reluctance. He said, "Human beings initiate actions either for promoting common welfare or for acquisition of personal possessions to enjoy life. The wise ones prefer to serve common cause rather than succumbing to pleasure enhancing deeds. Those who relentlessly pursue material wealth and positions fail to reap the rewards of knowledge.

Nachiketa, you chose wisdom over worldly pleasures that I offered in abundance. If one wants to wallow in ignorance, the endless chain of life and death becomes the burden of his destiny. Only intelligent persons like you seek the truth of reality, devotedly, for enlightenment. They try to learn all about the Supreme Self from a competent teacher. The assimilation of knowledge will, of course, depend on the level of eagerness of the learner."

He added, "Brahman or the Supreme Self, is the most subtle entity, comparable to an invisible form of energy. It is beyond all forms and descriptions. Gifted persons spontaneously get intelligent perception of its presence. The pathfinder from an enlightened person can speed up the long and arduous process of self-realization. It can be conveyed more effectively with suitable illustrations, anecdotes, and allegories. The student should live an austere life, as indulgence in sensory pleasures causes distraction in the rigorous process of learning. Nachiketa, you are eminently suitable to receive the supreme knowledge as you rejected my tempting offers with firm resolve."

"It is extremely difficult to understand the true nature of the ultimate entity called 'Brahman' or 'the Supreme Self'. Even though it is an all-pervading entity, words cannot describe its qualities and capabilities. Since physical forces of the phenomenal world do not apply to it, we can only feel its nearest presence as an observer of dreams. It is definitely not a part of the body or the material that creates the brain and the mind. Through sustained meditation, the true nature of Brahman may sometimes become intelligible to genuine seekers of knowledge. Some mystics feel its presence always in their unwavering minds.

When the mind is liberated from endless desires arising from body-related needs, Brahman becomes an unshakable faith of the enlightened. It is beyond our conception of what is right or wrong, success or failure and also time and space. The past, the present, and the future are all dimensions of our thoughts which do not affect the Supreme Being that includes all such concepts in its holistic ambit."

The Terminator revealed the secret of Brahman as the syllable "Om". He said, "It symbolizes the unborn and the eternal energy of the universe. The entire phenomenal world is the material manifestation of its existence. It embodies all kinds and forms of matter and forces, which are destined to perish with the passage of time. But the immortal energy does not have any beginning or end. In fact, different terms like Brahman, the Supreme Self, Universal Consciousness, and so on, refer to the same energy, which cannot be considered as a definite entity. In the primal state, it included everything in its eternal existence."

He went on describing some attributes of the Supreme Being to convey a broad representation of its immense presence.

'The universal energy known as Brahman dwells in all persons independently. In fact, the individual self exists side by side with the universal Self, as space exists both inside as well as outside of a pot. The enlightened ones see it as the sun and his own self as a localised sunbeam."

Yama continued, "We feel its presence when body awareness is minimised. In the purified mind, one can perceive the glory of the all-pervading Brahman. Its eternal wisdom transcends all boundaries of human thoughts and actions. The self-realized ones spontaneously become its integral part and enjoy blissful existence."

M: What exactly is this Brahman or the Supreme Self? Is it something like the concept of dark energy that neutralizes gravity and keeps the universe on an infinite expansion course? The recent study of a Princeton scientist confirms the existence of an unknown kind of energy. It probably permeates the entire universe and causes cyclical big bangs or infinite expansion.

P: My dear, these are all names coined by us to describe the unknown. Imagine Brahman, as the rider of a chariot, which is your body. The mind is the charioteer, holding on the reins of horses, which try to take the body on the path of pleasure. Brahman is not affected by the endless desires of the body and the mind. The mind creates an illusion of reality in which all deeds and thoughts appear to emanate from its own faculties. In fact, it is cleverly camouflaged, in the complexities of body-related activities. When it is uncontrolled, the senses get full freedom for pleasure hunting. The discriminatory power of the mind to do good deeds would be lost if it follows only pleasure enhancing activities. It would eventually lead to innumerable miseries of life.

M: How do you find the right path?

P: Have more patience, Mike. Listen to what the terminator told Nachiketa.

He said, "Life is evolved from Brahman, which is the un-manifested seed of all existence. It is both the cause and the effect of all events in the universe. The same entity contains and also controls stars, planets, and life. Our identity and the mind are all manifestations of its unknown kind of intelligence. The physical forces, the biological and non-biological matter and, in short, everything that we have known so far exists only inside its infinite space.

It is the ultimate goal of all quests for knowledge. The genuine seekers of existential wisdom find the reflection of their identity in the mirror of Brahman. People craving for sensory pleasures fail to feel its glorious presence. The process of discovery begins with an understanding of one's own mind and its fluctuations in relation to the body, like pain and pleasure. It culminates in correct perception of the meaning and purpose of existence."

M: Oh, now I see why you want to give a long sermon on the modern mind. Please proceed.

P: The god of death continued the elucidation. "When we are awake, the senses are turned outward for seeing objects and events of the external world. The attractions and challenges in the world keeps the mind fully occupied. It has no time for anything other than sorting out the endless stream of sensory data, which ensures survival. Consequently, it never looks inwards to see the effulgent Brahman that shines in its own innermost space.

Brahman is the lord of time that merges both forward and backward motions in its ambit. We become aware of our actions and all events in the phenomenal world, only when it lights up our perception with consciousness. The mortals can only see passage of time from the past to the future but the creator of time has no such limitations. The atoms, molecules and the wide varieties of proteins, enzymes, and so on, are all proof of its immense capacity to make an amazing phenomenal world. It is also in fire, in water, in the sun and stars and in all conceivable forms of matter. Many huge galaxies exist in it and perish, ultimately to fuse with its formless existence".

Yama added, "Existence is the same inside us, as well as in the external world. When one sees no difference between the external and the internal, the ultimate truth of unity of all forms of life becomes self-evident. The perception of differences, based on race, gender, intellectual and physical abilities and so on, is indicative of utter ignorance. With true knowledge, the feeling of separateness as also the distinction between life and death comes to an end. The eternal chain of being and becoming is relevant only for those who cannot see the unity of all existence in Brahman. The wise ones who understand this secret of life are never afraid of death. They know that it cannot separate them from Brahman."

He went on to explain death in more detail. "Death is only the loss of a transient identity attached to a particular form of matter. The form has to perish on the expiry of its span of life. When the mind is clouded by all kinds of distractions, it becomes blind to the infinite existence of all beings, in the ocean of consciousness. For the invisible Brahman alone, the existence is immortal, since it is the cause of all changes in form and dimension.

The enlightened person knows that it is the reflection   •

of the Supreme Spirit in him that enables him to experience the world. The physical body without consciousness has no means to experience the pleasures and pains of life nor has the capability to delve deep into the treasure of knowledge. The destruction or creation of a physical form does not add or subtract anything from the totality of existence. The immortal Self is the sole and supreme ruler of all subjects; the container as well as the content."

He added "The ignorant ones may continue to experience, even after death, all the miseries of material existence in some form or the other. They may enter another womb or become a part of the plant or animal kingdom. But the self-realized knows well in advance that he is ever existent despite changes in form. The Supreme Spirit is what remains awake in us when we sleep. It creates dreams showing up desirable objects that the body craves for. The destruction of the body is like falling into a deep slumber. Brahman simply passes through all states of our existence without changing its immortal stature and intrinsic nature.

In the endless sea of life, we are just like waves that rise and fall on the will of the wind. Those who fail to see this truth are afraid of death, disease, and deprivation. In fact, waves have no independent existence outside the sea, as its fleeting form is a cleverly created visual illusion.

The fact is that death cannot do anything to the Supreme Spirit residing in a body. Even I, the god of death, cannot harm the one who knows that he is an integral part of Brahman. Only ignorant ones fear me, for they take earthly existence as the most precious possession. The very thought of death drives them to hell as they want to enjoy sensory pleasures, and material wealth ad infinitum. One who reaches the zenith of knowledge would neither care for the continuation nor termination of the chain of existence. They are all irrelevant, to the one enlightened with the knowledge that the end of one form is actually the beginning of another. The essence of all forms is in the imperishable consciousness that continues even after it leaves one physical body.

The evils of the world do not affect the person, who transcends conceptual confusions like polarities, with the true knowledge of unity. He experiences the presence of Brahman in his own consciousness. The achievement of acquiring true knowledge liberates him from the chain of rebirths. A profound sense of peace and contentedness descends in his mind, which is fixed unwaveringly on the Supreme Self. He does not experience pain or pleasure in any event or circumstances in which he is placed," Yama said.

"Brahman becomes visible once the veil of ignorance is lifted as its sheen is then seen everywhere and in all forms of life. Its presence is in our thoughts and in all objects like the sun, the moon, and the stars. They all reflect the eternal glory of the Supreme Self, that is the root of the tree of existence. If we follow its reflection in the mirror of the mind, we reach the right path.

We take correct decisions, become tolerant and compassionate only when we know the essence of all existential wisdom. Once the ultimate reality of Brahman is understood, we get truly integrated with its undifferentiated presence. But, if we simply go on gratifying the needs of the pleasure centers of the body, the Supreme Spirit remains unrevealed. It is relegated to the backyard of the mind, and becomes dormant and ineffectual. The ignorant are always involved in activities to acquire more material comforts. When we understand what life is all about, we are instantly liberated from the fear of death. The mortal form and time-bound existence are seen as mirages by the one who lives in infinity.

Eyes cannot see it nor can ears hear its voice. The wise ones alone experience its presence in all kinds of sensory perceptions. When senses are calmed, and the mind is set at rest without any distraction from random thoughts, we reach unity with the universal existence of Brahman. In that state of awareness, all delusions of separateness disappear from the mind. Some people claim that they can reach this goal through the path of yoga or meditation. Some others achieve higher levels of awareness occasionally by performing penances, meditation or religious rites.

Even mind-altering drugs are taken by more adventurous ones to achieve ultimate knowledge. But after the drug-effect wears off, they fall back into the ignorance of material existence. Such short cuts that give glimpses of the transcendental states of the mind, do not take us to the knowledge of Brahman.

True knowledge alone can give the mind the enhanced awareness in which all existence is seen in the underlying essence of a Universal Spirit. Only self-realization can remove forever, the darkness of ignorance, the fear of death, diseases, loss of relations and so on. My advice to you is to seek Brahman in your own mind. This is the ultimate truth of existence," added the god of death.

After narrating the gist of Katha Upanishad in a manner intelligible to the modern mind, I asked Mike, "Can't we use this wisdom to make the youth see the futility of fear and terror?"

M: Well it depends. If educational institutions accept such books as part of the syllabi, we may get some positive results. The hardcore hate mongers are not likely to give up their views in spite of such fine lessons on existence. It is definitely a laudable attempt that can save the future generations from *the jaws of terror and ignorance.*

P: Let us now go through some more Upanishads before we conceive a viable action plan to spread the wisdom of the Upanishads.

CHAPTER TWO
PAINLESS PARTING

"The mind is spontaneously liberated when its bondage with the visible world, its objects, events and thoughts are terminated. It enters the realm of pure awareness free from the memory of the past and unconcerned about the uncertain future."

[Yogavaasishtha]

"Excessive desire and attachment will cost you dearly in the end."

[Tao Teh Ching]

"When one is united with the beloved, all physical and mental boundaries disappear. Likewise, in self-realization, we forget separateness and merge with the Supreme Self."

[Brihadaranyaka Upanishad]

"Glory is fleeting, but obscurity is forever."

[Napoleon Bonaparte]

P: Having overcome the fear of death, let us now learn how to get rid of the pain of losing near and dear ones. We have one such learning situation in 'Brihadaranyaka Upanishad'.

The sage Yajnavalkya, being an enlightened soul, decided to renounce all worldly attachments and possessions for more intense and uninterrupted meditation. He wanted to divide assets between his two wives in a mutually agreed manner. He discussed the matter with his first wife, Maitreyi, who asked, " Lord, if I get all the wealth in the World, can I live for ever?"

Yajnavalkya said, " My beloved, all the wealth in the world cannot give you immortality." She then requested him to instruct her how to transcend death rather than giving her some property that would become useless at the end.

The sage explained, "The intimate relationship of the kind between wife and husband, children and parents, brothers, sisters, and so on should not be only for the sake of complying with the natural requirements of personal attachments. The presence of the Supreme Spirit in beings should be the basic consideration for attachments. In fact, even inanimate objects like wealth are created by the grace of God. The various elements of nature deserve respect and worship for the sake of what is intrinsic in them.

In short, everything in the world should be loved not only for fulfilling the physical needs of a person but also for the Universal Self that exists in all of them. Meditating upon it and internalizing the indisputable fact that the entire universe contains only its manifestations, in various forms with different properties alone, will give you unlimited bliss and immortality. Ignorance is in the perception of a separate state of existence, that is detached from the universal Self".

The sage further explained with more illuminating illustrations. He said, "We cannot understand the sound of a drum without having some knowledge about the drum and the drummer. Similarly, the sound of a conch can be understood only by knowing more about the conch and the person who blows it.

The same is the case with all kinds of music. The vast wealth of knowledge in the Vedas, arts, sciences, and poetry emanates from the Self, and without knowing about its origin and infinite capabilities, we can never have a correct and complete comprehension."

"For example", he added, "the sea is necessary for the presence of water and, similarly, we need the skin for feeling the sensation of touch. Without the nose, we cannot smell anything nor can we enjoy the sense of taste without the tongue. We cannot see things without the eyes and no thought can arise without the mind.

All scriptures could have been written only if appropriate words were available to describe objects and events. Likewise, the universe and its structures such as galaxies, stars, planets, and various other manifestations of matter exist only because of Brahman. It is undoubtedly the origin of everything, imperishable, and without a beginning.

At the time of death, the individual awareness merges with universal consciousness like a lump of salt fallen into the sea. It gets dissolved in seawater and cannot be taken out again in the same shape or size. However, seawater has all the individual properties that the lump of salt once possessed. Similarly, the awareness that gives us a separate mind and identity gets totally dissolved in infinite consciousness".

M: It is true that biological life found in different kinds of bodies are all made up of the same type of atoms and molecules.

In fact, the entire visible universe is created out of the permutations and combinations of only 92 kinds of atoms. So, when physical existence is extinguished, the separate identity of the body dissolves in the ocean of pure consciousness. We do not perish nor does our consciousness; only physical form and the egoistic assumption of an identity are erased. The atoms and molecules continue their existence in other forms of matter.

P: Let us get back to the sage. He explained further, the idea of infinite existence. "As long as separateness from the infinite persists, the perceiver and the perceived are seen as different entities. We hear, smell, speak, and perform various functions by assuming that each one of us has a separate identity created by body awareness. But once it is understood that we are all integral ingredients in the infinite existence of consciousness, the difference between knowledge, the object of knowledge and the knower ceases to exist.

All of us evolved from just one primordial source and eventually we have to return to the same entity. When this undeniable faith motivates our actions and thoughts, the artificial distinction created by differences in form disappears like darkness melting away at dawn."

The sage concluded, "The Supreme Self is unlimited consciousness. It is temporarily attached to various individual manifestations of matter but with cessation of life it goes back to the ocean of infinite awareness. That is why no consciousness subsists in a dead body which decays into elementary particles in no time."

The lucid explanation on the mystery of life and relationships in terms of transient manifestation in the ocean of universal consciousness made Maitreyi immensely happy and content. The sage enlightened her further, "Duality, is the source of all painful thoughts of losing dear and near ones. Once death removes body awareness, how can one know anything about relatives left behind or about their prospects in this world? In supreme consciousness, knowledge and the knower become one, leaving no room for separateness. One who realizes this truth is not afraid of death or any other physical calamities."

Thus Maitreyi got fully enlightened with the wisdom of eternal existence. She did not feel any strong emotions when Yajnavalkya finally took leave of her to pursue a purely ascetic life of detachment.

M: When you put it logically, the idea of the Supreme Self appears simple and convincing. I would like to hear more about other episodes in the Upanishads that explain existence in different contexts.

P: Before we move further, let us see what the latest scientific discoveries indicate on the existence of an eternal and intelligent energy like the concept of Brahman or Supreme Self. It is now evident, that the universe was created from some form of intense energy that existed even before the big bang. That primordial energy is undeniably the substratum of everything that came into existence in the universe. There is ample proof that at the micro level, the all pervasive energy is intelligent and interactive. Elementary particles do not require any local force or medium for propagation. Quantum mechanics supports the view that at the particle level it is possible to have instant exchange of information across all barriers, like space and time.

The intelligent energy that created the universe and different structures like galaxies, stars, and planets can be called nature, God, destiny or some kind of supernatural Being. The Upanishads just call it the Supreme Self or Brahman. Ashtavakra calls it "universal consciousness".

What is really surprising is that scholars, who compiled the Upanishads, had correctly identified the intelligent energy that created us and continue to guide our actions and thoughts.

M: *But scientists assume an inexplicable kind of cosmic coincidence as the cause of creation of all kinds of matter and forces. The galaxies, stars, planets and even micro world of atoms and molecules could not have come into being without certain basic physical values, ratios and thermal contexts to facilitate interaction of particles. Since coincidence cannot be explained and the role of providence is clearly unacceptable to science, some have gone to the extent of conceptualizing a 'multiverse' containing millions of universes. According to them, ours is just one among the vast multitude of universes created probably in black holes or similar dense vacuums. Only our universe happens to have all the correct parameters necessary for creating and sustaining structures including human life. Do you think, so called scientific explanations like coincidence and multiverse are consistent with the wisdom of the Upanishads?*

P: I will give you my views about coincidence, providence and even multiverse in the concluding part. Now, let us try to understand more about the complex question of human relationships. How they arise in humans and are sustained, in spite of the genetic inclination for selfish actions.

The Upanishads conceive that all of us are manifestations of an eternal energy in different biological forms. In fact, all of them try to expound the fundamental principle of unity of all existence in that eternal energy. It is explained in the different contexts of human relationships to convince the uninitiated. The consciousness that leaves us on death can be scientifically accepted as energy that gives us life and perpetual abilities. It continues to exist in new manifestations, even after the death of an organism or extinction of a large number of species. We now know that individual differences arise out of just 0.2% variation in neural connections. The great gender differences that agitate many people are the outcome of the presence of just one different chromosome. We can say that God has been very equitable in gifting the elixir of life.

M: *The latest scientific discoveries show that the genetic base for gender difference is the predominance of certain hormones. The male hormones 'testosterone' and 'vasopressin' give the drive for mating and fighting. It induces aggressive instincts to protect a particular territory and to ensure sufficient supply of food and mates. In the modern world, male ego seeks to prove self-worth by establishing better positions in highly competitive and discriminating peer groups. According to Michael Gurian, the reputed author of "The Wonder of Boys", men become more workaholic once they have kids to show their progeny that they are not just worthless donors of sperms. The dominant hormone in female called 'oxytocin' creates a strong urge for attachments and long-term relationships. How come such relationships are established by chemical drives? Do you think chemicals are capable of choosing the correct combinations of hormones for males and females to ensure survival?*

P: Since you have brought up the subject, I would like to take you to the origin of gender differences. Some recent discoveries indicate that males actually are evolutionary products from female ancestors but we have no clear idea about the changes that occurred in the reproductive process. The 'X' and 'Y' chromosomes that define gender could have probably evolved from the mutations in unisex autosomes in the early days of life. 'Y' chromosome is sometimes called 'degenerate X' chromosome. What it means is that gender differences arise from slight alteration in the original text. We can call the male, a highly evolvable eve-mutant, as 'Y' chromosome has been the main arena of evolutionary changes. It may explain the rapid developments in the left hemisphere of the male brain while females carry on with the happy and holistic experiences delivered by dominance of the right hemisphere and oxytocin. No wonder, they chill out more easily with emotional conversations and soap operas.

We do not know the genetic compulsion that made the 'Y' chromosome, an anchorite for evolution. Possibly, it could have been for better propagation of the species and migration to distant lands. We can also assume that constant exchange of information with the environment could have resulted in genetic algorithm that produced a stronger and more focused variety of the same species. The predominance of hormones like testosterone and oxytocin are probably consequences of genetic adaptations made in consultation with the chemical signals of nature. It could have chosen the male for more hazardous tasks of defending habitat and hunting for big game.

The dominant chemical drives of oxytocin and serotonin in the females, ensured less of child mortality and more rapid propagation of the species. The emotional bonds powered by oxytocin probably laid the foundation for the joint family system and hierarchal social order. The male brain with less oxytocin and serotonin compels them to engage in high-risk sports and action-oriented outdoor games. It cannot sort out patiently the sensory inputs from the environment like the female, or settle down comfortably in congenial habitats. The male is condemned to achieve an outstanding career and excel in competitive events without enjoying a relaxing break over some emotional diversions.

Here, I would like to explain the significance of an astonishing physiological change that occurred in the female hominid during the evolutionary process. It was the loss of 'estrus', which happened to no female of any other species. Nature makes the females of other species to undergo periodical chemical tuning up for sexual activity. It is probably required for frequent mating to compensate the high mortality rate. In the animal kingdom, the reproductive act is not an enjoyable, leisurely activity. In some extreme cases like cats, it is a very painful process for the female.

Nature seems to have mercifully spared the hominid female from the vagaries of estrus, which would have interfered with prolonged periods of child rearing. The human offspring becomes self-sufficient very late and if the mother gets into the cycles of estrus at frequent intervals, the mortality rate could be very high with malnutrition and neglect. The loss of estrus was definitely an evolutionary achievement that ensured survival of humans.

We may also say that the human female made the biggest sacrifice of estrus for the sake of perpetuation of the species. It also created a context for the emergence of family as the basic social institution built upon enduring relationships. The great civilizations emerged, thanks to the missionary zeal of our female ancestors. And please remember that all such physical changes occurred, much before the scientists who attributed them to molecular wisdom were born.

The practice of monogamy can also be traced to the disappearance of estrus, which made the females receptive for sex at any time without chemical compulsions. We can also find in the loss of estrus the beginning of incest taboos. Social control on prohibited relationships must have been conceived to check uncontrolled population growth and social tensions particularly when sexually matured adult males and females live in close proximity. Another evolutionary feather in the cap of the creator!

In other words, we can say that stable family relationships emerged when nature removed the timing mechanism of estrus for the sexual act. The physical union, which was originally designed only for reproduction was converted by nature into an intense emotional experience leading to prolonged companionship. It is now evident that Homo erectus actually started the sexual revolution in their tribal settlements. They created stable family relationships essential for social life. The rest is history. But what is intriguing is how nature knew all our social and personal requirements for successful survival? That is where the role of 'intelligent energy' or 'Supreme Self' becomes self-evident.

The great transition from foraging tribal societies to modern civilizations has been possible thanks to the incredible sublimation in the basic chemical urges in human beings. The biological instinct of extreme aggressiveness and obsession with sex are now elevated to achieve socio-centric objectives like better career opportunities and more accomplished spouses. But evolutionary modifications in females are much less and they still get flooded with oxytocin to establish a focused and enduring attachment with off springs and others. It also creates enduring social relationships, which reduces the egocentric motive of seeking consideration for every action. Admittedly, the egocentric thoughts in the female mindset create the greatest hurdle to self-realization.

Whether modern or hominid, the female personality is defined by oxytocin and serotonin that nurture relationships. With changes in sexual practices and social hierarchy, hormonal effect in the human male has also undergone a considerable change. They don't have to fight aggressively for mating and securing territorial rights. Presently, we find more and more females clamouring for top positions in the job market and males performing paternal duties with great devotion and care.

The traditional gender roles dictated by chemicals are not fully reversed, but signs of some significant departures from the domains created by nature are clearly visible. It shows that cultural evolution has taken humans far beyond the paradigms created by biological compulsions. The gender revolution is definitely leading us to a better and more equitable social order with decreasing dominance of the males. Although it creates certain grey areas in well-defined roles, the overall impact will definitely be conducive for better co-existence. It takes us back to the dictum that nature knows better.

M: It is true that the role reversal or narrowing of gender differences will not in any way affect the basic assumption on the unity of existence propagated in the Upanishads? In fact it only enforces the argument that the intelligent energy that pervades the universe is capable of understanding the needs of every form of life in a given context. It mutates or modifies the genetic algorithm to accommodate even changes required for cultural evolution. If scientific knowledge also accepts that God knows everything, it is definitely reassuring in modern times. We are coming closer to such a conclusion in the idea of multiverse.

P: We can observe an underlying unity in all kinds of life on earth, despite variations in chemical drives. Almost sixty per cent of DNA is common for higher forms of life. A part of what makes a human is similar to the stuff that gives life to a monkey, mouse or fly. The differences in size, shape and capabilities are not based on major DNA variations. The context and probably the time, create the subtle differences. Switching on or off certain sequences in DNA and fine-tuned variations in the spatial arrangement of the embryo can produce a different organism, even from the same basic stock.

Once death removes consciousness from any form of life, what is left is the original stuff that contains only inanimate matter. We can assume that consciousness returns to Brahman or more scientifically to a Universal Pool of Consciousness. All faiths can accept that the basic cause of creation is something like consciousness that can be worshipped or admired in whatever form or name. Differences in individual perceptions cannot deny the fact that all creatures emerged from the same entity. We should see in all relationships, the trace of the Supreme Self that calls for respect and compassion for other persons. The gender controversy is a myth created by our ignorance of the basic unity of existence. All genders in all species contain the same undeniable spark of consciousness donated by the intelligent energy. No sensible person can deny the obvious.

CHAPTER THREE
TEST FOR THE BEST

"Unknowingly every night we enter the heavenly world of Brahman and sleep like children in his embrace. But while awake, the mind leads us to miserable deeds and a sinful life."

[Chandogya Upanishad]

"He who knows what is enough will always have enough."

[Tao Teh Ching]

"Only those who know the secret of the visible world, get a glimpse of the invisible that created all worlds."

[Atharva Veda]

"It is better to deserve honours and not have them, than to have them and not deserve them."

[Mark Twain]

P: In modern times, we adjudge the best in sports and games by holding competitive events like the World Cup, Olympic games and other contests. Excellent performance in literature, science, technology and so on also get recognition with awards and prizes. But in ancient days, such events were rare, and award for highly accomplished persons was only an occasional gift from the ruler of the land or reward of a position in the royal court. Scholars used to vie with each other to catch the eyes of the king by all means. With no steady income from land or labour, academic pursuits granted them only a frugal existence. No wonder, in the past very few were interested in devoting their entire life for propagating elitist ideals.

Ceremonial occasions invariably attracted many learned persons, who tried to expound their wisdom to the huge gathering. At times, celebrities like kings or chieftains witnessed keen intellectual combats. Such occasions were marked by heated debates that excited the audience. In Brihadaranyaka Upanishad, we get glimpses of a great clash of the cerebral titans of ancient days.

In the previous chapter, we saw the great sage Yajnavalkya explaining existential wisdom to his beloved. Here we find the same scholar in a heated spiritual debate conducted in connection with a sacrificial ceremony. Janaka, the venerable King of Videha, distributed many expensive gifts to the learned participants. He was eager to find out the wisest among the multitude of scholars. So, he kept a thousand cows in a pen and tied ten gold coins across the horns of each one.

He then told them, "These cows are for the wisest among you. Let the best take them away."

The huge gathering of scholars was dumbstruck as many of them were not confident enough to stake claim to the title of the wisest. They all had some self-doubt except the great sage Yajnavalkya. He calmly told his son to drive the cows home. The son happily complied with the command.

Then all hell broke loose. The assembly of learned seers was aghast at the audacity of Yajnavalkya. They shouted, "How dare you be so presumptuous? Do you think all others present here are in any way inferior to you?"

The sage coolly replied, "Whoever is the wisest, I salute him. But all I want is the royal gift of cows and gold."

First, the royal priest Aswala questioned him. He asked, "Since everything related to sacrificial rites is subject to death and pervaded by thoughts of death, how can the worshipper overcome the fear of death?"

Yajnavalkya replied, "One could overcome death, by knowing the identity of the worshipper, the sacred fire and the ritual words. As all the three are forms derived from Brahman, which pervades the entire universe, the correct knowledge of existence would make one overcome the fear of death."

Another scholar asked Yajnavalkya, "Everything is seemingly destroyed by death. Tell us, is there any power which can consume death itself?" Yajnavalkya replied, "Fire destroys everything. But it is extinguished by water. Similarly, death is defied by the one who knows the truth of Brahman and its eternal existence."

He was again quizzed about the perceptive faculty of a dying man. He wanted to know whether it goes out along with the mind or continues to dwell within the body. Yajnavalkya said, "It merges with the final cause, which is the all pervading universal spirit. The lifeless body has no perceptive faculty or a mind left in it."

Another reputed scholar brought up a difficult

question. He asked, "Yajnavalkya, tell me what is the ultimate?"

He wanted to know whether the ultimate was the immediate Brahman or Brahman directly realized as such or the Supreme Self, which dwells in all beings. Yajnavalkya affirmed that the ultimate is the Supreme Self, which is present in all beings. He further elaborated, "The self in a body is that which breathes in as well as out and the one which diffuses breath in the body. It is the same Universal Self that is the ultimate and present in all beings."

On further questioning, he explained the concept of the ultimate. Brahman or the Supreme Self is the universal Spirit that sees the sight, hears the sound, and thinks up all thoughts. It is also the knower of knowledge. It doesn't perish even after the body decays. He added, "It is beyond hunger, thirst, grief, delusions, and death.

With self-realization, the enlightened person spontaneously abandons all cravings for material wealth, pleasures of other worlds after death, welfare of the progeny and such egocentric thoughts. He is like a mendicant devoting entire time on contemplation in the wonderland of the Self Supreme. All distracting thoughts disappear from the mind that understands true nature of existence. His knowledge that manifestations of matter perish at some time or other, extinguishes all desires and gives him total peace in the realization of the ultimate."

Many scholars in the audience were still restless and did not accept Yajnavalkya as the best. One of them called Uddalaka asked, "Do you know what is the thread that connects this life, the next life, and all beings together? Can you tell us who is the inner ruler who controls from within this life, the next life, and all beings?"

Yajnavalkya said, "The subtle principle of life is the

thread that connects this life and all other life and all beings together and the inner ruler is the one who dwells on earth but it doesn't know anything about him. Earth is his body and he controls it from within and yet he is immortal. The same way, he dwells in water but is totally different from water. Water doesn't know anything about him, although his body is water and he controls it from within."

Using apt analogies, Yajnavalkya illustrated the nature of the inner ruler that controls everything without our knowledge. He told them, "It is universal consciousness, which is imperishable, and present in all beings as the ruler."

After a while, Gargi, a woman scholar of great repute, challenged him. She said, "I shall ask you only two questions. If you answer them correctly, I will accept you as the best among all of us". The first question is: "What is that above the heaven and below the earth which also exists between heaven and earth as well as in the past, present and the future? In what is that woven, warp and weft?"

Yajnavalkya readily answered, "It is space, which is above heaven and below earth and also between the heaven and the earth. On the same space the past, the present and the future are woven, warp and weft".

Gargi was satisfied with the answer. She then asked the second question: "In what is the space woven, warp and weft?"

Yajnavalkya said, " Mystics call it the 'Akshara'. It is an indefinable, changeless reality, which is neither fine nor gross, neither short nor long, neither hot nor cold, neither light nor dark, and such vague descriptions can go on and on. No causal relations, senses, and perceptions are attributable to this entity, which exists both inside and outside of all beings. It does not enjoy anything nor can anything enjoy it."

"According to its command, the sun and the moon deploy their forces. It keeps heaven and earth in their orbits and makes time move forward and makes the rivers flow into the sea. It is Brahman that exists in all. The knowledge of the imperishable "Akshara" is essential for proper understanding of life. It is unseen; but it is the seer in all beings; it is unheard; but is the hearer of all sounds, it is unthinkable; but is the thinker of all thoughts. The space is woven, warp and weft, in Akshara."

On hearing the answer, Gargi said, " All of you can now go home as none knows about the Universal Spirit better than Yajnavalkya."

Then, Yajnavalkya invited further questions but the spellbound scholars did not utter a word.

This episode reveals the utter futility of wasteful spiritual debates. What we really need is true knowledge of existence, and all spiritual mumbo jumbo on various attributes of God, is of no practical use in the modern world. The meaning and purpose of life cannot be understood in the current ambience without a rational explanation of the being and the becoming. If the underlying universal Spirit is accepted as the reality that exists in all beings, our confusions about different faiths would spontaneously disappear.

Yajnavalkya logically explained death, as the process of return of perceptive faculties to the universal spirit. Similarly, he also established how the whole universe is woven on space and how space is woven on the universal spirit. It is a great lesson for aspirants of spiritual knowledge who are normally carried away by academic achievements in some small area of enquiry. This episode explains existence cogently and makes us feel relieved that death is only a semicolon and not a full stop.

M: *Yes, the logic is irrefutable. Scientific knowledge has now established the imperishable nature of energy. Death can only bring about a transformation in the configuration of atoms and molecules. They get recycled in new forms of existence. Everything returns to the warehouse of the universal energy and sets out again for playing different roles in new manifestations. Maybe what the sage explained to his competitors is the current scientific wisdom. The amazing fact is that such accurate insight was acquired without the aid of any modern scientific tools of observations and analysis.*

P: Let us see some more learning situations in which the same sage explains the wisdom of existence in different interesting contexts. It is an effective way to convey the message of unity to the seekers of knowledge.

M: *Yes, it is time to leave death and competition to learn more fascinating things.*

CHAPTER FOUR
ROYAL SALUTE

"The self-realized transcends time and space and abides in pure consciousness. No evil thoughts, desires or fear can ever enter his enlightened mind."

[Ashtavakra Gita]

"The best ruler is the one whose existence is not known to his subjects."

[Tao Teh Ching]

"By knowing a few names and qualities of finite matter nothing can be achieved in life. The awareness of the infinite qualities of the cause of life alone can give enduring enlightenment."

[Chandogya Upanishad]

"Humility is a strange thing. The moment you think you've got it, you've lost it.

[Groucho Marx]

P: As you now know, in ancient days, great intellectual accomplishments were essential to become a renowned teacher. Many illustrative examples had to be given to convince disciples about the infinite qualities of the Supreme Self. Some of them were adept in telling stories using familiar metaphors and anecdotes. On many occasions, they instructed through dialogues between mythological characters. The disciples were mostly young students eager to learn from a competent master. They readily absorbed the stories and dialogues and remembered the moral of the lesson for a very long time.

But amongst them were also elderly disciples, like "Janaka", the king of Videha who was a highly respected ruler and scholar. One day he saw Yajnavalkya in the royal court and sought permission to ask questions about the concept of Brahman. We have seen in the preceding chapter how Yajnavalkya won the 'test for the best' conducted by the same king. He also figures prominently in several Upanishads as a keen observer and an avid learner. In addition, he had been famous for being generous to scholars seeking material assistance.

In this interesting dialogue in the Brihadaranyaka Upanishad, Janaka asks the first question, " Yajnavalkya, what is the light of man?"

"It is the sun, ·O, king. We work, walk, and rest by that light," he replied.

The king asked, "What is the light of man when the sun sets?"

"It is the moon that becomes our light. We work, go out, rest, and return in that light," replied Yajnavalkya.

"When both the sun and the moon set, what is our light?" asked the king.

"The fire is our light. We work, walk, and rest in its light," said the teacher.

The king probed further, " When the sun and the moon set, and the fire is out, what is our light?"

"The speech is our light. It gives us directions to move about safely, work, go out, come back, and rest."

"When speech also stops, what is our light?" asked the king.

"The Self Supreme is the light of man. We work, move about, and rest in its light," replied Yajnavalkya.

"What is that Supreme Self?" questioned the king.

"Your Majesty, it is pure awareness embedded in the body as the light of the heart. Surrounded by senses, it ignites our consciousness and illuminates the entire world. No action, thought or sleep emanates from this entity, which assumes all frailties of a body as long as it is there. When it leaves a body, all body-related burdens are extinguished and consciousness returns to the cosmos," said Yajnavalkya.

He explained the concept of the Supreme Self further. "Death destroys only physical body from its given form. Consciousness continues in non-physical realms like thoughts and dreams. It carries the memory of past life and aspirations for the future. Oh, Your Majesty, the Supreme Self that you are seeking is there in all your states of consciousness and beyond. The seeker finds it, understands it as the ultimate truth of reality, and dissolves his separate identity in its infinite existence."

M: You mean consciousness is carried forward by DNA to the next generation? Isn't it?

P: The exact relationship between biological entities and consciousness is not known nor is it our subject of enquiry here. We are looking at the broad spectrum of human life and the role of Consciousness in shaping its course. When we sleep, who is watching our dreams? We are not conscious enough to do that. But all the same, we remember sequences and content of at least some of the dreams.

Who keeps the body alive with all vital systems working in perfect condition even when we are fast asleep? The spark of the Self Supreme in you does not sleep. In dreamless sleep, it remains dormant to take us back to waking awareness. When we are in extreme states of pleasure and pain, we forget our separateness from its presence. It is totally free from desire, fear and all evils of the world. Simply stated, it is far, far above our emotional bonds and concept of karma that arise from localized thoughts and actions in a mortal form of biological matter.

M: *Tell me what happens to the Supreme Self in a hypnotic trance? Does it go to the hypnotist or remain dormant in the body, as if the subject was asleep? Can Yajnavalkya's wisdom throw some light on this puzzle?*

P: It is somewhat similar to the state of unity mentioned in the Upanishads. In dreamless sleep, we exist in a dormant state. The brain is active but consciousness that creates separateness or identity is held in abeyance. Hypnotic suggestions are received and processed by the brain as if they originated from the conscious mind. But they are not acted upon in the trance state. If suggestions are contrary to the moral convictions of the subject, they will not be obeyed in the conscious state. Consciousness is neither removed from the subject nor transferred to the hypnotist. What the hypnotist does is to give a powerful suggestion to induce a mild state of sleep, but all processes in the brain go on without interruption.

M: *But is it not the autonomous nervous system that keeps the organs functioning in our sleep? Can we call it the abode of the Supreme Self?*

P: Whatever keeps the heart's rhythm; breathing and metabolic functions should have intelligence to know the correct parameters. Do you think atoms and molecules can have advance knowledge on the correct rate of heartbeat and other such rhythms that run the body? That is where we find the wisdom of the Supreme Self and its infinite creativity. You may not readily accept this view, but without its presence, can anything work? Utter chaos will prevail in the body if every organ starts functioning independently. Ultimately, life will altogether cease forever.

M: *Well that makes sense, but tell me how reflection of the Supreme Self worked in Siamese twins?*

P: It is true that Siamese twins behaved as if they had two minds in one body. Identical twins, derived from the division of a single fertilized egg also develop different personalities. Since they have two bodies and distinct brains, each one has the Supreme Self, embedded in the mind. But Siamese twins present a unique case of two minds emerging from the same body awareness. The dual neural networks in the brain give them different identities. The mind arises in the brain, only when we are conscious. Siamese twins not only have two minds but also show separate capacities to become conscious. It is an interesting puzzle for scientists to ponder.

The state of unity between an individual mind and the entity that we call the Supreme Self or consciousness is achieved only at the highest level of enlightenment, which some people call cosmic awareness. Mystics meditate to reach the exalted state of perception in which nothing separates the mind from external reality. All sensory organs and thoughts and emotions work spontaneously, without assuming the identity of a separate conscious entity. According to Yajnavalkya, the world of Brahman is the supreme goal of life and the greatest bliss, a human can achieve. In that state of unity, we get immense happiness and mental stability.

M: *Please continue with the royal lessons. It is getting more and more absorbing.*

P: At that point, the king offered Yajnavalkya more cows and sought deeper knowledge on Brahman.

Yajnavalkya continued: "Like a ripe mango or a fig separates from the stalk and falls to the ground to begin a new life, the individual self leaves the body weakened by old age and disease. All our physical and mental powers leave along with consciousness; no faculties of sight, hearing, and feeling can function in a dead body. Consciousness merges with the universal energy, and along with it all memories, experiences and knowledge go to the common warehouse of existence. Only fools think that they have succeeded in life by amassing wealth and getting into lasting relationships. The dead man tells no tales.

Actually, we have nothing enduring in us other than consciousness that is also a shared experience. The Supreme Self continues to care other bodies that can function better. It leaves a dilapidated abode, but the drama of life goes on with new episodes. Through ignorance, we take individual self as the composite entity containing the mind, senses, desires and all physical attributes of a person. The truth is that, it is beyond all these, although it exists in everything. In fact, the Supreme Self contains everything in the visible and invisible worlds. The kind of life one lives depends on the quality of thought and action. Those who choose good deeds and make correct choices become an asset to society, while evildoers not only harm others but endanger their own chances of acquiring wisdom."

Yajnavalkya explained further: "When we achieve the goal of self-realization, all desires, fears and anxieties disappear. No further urge for rebirth to experience another round of earthly existence will torment the mind. Another tryst with life is necessary only for those who desperately long for eternal enjoyment of worldly pleasures. When desires are extinguished with the knowledge of Brahman, death becomes a celebration of reunion. The individual self goes back to the vast ocean of consciousness, which actually means a blissful reunion with immortal Brahman.

Janaka offered another one thousand cows for further knowledge on self-realization.

M: The cow was probably the only reward for wise men of the ancient world. Maybe it was the most useful gift to the teacher, to sustain his austere existence.

P: Even today, Hindus consider cow as a goddess and mother figure. It gives them not only milk but also fuel for the hearth. Sun-dried cow dung, which is an environmental friendly fuel, is used for cooking in Indian villages. Cow dung is also a wonderful organic manure and cow's urine has several antiseptic properties. The animal that gives so many goodies deserves to be adored as a divine creature. In fact, cow slaughter is banned in many places to respect the sentiments of its worshippers. Anyway, let us get back to the king and his teacher.

Yajnavalkya continued: "Self-realization gives us perfect peace and happiness. It enables us to see the reflection of the Supreme Self in all beings. In addition, we gain the true knowledge that everything exists only in its eternal presence. Evil thoughts do not emanate from such wise and compassionate persons who have overcome all desires with proper understanding of the meaning of life. The enlightened ones do not commit any sins or wrong deeds. When we understand that our existence is only in the Universal Spirit, we achieve total harmony with its glorious, all pervading presence."

M: *So, indirectly the teacher instructed the royal disciple that true knowledge would lead him to correct decisions. In other words, peace and prosperity of the country would depend on the existential wisdom of the ruler. It is a good advice applicable to rulers at all times. Before they aspire for powerful offices, they should acquire some true knowledge. Good governance is possible only with proper understanding of people, their attitudes and motivations.*

P: Then they may not seek any electoral offices, as the greatest wisdom may make them ascetics. But as you correctly put it, no harm will come if they get initiated into such ideas before trying to run the affairs of a country.

On another occasion, when Janaka saw Yajnavalkya in his royal court, he asked, "This time have you come for cattle or for teaching philosophy?"

The sage replied that he wanted both and started questioning the king on what he had already learnt from other scholars.

Janaka said, "Jitwa told me the word is Brahman." Yajnavalkya agreed that it was the correct knowledge, since without the word there is no existence and the word is nothing but Brahman.

He then found that Janaka had not been taught on the abode and support of Brahman. Yajnavalkya told him more about Brahman. He said, "the abode of Brahman is the organ of speech and space is its support. You meditate upon the word as knowledge."

The king then wanted to know the meaning of knowledge.

Yajnavalkya said, "Word is knowledge, as one can know all about the world only through the word. It gives spiritual, material, and all kinds of knowledge. Words symbolically convey the meaning of existence to make it intelligible to us. The word indeed is Brahman."

As usual, the king offered thousand cows. But this time, the teacher was reluctant to accept the gift without instructing the king more about existence. For further lessons, he wanted to know what the king had learnt from others.

The king said, "Udanka taught me that primal energy is Brahman. But he gave me no instructions on its abode and support."

Yajnavalkya said, "Breath is its abode and space is its support. One should meditate upon it as Brahman. Tell me what further knowledge you got from others."

"Barku taught me sight is Brahman," said Janaka. "But I was not instructed on its abode and support."

Yajnavalkya told him that if sight is taken as Brahman, the eye is its abode and space is its support. If hearing is Brahman, ear is its abode and space is its support. But if the mind is considered Brahman, the mind itself is its abode and space is its support. It should be meditated upon as happiness, as without the mind, we have no knowledge or happiness. The heart is also Brahman, as all beings find rest in the heart.

The king was profusely confused with several versions of the knowledge of Brahman. He said, "I bow down to you, Yajnavalkya, please give me the correct and complete knowledge of Brahman or the Supreme Self."

Yajnavalkya told him that in dreamless sleep, it dwells in the mind in the form of a vital force. It makes the body function harmoniously and opens the window of consciousness, to access the outside world. When we sleep, it keeps the window temporarily closed. Actually, it is a part of Universal spirit or Brahman that cannot be described or comprehended. On death, it merges with Brahman and the physical body perishes to join the elements. By knowing about it, one goes beyond the bondage of relationships and chronic fear of death.

Yajnavalkya concluded, "Oh revered king, with this knowledge, you have now transcended death and achieved eternal existence in Brahman."

The king bowed again and said, "The entire kingdom and the king are at your service, Sir, please demand whatever you want."

M: So by giving a few thousand cows the king got true knowledge. Not a bad bargain, I say.

P: Mike, your mindset is highly materialistic. You always think in terms of the consideration involved in any kind of exchange. For you, even spiritual ideas do not come free. You put a price tag on everything, claim copyright and intellectual property right for every word uttered as if you created them. Do you think anything really belongs to any one of us in this biosphere? You are connected to global culture through consciousness. It is consciousness that makes the entire world visible to your perception. It survives even after your death. Can you claim an exclusive right to your consciousness? As somebody put it, originality is undetected plagiarism. There is only one original architect; all others are clever imitators claiming creativity.

M: I didn't mean that the knowledge of consciousness was given as a consideration for cattle. I know it is a symbolic gesture of showing respect to a reputed scholar. Now, please take me through the other lessons.

CHAPTER FIVE
MANY PATHS: ONE GOAL

"The Supreme Self is the hub of the wheel of life, the elements and senses are its sixteen spokes that created the material universe. Reach out for unity with that reality to transcend death, fear and rebirth."

[Prashna Upanishad]

"Tao is an elusive concept that signifies a core of intelligent energy showing an unknown purpose of creativity."

[Tao Teh Ching]

"Knowledge, scriptures and discourses cannot disclose the cause of life. Search for the wisdom of existence in the eternal reality that unites all life."

[Mundaka Upanishad]

"Never express yourself more clearly than you think."

[Niels Bohr]

VOYAGE-1
WHEEL WITH SIXTEEN SPOKES

P: I told you elsewhere that some of the stories of the Upanishads might appear repetitive, because of the same core theme. The qualities of Brahman being infinite, all major Upanishads try to narrate its unchanging common attributes. Different teaching methods are used to make sure that disciples do not miss out on the main features of the central subject of Brahman.

In Prashna Upanishad, a learning situation is given where we find six disciples approaching the teacher 'Pippalada' for enlightenment. He asked them to live with him for one year practicing control of senses and complete trust. He promised to answer their questions thereafter.

After one year, a disciple asked, "Master, who created the universe?"

The sage replied: "The Lord of all beings meditated and created Prana, the primal energy with Rayi, the giver of name and form. They represent the male and female forms so that they could bring forth several creatures for the Lord. Prana is the sun that gives light and life to the universe.

"Wise men see in the sun the Lord of love, life, and light. They seek self-realization through meditation, control, and total faith in the Lord. They take the northern path after death to the solar world of immortality. The cycle of birth and death cannot trap such fearless souls."

M: *I find it difficult to follow the logic of the sun and the moon in explaining existence. The metaphor really confuses the issue, without clarifying its intent.*

P: The metaphor is indeed far-fetched. But students of

that period probably related a lot more to the sun and the moon, as they gave light, brought change in seasons, helped agricultural operations, and so on. They attributed wisdom and knowledge to the bright half of the day that belongs to the sun. Sex, ignorance, and all kinds of evils arise with the moon that presides over affairs of the night. The creator is seen by the wise, in the light of the sun, and in all kinds of food that sustains life. Those who live for sex alone are the ignorant ones, taking the path of darkness. Practice of austerity, self-control, and truthfulness takes us to the region of sunshine, the abode of the Supreme Lord of all life. This, in brief, is the meaning of the dialogue.

Another disciple asked the sage, "Master, what are the various forces that keep the physical body alive, and which is the dominant and most potent one?"

The Sage replied, "The powers that create the body are space, air, fire, water and earth. Besides them, speech, mind, eye, ear and the other sense organs also support the body. Once, all of them claimed that their support to the body is exclusive and without them the body would not exist. But the vital energy called Prana told them that the body is held together by its power.

Since they did not accept the claim, Prana, demonstrated its power by leaving the body. Then all the other forces became impotent and had to leave the body. They could return only when Prana re-entered. It is like bees following the queen wherever she goes. All of them were convinced that the power of Prana was supreme. They accepted the fact that everything exists in Prana and depends on it for sustenance. Prana also prevails in the mind and in all its emergent qualities."

Here, the teacher becomes very eloquent while describing the omnipotence of Prana, the primal energy. He finds it burning in the fire, shining in the sun, in thunder, clouds, and in all forms of life and even in formless existence. Finally, he prays to Prana to look after all existence as a mother tends her child.

Then another disciple, Kausalya, asked the question, "Master, what is the origin of Prana? How does it enter the body and how does it leave at the time of death?"

The sage said, "Prana is born of the Supreme Self and it enters the body at the time of birth. It is like the casting of a shadow. We can say that Brahman puts its shadow on all beings. It also works through other forces for carrying out specific functions."

The sage explained the role of Prana by many illustrations and concluded that consciousness that leaves us at the time of death is what unites us to Prana.

More explanations with mythical metaphors and analogies may confuse you at this stage. All that is relevant to our understanding of the concept of Prana is that it is the localized presence of universal consciousness or Brahman that enters the physical body at the time of birth. It is the vital energy that activates organs and systems in the body for effective performance. At the time of death, the organs fail to maintain life, as it leaves the body.

Another disciple asked the sage, "Master, when a man sleeps, who is with him? Who sees the dreams? When he wakes up, who wakes him up and lights up the lamp of awareness? Who is the one enjoying the fruits of our physical labour and in whom do the faculties rest?"

The master replied, "The mind is the master of all senses. When we sleep, the senses rest and all activities stop. Only Prana is awake keeping the body alive, and the mind is united to the Supreme Self. In dreams, the mind revives memories of the past and desires of the future. But when we are in deep sleep, memories, desires and actions are all extinguished. In fact, we sleep in the caring hands of Brahman.

The elements and faculties also take rest in the Supreme intelligence, which receives sensory inputs and creates knowledge for our survival. One who understands that it is in the eternal Supreme Self that the mind, the senses, Prana and the elements exist requires no further enlightenment."

Finally, Satyakama arose and asked, "If a person meditates on the syllable "OM" throughout his life, what will be his reward after death?"

The master said, "OM is the symbol that stands for Brahman or the Supreme Self. By meditating on it, you get different kinds of rewards depending on your knowledge of the meaning of the word. If you don't know the meaning, even then you will be enlightened by meditation. But after death, you will be born again and strive to attain higher spiritual knowledge.

If with more knowledge you meditate on the word "OM", after death you will enjoy the pleasures of heaven but you will be reborn for continuing earthly life. But if meditation is done with full knowledge of the meaning of the word that it stands for the Supreme Self, after death you will be united with its infinite existence. You will be set free from all burdens of life. When true knowledge removes fear of death, one achieves immortality in this life itself."

M: So, 'OM' is the syllable or symbol used for meditation in the Vedic period?

P: Yes, in ancient times, they wanted some symbolic representation to focus attention on a formless entity like Brahman. But once it is realized, no symbols are required to sustain the unwavering faith in its omnipresence. The rewards mentioned in the story are for easy comprehension of the concept of Supreme Self as compared to the individual self.

Another disciple, Sukesa, requested the sage to explain the Supreme Self and its sixteen forms. The sage replied, "The Supreme Self, with its sixteen forms, dwells within the body. It created sixteen parts of the universe by reflecting upon its position in the creations. All the sixteen forms, including the senses, elements, Prana, desire, Veda and so on lose their name and identity when they reach the Supreme Self. It is like sixteen rivers flowing into the sea and irretrievably merging into it, without any trace of individual identity. Ultimately, only the infinite Self exists. The sixteen forms are the spokes projecting from the Self which act like the hub of a giant wheel of life."

He told the disciples that the lessons they had learnt contained all that could be said about the Supreme Self. No further explanation was possible on the cause or purpose of our existence. The disciples saluted the sage and said, "You are our father. You have taken us across the sea of ignorance to the domain of the eternal Self."

M: It is indeed a great explanation on the complex process of creation and existence. I wish we had teachers like Pippalada to impart knowledge of the unity of human kind to the modern mind!

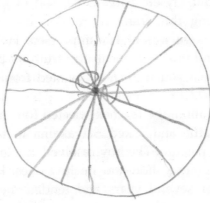

VOYAGE - 2
UNWED MOTHER, UNKNOWN FATHER

Chandogya Upanishad narrates an interesting story to introduce the concept of Brahman. It is about a boy who was eager to learn the Holy Scriptures. He did not belong to Brahmin caste, which was the only one entitled to receive spiritual instructions. But, the boy wanted to get true knowledge at any cost. He enquired about his family name so that a competent teacher could be approached for learning vedas.

The mother said, "Having worked in several places as a young maid, I do not remember the name of your father. You tell the teacher that you are Satyakama, the son of Jabala."

The boy went to Gautama, a renowned teacher of scriptures. He asked, "To which family do you belong to, young one?"

The boy said, "I asked my mother about my family name. In her youth, she worked as a maid in several houses. She did not remember the name of my father. She told me to call myself 'Satyakama, son of Jabala'.

On hearing this frank admission on his uncertain ancestry, the sage was highly impressed. He said, "None but a true Brahmin will speak the truth so boldly. I will teach you since you have not deviated from the path of truth."

After initiation, the teacher selected four hundred lean and sickly cattle and asked Satyakama to take them to the jungle to pasture. The boy resolved not to return until the cattle became a thousand healthy ones. He stayed in the jungle for several years and tended the cattle with care and devotion. One day the leading bull of the herd approached the boy and said, "Satyakama, we have become one thousand strong and healthy cattle. Now you can take us to the house of our master but before that, I shall teach you about one of the four feet of Brahman. All the four quarters of space, namely, east, west, south, and north, constitute one foot of Brahman. If you meditate on this, you will be enlightened and gain mastery on the heavenly regions of the cosmos. About the rest, the fire will tell you as you go further."

Satyakama and his entourage of cattle then began their return journey to the house of the teacher. In the evening, he lit a fire, put the cattle in a pen, and sat facing the east. Then the fire spoke, "I can teach you about another foot of Brahman which is earth, sky, heaven, and the ocean. These four quarters constitute one foot of Brahman, which is the endless entity. If you meditate on this reality, life will be endless for you on this earth. Now a swan will tell you more about Brahman."

Satyakama continued his journey. On the next evening, when he lit a fire and sat facing the east, a swan approached him and said, "The fire, the sun, the moon, and the lightning are the four quarters of another foot of Brahman. If you meditate on this reality, you will become master of the world of light. Another bird will tell you all about the other foot of Brahman."

The next day, at the same time, a bird came to him and said, "The breath, the ear, the eye, and mind form another foot of Brahman. If you meditate on this foot of Brahman, you will become the master of space and will be known as established."

When Satyakama returned to his teacher's house, the teacher said, "You shine like an enlightened person. Tell me, who taught you the secret of Brahman?" Satyakama narrated his adventures in the jungle and requested the sage to instruct him on ultimate wisdom. The teacher obliged and taught him all about the eternal existence of Brahman, without holding back anything.

In another story, the same Satyakama takes on the role of a teacher.

One student called Upakosala lived with him for twelve years. The teacher allowed all students, except Upakosala, to return home after they were initiated and instructed on the wisdom of life. Even the teacher's wife pleaded for the release of Upakosala. Without giving him permission to leave, Satyakama went on a long journey. The boy could neither eat nor sleep, as he felt desolate, impure and inadequate.

He then heard a voice from the fire, which said, "Life is Brahman, the sky is Brahman, bliss is Brahman, and you are also Brahman."

The voice explained further, "The sky means lotus of the heart where Brahman dwells, and bliss means the bliss of Brahman. The earth, the fire, the sun, and all the elements we worship are different forms of Brahman. Slowly, the true nature of existence became evident to the boy who had been very unhappy for the unreasonable detention.

When Satyakama returned, he looked at the boy and said, "You shine like the one who knows all about Brahman."

The boy narrated his encounter with the ethereal voice. Satyakama said, "My dear boy, what you have learnt now is absolutely true. I will now tell you more about Brahman. What shines in the depth of your eye is Brahman. That is the self in you, the shadow of the universal energy that gives you life. He is beautiful forever and illuminates all worlds."

Enlightened on the true nature of existence, the boy returned home fully contented and confident enough to meet all challenges of life.

M: It is surprising that in all these stories, nature is the main instructor. The human hand is only instrumental in making the disciple observe nature and learn the lessons of life. In fact, jungle is the school, and birds and animals are the main sources of knowledge. The enlightened teacher who lives the simple life of an ascetic gives only final touches to make the student competent to bear the responsibilities of life. If only our educational systems followed such nature-oriented instructions, we could have turned out better human beings having respect for all forms of life and nature.

P: Let us go through some more lessons. In the next story, we find an erudite father stepping in to make up the shortcomings of an incompetent teacher.

VOYAGE - 3
TEACH ME MORE, DAD

The story of Shvetaketu, the son of Uddalaka, tells us that even ancient times had many inept teachers. When the boy returned home after living with a Vedic teacher for twelve years, Uddalaka tested his level of learning.

The father asked, "Have you received the spiritual wisdom from your teacher, which enables you to hear the unheard, think the un-thought, and know the unknown?" The son said that he knew how to chant many mantras, but not wisdom of the unknown. He entreated for instructions on the ultimate knowledge. Uddalaka taught his son the truth of reality by using several interesting metaphors.

Uddalaka said, "Son, from the knowledge of one lump of clay, we come to know all about the composition and quality of everything made of clay. The difference is only in names and forms, not in the inner substance, which is the same. Similarly, by knowing everything about one piece of gold, we learn about all things made of gold. The same applies to all manifestations of matter. Spiritual wisdom gives the knowledge that all kinds of life has one origin and that the difference is only in the names and forms."

Shvetaketu felt very unhappy that his master did not teach him the basic wisdom of the unity of existence during his twelve long years of stay. He requested Uddalaka to tell him more about existence.

Uddalaka started from genesis. He said, "In the beginning there was only one Being, without any cause or effect. It was an unborn, pure, and indefinable entity.

From its thoughts came the cosmos and various structures like galaxies, stars, and planets. It entered into all emergent manifestations. The fact is that everything visible and invisible in the world is its creative expressions and it also exists in the innermost core of all beings. It is the ultimate cause of all reality and we are an integral part of that infinity."

The father then explained more about Brahman. "In dreamless sleep, we are united with it without any such awareness. As a tethered bird gets tired of trying to get away, in sleep, the weary mind finally settles down in the Supreme Self. For all creatures in the universe, it is the ultimate shelter as well as the inner strength.

Let me tell you what is death. When a man dies, speech merges with the mind and the mind goes to Prana. Prana enters the fire and the fire unites with the Supreme Being. It is that Supreme Self that exists both inside and outside us. With that basic knowledge, learn to live happily in this world.

Son, you know that the honey sucked by the bees from different kinds of flowers eventually becomes one lot. Can any drop of honey claim an exclusive origin to a particular flower?

Like that, the feeling of separateness, arising from difference in sources, is just an illusion created by the mind. All creatures belong to the Supreme Self that makes them function in a variety of forms. Like rivers flowing into the sea eventually become one without any trace of original identity, all creatures when they finally merge with the Supreme Self reach total unity. There is no exception to this universal rule.

It creates new biological forms of life like trees, cows, human beings and so on and keeps them functioning in perfect harmony. When it leaves, they perish, but the infinite Self continues its existence. Death is only a signal of its departure from one's body. No memory of any past deeds or experiences remains in the dead body. It cannot recognize the near and dear ones. The Supreme Self knows everything but that knowledge is available to manifestations if they diligently pursue it. The fact is that the supreme Self is the sole cause for multifarious manifestations of existence.

Son, when we cut a fruit, we find seeds. If a seed is further cut into smaller and smaller pieces, it reaches a stage where we cannot find anything. But as we know, a whole tree grows out of that seed. The individual self is like the hidden essence of the seed, that is invisible but can create a whole life.

I will now give you another example of the Supreme Self. Take this lump of salt and put it into a cup of water and bring it back tomorrow."

The next day Shvetaketu brought back the cup of water.

"Where is the lump of salt, son?" asked the father.

"It got dissolved in the water," said the son.

"Now taste the water from different parts of the cup. Don't you find that it is salty everywhere. Just like that, the Supreme Being is everywhere and in all beings. An enlightened teacher removes your blindfold created by instincts. He shows you the path towards the goal of understanding the ultimate. Once you reach the right course, life is just a song. You become the happiest person, finding peace in the knowledge of the truth of existence."

Shvetaketu understood that he was nothing but another manifestation of the Supreme Self. At last, his own father completed his spiritual education.

VOYAGE - 4
REVEAL THE REAL ONE

M: *Parental influence might have been very strong in ancient India. They took keen interest in the all-round development of the child. After completing several years of learning with competent teachers, Shvetaketu learnt the final lesson only from his father. It shows that parents were also well instructed in spiritual matters.*

P: Yes. In fact, in Vedic times, parents and teachers were considered equivalent to God. It was assumed that if they were served faithfully, worship of God was not necessary. Traditionally, children looked after old parents with great devotion. There was no concept of old age homes in ancient times and the elderly people normally proceeded on long pilgrimages or continued to enjoy the company of their children and grand children. Their advice was frequently sought on important matters. The great advantage of the joint family system was that many generations coexisted as a well-knit unit. The common interests of the family bound them with a sense of purpose, pride, and belonging. The great feeling of close relationship is fast disappearing even in India. The advent of nuclear family deprived them of an important source of spiritual counsel.

In this story, we see Bhrigu, the son of Varuna, the god of Water, seeking knowledge on Brahman.

Varuna said, "First you learn all about food, speech, breath, eye, ear, and the mind. Then you will find out from what these things emerge, how they function, what they search for, and ultimately where they all end up. That source is called Brahman."

The boy thought it over and, in his meditation, he found out that food is Brahman. All creatures are born out of food and they grow by consuming it. Finally, when they die they become food for other creatures to sustain the chain of existence. But he was not satisfied with this inference. He went back to his father for more knowledge about Brahman. Then he was told to find out Brahman through meditation. He said, "Meditation is Brahman."

The boy underwent a long spell of meditation. He found that all creatures grow because they are alive. Even after death, they continue to live in new forms of life. But this knowledge also, did not satisfy him. When he approached Varuna again to know more about Brahman, he got the same advice, "Meditate more, because meditation is Brahman."

On further meditation, he found that the mind is Brahman, as all creatures are born out of the mind and they grow because of the mind and on death they return to the mind. This knowledge also did not fulfill his desire for the ultimate wisdom. He requested Varuna to give more enlightenment. He was advised again to meditate more and discover all about Brahman.

Further meditation gave the boy the idea that wisdom is Brahman, because out of wisdom arise all creatures and it makes them grow further. Ultimately, everything returns to the wisdom of existence. This knowledge also did not satisfy his spiritual quest. He was again asked to meditate more and find out for himself the true nature of Brahman.

He then found that Brahman is joy, because from joy all creatures are born and they grow in joy and return to life to seek more experiences on enjoyment. But it was not enough to satiate his quest.

On further meditation, he understood that self-realization means respect for food or other materials like water or fire and not wasting them. The self-realized person stands firm in all circumstances; he becomes prosperous and shows compassion to all persons. In turn, he also receives love and respect from everyone. He never refuses food to the hungry and helps the needy, as serving the poor means worshiping God. On further meditation, Bhrigu found that self-realization makes one's speech more pleasant, breath deeper, and the body healthier. This enables the person to serve all creations of Brahman more effectively.

Understanding Brahman gives the seeker a sense of harmony in thought and action. Our approach to life undergoes a profound change. Every object and event in the world is seen as expressions of the creativity of Brahman. The enlightened person has no enemy or competitor, as he knows that all of them belong to the same Supreme Self. Those who gain this true knowledge go beyond ordinary perception and realize the ultimate unity of all beings. They are at peace in all situations as every moment of existence gives them an opportunity to serve Brahman through less endowed creations. Even while alive, they are far above the ordinary mortals wallowing in the miseries of materialistic life and endless desires. The father said, "This is the correct vision that will help you live happily."

M: I never heard a more lucid presentation of spiritual knowledge. It gives me a purposeful life full of peace and bliss. In fact, the concept of self-realization explained so well in this story makes me happy with a definite goal to serve the cause of Brahman or Supreme Self, whatever you call it.

P: I see that you are already basking in the glory of genuine enlightenment. A spiritual glow is visible on your face.

VOYAGE - 5
GOD IS BEYOND WORDS

In Hindu mythology, sage Narada is shown as a compulsive gossiper carrying tales and creating conflicts. He cleverly exploits the vanity of gods, demons and even humans. But finally, all the episodes end up with the victory of good over evil. Chandogya Upanishad narrates the story of Narada approaching Sanathkumara, a sage of great renown, for more spiritual wisdom. Sanathkumara asked him, "Tell me, what have you already learnt from others?"

Narada replied, "I know the four Vedas and I have also studied grammar, rituals, mathematics, astronomy and so on, including even snake-charming. But all the knowledge gained from competent teachers does not show the way to get over the feeling of sadness. I was told that only self-realization could remove negative thoughts from the mind. Please instruct me on the true knowledge of the Supreme Self."

Sanathkumara told him, "Whatever you have learnt so far are just words describing some finite phenomena. The 'infinite' is the source of ultimate peace and enduring happiness. It is not subject to any change and true knowledge about its immortal stature is the only source of unlimited bliss."

Narada then requested for more instructions about the infinite.

Sanathkumara said, "The infinite can be realized only when one understands the indivisibility of existence. It is for the faculty to see, hear and know things beyond the material world. If one sees separateness or tries to create more divisions, he knows only the finite. The phenomenal world will perish in course of time but the infinite will continue beyond death and decay."

Narada then wanted to know the actual basis or support of the infinite.

Sanathkumara said, "It is the only entity that depends on its own glorious existence. The mortals depend on worldly possessions like cows, horses, elephants, servants, wealth, and other things for sustenance. But all such objects derive support from others for maintaining life. The infinite does not need the support of anything for its existence."

"It is totally and truly independent. Those who meditate upon it can see its indivisible presence everywhere. The enlightened one is free from all fetters like fear, relationships, and possessions. He knows that everything, including his mind and the world, comes from Brahman. It controls the senses and makes the mind see its undifferentiated existence. Those who only seek the pleasures from finite possessions become blind to reality and suffer from fear of death and loss of relationships."

Narada thanked the teacher for the true knowledge of the infinite. He transcended the finite and reached the realm of the Supreme Self.

VOYAGE - 6
HUNDRED AND ONE YEARS OF LEARNING

P: Many people in Vedic times heard lots of wonderful things about Brahman. They were amazed at its qualities such as immortality, freedom from hunger, greed, and desire. The good as well as the evil were eager to acquire ultimate knowledge, which they assumed would give them all the great attributes of Brahman. They wanted to be invincible and enjoy life forever.

The good and the evil are designated in Hindu mythology as gods and demons. Here is a story of the gods and demons trying to learn all about the Supreme Self from a renowned teacher called Prajapathi. The leader of the gods was Indra, and Virochana was the chief of demons. They carried some fuel to show their desire to become disciples. Prajapathi allowed them to live with him for thirty-two years. After the thirty-second year, he asked them why they stayed for so long and what exactly they wanted to learn.

They said, "Sir, we have heard from sages like you that one who learns about the Supreme Self achieves all desires. It is pure, beyond death, fear, hunger and thirst. We lived with you to learn all about it."

Prajapathi said, " When you look into another person's eyes, what you see is the Supreme Self, that is beyond death and desires. It is also known as Brahman."

The disciples enquired further. "Great teacher, do we see it when we look into water or a mirror?"

Prajapathi said, "Yes, you see the same Supreme Self in all these reflections. Take a bowl of water and look at the image."

They looked into the bowl of water and saw their own reflections and said, "We see the Supreme Self, even the hair and nails are visible."

"Now, you put on ornaments and a good dress and look again, then tell me what you see," said the teacher.

They decorated themselves and looked at their reflections and said, "It is now well dressed with nice clothes and glittering jewellery."

Prajapathi told them, "What you have seen is the Supreme Being or Brahman. It is beyond fear and death, and free from all desires, thirst and hunger."

The disciples went away with a great sense of achievement and satisfaction. But the teacher was dismayed. He said to himself, 'Poor fools, they saw the Supreme Self, but did not recognize it. All that they learnt was that it is the body and with that false knowledge, they will indulge in all sensory pleasures. They will assume that the Self is enjoying all body-related functions."

The teacher was right. Virochana, the leader of demons, went back and told his fellow demons to worship the body, as it is the Self Supreme. He asked them to adore it and enjoy all sensory pleasures that give happiness. They forgot all about compassion and failed to see the same Self Supreme existing in all beings. That is how demons became utterly selfish and committed many atrocities for enriching themselves.

Indra, the leader of the gods representing various natural elements and virtues, felt some doubts about such knowledge. He thought, 'If the Supreme Self is the body, it would also suffer physical infirmities and all kinds of desires, death and decay. I don't find any wisdom in this knowledge. Something is amiss. I am being carried away by ignorance and a misplaced sense of achievement.'

So he went back to the teacher with more fuel for

further instructions.

Prajapati said, "Indra, you had gone away fully satisfied with my teachings. Then why have you returned seeking for more?"

Indra explained his doubts about what he had learnt.

The teacher was happy that Indra was thinking more clearly. He told him to live with him for another thirty-two years to learn more about the infinite Self.

After thirty-two years, Prajapathi said, "Indra, the Supreme Self is that which is watching you in dreams; it is fearless and beyond death and decay. It is also called Brahman."

Indra was highly pleased. He assumed that he had acquired the supreme wisdom. He went back to his fellow gods and taught them the newly acquired knowledge.

But when he thought more and more about the dreams. 'Well, it is true that what is watching the dreams does not suffer the infirmities and miseries of the body. But in dreams it suffers from fright, fears and desires. This knowledge is also meaningless.'

So, Indra went back with fuel and explained his doubts about accepting the dreaming self as Brahman. The teacher asked him to stay for the same span of time for attaining a higher level of knowledge.

After the stipulated time, Indra was given further existential wisdom. Prajapathi said, "The Supreme Self is the one who is in dreamless sleep when the mind is in a restful state. It is free from fear, death and desires and is called Brahman."

On his way back, Indra began some introspection. He thought, 'in the state of dreamless sleep, we lose awareness. We are as good as dead and gone. This knowledge is also imperfect as the Supreme Self is beyond any kind of extinction'.

He returned to the teacher to clear up his confusion. This time Prajapathi was more considerate. He asked Indra to stay with him for five more years for attaining ultimate knowledge. His total stay with the master was now one hundred and one years, which shows the tremendous perseverance required for self-realization.

This time, the teacher revealed the whole truth about Brahman.

"Dear Indra, your doubts are well-founded. It is true that Supreme Self subsists within your body. What you think, see, smell or feel are all done by its intelligence. The body and senses are only perishable instruments. They create an illusion that all these activities are done by the body. It is acute body awareness that keeps us away from self-realization.

When you rise above the powerful hold of bodily attachments, you will find real, transcendental nature of the Self Supreme. The one who understands this truth conquers the fear of death and desire for body-related pleasures. Brahman is consciousness that guides us from within, so long as life lasts. It leaves at the time of death, as pure and unattached as it entered the body on birth. The fact is that consciousness alone is eternal, and the one who realizes this truth overcomes the fear of death."

Finally, Indra understood the truth of existence, which he conveyed to other gods. They achieved the ultimate knowledge that fulfilled all desires and assumed compassionate wisdom as the guiding principle of life.

M: It is a wonderful way to reach the true understanding of reality. Indra took more than a hundred years of rigorous, ascetic grind to reach this goal. Those who are satisfied with limited and imperfect information cannot understand the meaning of existence. One should be motivated to pursue the spirit of inquiry and a competent teacher should guide through the maze of conflicting ideas. It is a long pilgrimage, but the reward of a life free from fear and full of joy is worth all the hard work.

P: Let us go through some more situations before we enter genesis.

VOYAGE - 7
MANAGER OF THE MIND

P: Kena Upanishad contains dialogues between a student and his teacher in a forthright manner. It doesn't create any context for initiation of the dialogue.

The student asks, "Tell me, sir, who makes my mind think, fills my body with the vital energy to work? Who sees and hears the world through my eyes and ears? Whose invisible hand makes my tongue utter these words?

I am really confused. Am I the doer, performer, and the cause of all my thoughts and actions?"

The teacher replies, "The one who sees and hears for you, thinks all your thoughts, and in short, guides your life, is the deathless Supreme Self. It is transcendent reality that is above the senses, mind, and matter. We can't describe its attributes nor can we comprehend and communicate its qualities. Being different from all that we have seen, heard and known, we can only experience its undeniable presence in all existence as the primal as well as the immediate cause and effect."

"I will try to make it clearer," the teacher continued. "It makes my tongue speak but I can't describe it. I simply do not know what it is. What is it made of, how does it create my thoughts, actions and understanding? No doubt, it is in me but where does it dwell, why is it there? I have only assumptions and approximations, no definite clues on its abode in my body or elsewhere."

The teacher said, "Those who think that they know the Supreme Being, are conceited persons carried away by limited understanding of external forms. There is only one way to know, meditate on it, and think about what it is not.

Only then you understand what it is. The empowered awareness to understand its absolute qualities is called self-realization. No teacher can tell you what it is. You will be convinced only when you experience it as a magnificent presence in your own mind. It cannot be realized so long as duality of the knower and the knowledge exists in the mind."

"How do I attain it?" asked the student.

"By upgrading awareness to a higher, undifferentiated level, by going beyond the separate identity of a perishable body and fickle mind," said the teacher.

"When you see the Self Supreme in all beings, you achieve the goal of self-realization. That leads you to a new vision of existence, seeing all beings in you and your presence in all kinds of life. When your ignorance is removed, what is left is only unlimited bliss of eternal existence," the teacher concluded.

M: Yes, I definitely feel its indescribable presence in my mind.

P: Maybe it is the beginning of your self-realization.

VOYAGE - 8
HERO NUMBER ONE

P: As I told you, in Hindu mythology, the gods do good deeds and demons indulge in destruction. The good and evil are always at each other's throats and hapless humans are placed in between. They pray for the victory of the gods over the evil demons. Every element in nature is represented in the pantheon of gods. They are worshipped with rituals and sacrifices to reap good harvests and success in all endeavors.

Don't mistake them for the real God who is indefinable, all pervading energy called Brahman. Below it, a second string of gods exists, which takes care of events like creation, maintenance, and destruction. The third level of gods represents various natural forces and life sustaining systems. This story gives us some more ideas on the real God who created the universe and controls all its manifestations.

In one of the many wars they fought, the gods defeated the demons. Actually, they won over evil-mongers with the help of Brahman. But in their ignorance, they boasted, "We, the mighty gods conquered the demons."

Brahman, the all-powerful, appeared before the gods. They did not even recognize it, as they were blinded by pride and ignorance. They sent the god of fire to find out what this mysterious form was and as to why it had appeared?

The mysterious form, asked the god of fire, "Who are you?"

"I am Agni, the god of fire. I am all powerful, I can burn down everything anywhere," boasted fire.

"Then try to burn this straw." Brahman placed a piece of straw before the god of fire.

Fire tried to burn down the straw, which is normally an easy task. But now, it remained un-burnt. Frightened, the god of fire ran back to the others and reported his failed mission.

Then they sent the god of air to find out the identity of the mysterious Being. He approached the unknown form.

"I am the god of air, the king of space. I am all powerful and I can blow away anything anywhere," he bragged.

Brahman placed a piece of straw in front of the god of air and asked him to blow it away.

With all his might, the god of air blew at the straw but it did not move even a little bit. He ran back to the other gods and told them the invincibility of the unknown being.

The new challenge upset the victory celebrations of the gods. They begged Indra, their king, to find out the true identity of the mysterious being.

Indra went to inquire but it disappeared instantly and in its place stood the goddess of wisdom. He asked her, "Who was that mysterious being?"

"That was Brahman, the one and only source of all power, glory and existence," she said. Indra realized that it is the power of Brahman that makes the mind think, desire and decide to act. The same power can be used to meditate and it is in the innermost part of the mind. The gods understood that Brahman alone is worthy of adulation, worship, and love. All other manifestations, whether good or bad, exist only in its infinite space.

M: This lesson is particularly useful in modern times. People try to achieve positions in life and material possessions by ruthless competition. They should realize that all achievements are worthless, in the absence of consciousness.

P: We will see that later; now let us go on to the last lesson.

VOYAGE - 9
FITTING FINALE

P: Now, we are on the last lap of our voyage of discovery. Before we consolidate the wisdom of Vedic thoughts, let us have one more short session.

The student after hearing the story of the straw requested the teacher to give him some more spiritual wisdom.

The teacher said, "I shall tell you whatever I know about Brahman. The body of spiritual wisdom consists of control of senses and desires, compassion, and selfless service to humanity. Scriptures are its limbs and truth is its heart. Those who understand the Supreme Self this way achieve eternal existence in universal consciousness. They conquer all evil thoughts and attain a state of undifferentiated awareness, in which all life is seen united with one thread. Follow the path of truth, compassion and selfless service. You reach not only the goal; you become an integral and indivisible part of it. That is the glorious life of the one who knows the ultimate truth of reality," the teacher concluded.

M: *Well, it was an exciting expedition, to the peak of knowledge. There is nothing left to know now and all my doubts are cleared. The essence of wisdom imparted in different situations reveal what existence is all about. The young and the old, the good and the evil, all can benefit from this ultimate wisdom. The concept of the Supreme Self doesn't find any parallels in human thought. It is truly the greatest human heritage.*

P: Now, let us move on to the mysterious domain of the mind. Our knowledge expedition will be incomplete without understanding the latest scientific discoveries on the mind. After all, we are trying to apply the wisdom of the Upanishads to the intolerant and competitive mindset of the modern world. In the next three chapters, we will see the physical basis of the mind and its capabilities. Then we will get back to the Upanishads for a more comprehensive evaluation of its relevance in the 21st century.

CHAPTER SIX
MARVELLOUS MOTHERBOARD

"The tree of mind bearing the creeper of thoughts has two roots. One is mobile bio-energy and the other is stable imagery. When bio-energy moves the nerves, the mind is born."

[Yogavaasishtha]

"But we have also acquired compassion for others, love for our children and children's children, a desire to learn from history and a great soaring passionate intelligence - the clear tool for our continued survival and prosperity."

[Carl Sagan]

"The universe exists only in your ignorant imagination. In reality, only you exist. There is no God or Universe other than the Supreme Self that gives you conscious perception."

[Ashtavakra Gita]

"Science is organized knowledge. Wisdom is organized life."

[Immanuel Kant]

M: *All right, let us see the distinct features of the modern mind that unleash terror and destruction. My understanding is that it is poverty, illiteracy and blind faith, which create a mindset that leads to excessive and unprovoked aggressiveness? •A terrorist is not born to kill; circumstances make him do it. That is conventional wisdom isn't it?*

P: That is an outdated assumption. In the past, outbursts of violence were invariably associated with immediate socio-economic causes. It gave a convincing explanation for any anti-social or inhuman act. Even popular and justifiable uprisings like the French Revolution arose as a protest against repression.

But the latest profile on violence, presents a different picture. A recent study by some Princeton scholars clearly reveals that indoctrination is the major cause for the spread of terrorism. It is incorrect to assume that the poor and illiterate are the only victims willing to die for any cause.

No doubt, in dire need, they might commit heinous crimes for a consideration. But, most of the modern terrorists are highly educated persons hailing from rich families. They are not the kind who can be bought out from the back streets of urban jungles. The fodder for the terror machines is far beyond material gains. They are also fully aware of grave personal risks involved in the operations and the enormous damage that can be inflicted anywhere.

M: *You mean to say; even today educated people are vulnerable to religious and political indoctrination? In fact, literacy and material prosperity should have strengthened the mind to resist brain washing for the cause of religion or nationality. What happened to the rational wisdom of science, which created all our technological wonders? Learning science is supposed to inculcate a spirit of unbiased inquiry into all features of life, isn't it?*

P: Mike you have an open mind evolved by liberal education available in a pluralistic society. There are still vast areas of poverty and ignorance on earth. The pockets of prosperity are definitely more literate but they are not capable of evolving an effective strategy to reduce intolerance. The problem with the mind is that, if the upbringing and education of a child in the formative years is not liberal, I mean, incorporating an attitude of benign tolerance for different viewpoints and value systems, it can acquire very dangerous and aggressive tendencies. The rigid social and religious instructions can induce powerful motivations to kill and die for a chosen cause.

In such situations, value systems imbibed through higher education remains solely cerebral without enabling the mind to question the exhortations of zealots. Instead, they invent clever justifications for any evil deed. Moreover, our current technical knowledge can extend the deadly reach of mental capabilities. The faith that promotes violence, also promises immunity from any kind of divine retribution. They are also assured of abundant happiness after death. The indoctrinated merchants of terror go on murdering the innocent and the defenseless without feeling any remorse or sadness. For them, death is not a deterrent; it is a stepping-stone to unlimited glory.

M: *So, you mean to say it is the tremendous power of indoctrination that holds them in something like a hypnotic trance. Do they truly believe that acts of wanton destruction can defend or promote a faith? Is it the right path to reach the kingdom of heaven ruled by a just and merciful God? What reward can they expect for destroying God's own creations?*

P: Mike, the fact is that we cannot treat the menace of intolerance simply by getting annoyed with it or by improving living conditions. We have to create a mindset capable of respecting other people's views. That is why we should know how the mind works and what motivates some of them to create havoc, while some others happily devote the entire life in the service of humanity. Remember, Mother Theresa lived only for serving the poor and sick in distant lands. She had no other objective in life.

M: *Agreed. Let us first get a general idea on the mind. Maybe it will enable us to identify the forces that take it either to the zenith of wisdom or keep it in a mire of ignorance. After all, what we wish to know is an effective way to make the mind more tolerant and compassionate. But keep it short and simple. You know, I am not a science freak like you!*

P: Mike, you cannot get a correct picture of the mind in a composite capsule. I shall try to keep hard science out, but you may have to put up with a little bit of jargon here and there. There is a glossary to guide you with some difficult expressions. I promise an exhaustive appendix that will give you the latest scientific knowledge on the brain and the mind.

You know, the mind is the ultimate biological boundary that sets us apart from other forms of life on earth. Historically, it has been kept at a higher pedestal from the physical body, which is subject to death and decay. In the west, pre-Socratics thought that the external reality was an illusion. But they considered the mind as an intelligent entity, capable of creating new ideas and executing them with finesse.

Later on, Plato and Descartes conceptualized the mind as a distinct and unique entity unrelated to frailties of the mortal body. They even attributed several celestial qualities to the mind and called it the spirit or the soul. Probably, they wanted to keep it away from the baser instincts of the body and its abominable afflictions.

The Eastern thinkers, particularly Vedic scholars, held a different view. The mind was an illusion for them; a bridge between external reality and the mortal body. They attributed the qualities of the mind to body awareness and needs and desires arising out of perceptual experiences. But they assumed that an external reality was underlying all objects of nature including the mind, which was considered eternal and unchanging.

They called it 'Brahman' or 'the Supreme Self' and propounded that its reflection in the physical body gave us consciousness, the mind and the idea of a separate identity. The material forms of existence are transient manifestations of an underlying objective reality. The spiritual attributes of the mind arise from the influence of an external reality that is entirely different from the mortal body and its short-lived capabilities. The potential for consciousness and higher mental faculties belong to the ethereal realm of universal consciousness.

After the Darwinian revolution that reduced human kind to well-dressed apes with bigger brains, Freud, began to unmask the mind that lies below consciousness. He divided it into two compartments. All socially unacceptable desires, like erotic thoughts, are usually consigned to an unconscious appendage of the mind that keeps evil tendencies beyond the reach of consciousness. Since it is inaccessible to the conscious mind, he conceived that we get only an occasional glimpse of its disgusting contents through dreams.

With the advent of more advanced knowledge and sophisticated probing devices, the mind is now laid bare and cold. Many disciplines like psychology, cognitive sciences, and neurosciences converged on it, to put an end to popular misconceptions on its mysterious qualities and ethereal capabilities. They used all the intelligence of the mind itself to prove that it is an unexciting non-entity.

The last few decades gave us immense insights into structural and functional features of the brain and emergence of the mind from its purely physical programs. Before proceeding further, let us first take a quick glance at the brain, which is the biological mother of the mind. It is the stage, where the mind performs all its cognitive and emotional magic shows. But, the pitiable truth is that the brain is just about three pounds of jelly-like biological matter. It doesn't contain any crystals that can create unknown capabilities or any niches, to nurture spiritual entities capable of transmigration to other bodies. In short, there are no phantoms in the mind.

M: That means the soul is dead.

P: Exactly. But it baffles not only soul searchers; the scientists are equally at sea, when it comes to mind watching.

The basic premise of scientific wisdom is that the output of a machine can be determined from functions of its constituent parts. But such physical laws completely break down in the realm of the mind. From the activities of the brain we cannot even remotely anticipate qualities of the mind that would emerge from its portals. Although we know that certain molecules like neurotransmitters do regulate our moods, it is not known how they influence the mind. The mechanical approach of science leads us to a dead end, where we scuttle between cells and molecules, in search of an explanation. The bits and pieces collected so far do not create a complete mind.

Now hold your breath. We are going a bit deeper into the brain. The first step towards a general understanding of the mind is that it emerges only in a conscious brain. The brain is undoubtedly the mother of the mind. The most important and recently evolved brain region is the cerebral cortex that gives rise to abstract thoughts. It contains the secret key to the mind and all its conscious capacities.

The brain comprises a vast network of about 100 billion basic functional units called neurons. They are specialized cells capable of conducting very complex activities, like processing of sensory and even extra-sensory inputs, maintenance and recall of memory, focusing attention and so on. Neurons normally function in clusters constituting exclusive micro worlds of network connections. They set up innumerable such columns that make bigger sub systems and systems. A system is generally meant for performing a specific function but some of them have the versatility to take over even unassigned tasks. Other structures like glial cells support neurons in many ways.

A neural column is something like a galaxy. Structures of different scales and properties like cells, microtubules, chemical and electrical pathways, communication cables and networks make it a beehive of innumerable activities. The cortex is the abode of all intelligent functions but there are other structures like hippocampus and thalamus that also perform vital tasks. Neural columns consisting of about one hundred thousand neurons each are the main workhorses of the brain. In the cortical area alone, about six hundred thousand columns function, to create the magnificent network of our mental world.

M: Are they not like computers processing information? I understand the brain is a biological kind of computer?

P: Not exactly. The neurons establish connectivity on the basis of our experiences. It is not at all like what happens inside fully wired computers we get from the market. The neural columns create a vast network of connections, which are evolved out of our perceptual experiences. The plasticity of the brain helps to make its own hardware to meet challenges of the external world. Out of the multitude of perceptions, tools are made for sorting out future experiences and planning for correct responses.

Even the most advanced digital machine cannot make its own blue print. A human mind has to tell it what to do, how to do it, and when to do it. With more and more experiences, neural columns of the brain can differentiate tasks to be performed and evolve smaller specialized columns to handle them. Simply stated, it creates its own tools for taking on the world.

That is not the end of neural complexity. Each neuron acts like an autonomous, miniature mind. Just imagine, approx one hundred billion mini-minds making up a mega mind! The neuron has several microtubules in its frame called "cytoskeleton". Inside the cell, genes command multifarious functions. They all behave in a semi-autonomous manner as if possessing some kind of free will. The chemical paths, electrical activities, memory storage, and many more mind-boggling mysteries make it a biological marvel.

The magnitude of the operations in the brain can be imagined, from the fact that on an average, a cortical column receives inputs from about two hundred thousand synapses. It sends about fifty thousand outputs. Unlike a computer, the brain does not rely on one mode of function. Neurons communicate, both chemically and electrically, which is beyond the capability of computers of the current generation.

Apart from a network of billions of neurons, the brain has several other structures, and cells. They are also involved in very important main line tasks. At the lower end of the brain, the brainstem regulates the basic functions of the body. Above the brainstem, the thalamus acts as a relay station for nerve signals. Hypothalamus is associated with activities like feelings of hunger, sex urge, feelings of pleasure and pain. It also sends specialized molecules to the endocrine systems for controlling production of various hormones.

The outer part of the brain has two separate lobes known as cerebral hemispheres, which are closely connected by a thick cable of nerve fibers. The temporal lobes of the brain are involved in hearing, memory, learning, and emotions. All higher functions of the mind and brain are performed by the cerebral cortex. It is the true custodian of our intelligence.

M: Please, tell me less about the structural organization of the brain. Rather briefly give me some ideas on its functions.

P: The organization of the brain begins between the third and fourth week after fertilization of the egg. The neural tubes developed during this period rapidly multiply to form the brain and the central nervous system. After the fourth week, cells at the top of the neural tubes form a curved structure that eventually becomes the brain. By the fifth month, the general outline of all-important features of the brain is established. The synapses between neurons develop after about the seventh month.

The neuron, which is the basic functional unit of the brain, is an ordinary cell containing certain additional features for performing cerebral functions. It has a tree like structure moving out of the central body with a lot of branches called 'dendrites'. They receive inputs from other neurons. The output junction of the neurons is another long fiber like structure called 'axon'. Nerve signals are exchanged through axons in a complicated process that involves both chemical and electrical signals.

M: It looks like a lot of scientific jargon to me. If required,

I will consult the appendix for more information. Let us now proceed to the mind. I will accept whatever you say about the brain as Gospel truth.

P: I will definitely give you much more information on the structural and functional features of the brain in the appendix. But now kindly listen to a little more on its basic chemistry for a better appreciation of the complexity of this mega computer.

Recently, lot of attention is focused on special type of molecules called 'neurotransmitters'. Now we have fairly accurate ideas on the functions being performed by such molecules and their consequential effects on the mind. They are ·actually responsible for creating perceptible changes in mental states.

Many of the maladies affecting the mind are now traceable to the deficiency of certain neurotransmitters. Simply stated, it is the chemistry of the brain that decides our perception, emotions and behavior. The study of the chemical messengers indicates that we are not any special creation, as we would like to presume. It is the chemical environment of the brain that decides the state of the mind and our destiny. The role of specific neuro-transmitters like dopamine and acetylcholine in Alzheimer's disease and Schizophrenia are now well established.

M: I understand that some of them are the real causes of chronic stress and anxieties.

P: Definitely. But as you said, let us not get involved in the affairs of neurotransmitters.

I have given you a very brief overview on the prominent features of the brain and its chemical conundrums. Let us now see how it functions to create a wonderful world for our existence. Unlike computers, the world of nature does not work on the basis of symbolic representations. Numbers and words do not run the brain, but patterns and images achieve the task more effectively. They collect data on objects and situations passively by creating stable impressions and storing them in neural nets. Consistencies in patterns help the network to recognize an object.

M: I am relieved to know that. Better to be human than a mindless machine.

P: In digital computation, words and numbers are used to create a super store of classified information. With such symbolic representations they can carry out certain given tasks, but cannot reach even the lowest level of consciousness, that we find in some animals. In more advanced neural net computing, we simulate the nervous system on a computer with a corrective feedback. Consistencies of responses and familiarities of object patterns recreate a miniature version of the real world in the system. These machines learn by experience and that knowledge is derived autonomously. Neural columns of animals also create similar conscious capacities by learning from experiences relevant to their existence. We cannot rule out the possibility of computers with neural nets becoming conscious, perhaps some time later in the distant future.

M: Let us hope that we will create metallic monsters only in fictions and films. We already have more than enough human problems to solve. The last thing I would like to see is the real life version of horror scenes in science fiction.

P: The neural network in our brain does both digital and analog computing. This capacity, we acquired some time late in our evolutionary ascend. We create symbols on the basis of analogue impressions and use them for faster and more powerful computing. The language we speak so effortlessly is an outcome of our capacity to create symbols.

It is like having two minds; one related to symbolic representation of reality and the other, emerging from storehouses of data collected in analog computing. The symbolizing mind is more proactive as it can go deep into the world of abstract thoughts by retrieving information from memory.

M: Tell me, how the brain creates a huge memory bank and uses it without making any conscious effort for retrieval? Where is the data parked?

P: In all probability, our memories are stored in neural nets, not in single neurons. It may be in electrical or chemical form or in a combined matrix. We do not know the exact mechanism used for storing data in different kinds of compartments. Most probably, strengthening of certain synaptic connections by the so called 'long-term potentations' does it. Enhancing the growth of neuronal contacts and keeping them in stable patterns by molecular activity creates what we call memory. For retrieval, a signal should reach the neural network to retrieve the stored data and place it in the narrow space of consciousness. The signal for retrieval may be given automatically without our awareness.

Nervous system of apes does not have the capacity for automatic recall. Computers do it by scrutinizing memory files. In our brain some molecular device acts like a ghost sorting out impressions, putting them in appropriate files and retrieving them on command. Maybe, our capacity for symbolic representation is the key to the secret of memory storage and retrieval.

Before we leave the brain, let me give you a brief account on its electrical activity, which has been extensively studied to trace the functioning of various systems. Beta waves appear during conscious functioning of the brain. They originate in ionic currents released by the activities of neurons. In relaxed state, alpha waves are seen and complex patterns are observed in the state of alertness. Undoubtedly, electrical activities are related to the level of attention. The electrical patterns of the brain appear as early as in the third foetal month. First it comes as regular slow theta and delta rhythms, which we see in children. Electrical rhythms also vary during different stages of sleep. The waves produced while dreaming are similar to the ones in conscious state.

Lastly, let me tell you something about a structure lying deep in the middle brain, which is not associated with both the hemispheres. It is the pineal gland that regulates our sleep and wakefulness. Descartes thought it was the seat of the soul. When 'melatonin', the hormone that it secretes, is at higher levels, we fall asleep. But in addition to the melatonin level, many other factors control our biological clock. All that it shows is that we cannot pin down the origin of consciousness to the activity in a particular area of the brain. Anyway, there is no soul or spirit hiding in the pineal gland. That is a certainty.

Now, that we know some basic features of the brain let us move on to the more intriguing avenue of awareness.

M: I hope for a more intelligible treat in your wonderland of consciousness.

CHAPTER SEVEN
IN THE WONDERLAND OF CONSCIOUSNESS

"Like the sun illuminates the earth, consciousness makes the world visible to us. The knowledge that it is the cause of all existence sets us free from the fear of death."

[*Ashtavakra Gita*]

"All elements, all creatures that walk, fly or crawl are guided by pure consciousness. The universe subsists in consciousness and those who realize this truth transcend death."

[*Aitareya Upanishad*]

"Self-realization is the vision of harmonious existence of all beings in the ocean of consciousness. It is the truth of reality that dispels all dichotomies from the mind."

[*Brihadaranyaka Upanishad*]

"God is subtle, but he is not malicious."

[*Albert Einstein*]

P: As you know, our awareness or consciousness lights up the arena where the mind emerges to perform fantastic magic shows. Let us have a look at the process that gives us the awareness to perceive the world and ourselves. Many people have the misconception that the mind itself is consciousness. The fact is that only when we are conscious, self-awareness, intelligence, and other known faculties of the mind get activated.

The all-important state of awareness is not an exclusive human property, but the mind more or less is. Every form of life, whether it is a worm or a whale, can be sensitive to certain environmental stimulation. Like humans, many animals also have sensory and memory equipments in the brain. What they definitely lack is the complexities of our cognitive capacities. It shows that the nature had the knowledge, that at least a rudimentary form of consciousness is absolutely necessary for survival of its creatures. Doesn't it suggest that   awareness is an innate quality of the initial entity? Otherwise, can it create a mechanism in a biological body to receive and respond to the trillions of signals from the environment?

M: I agree. It makes the mind more complex. More miles to go before we understand its mysteries; Well, let us see what exactly is consciousness?

P: Mike, there is no easy way to unravel consciousness. The evidences available so far indicate that awareness is a graded capacity gained by organisms commensurate with their evolutionary ascent. The primate nervous system that we inherited was designed about sixty-five million years ago. Humans with advanced cerebral capabilities are a very recent addition to about twenty million species of life sharing the biosphere. In fact, rapid development of the human brain and its conscious capacities are less than fifty thousand years old. In the cosmic time scale, such short spans may not matter. But here we are with a highly evolved mind trying to understand our own consciousness and its creative abilities. And it all happened in no real time. I don't know whether it is our achievement or it all belongs to the infinite qualities of consciousness.

M: *If human body and mind are the products of evolution, why don't we display all capabilities of other forms of life from which we emerged?*

P: Yes, you are right. Human body and its conscious capacities retain several common features of the chain of species that we passed through in our evolutionary adventure. Perceptual abilities of mammals and their awareness and memory show clearly that our consciousness is not a unique quality conferred by a benign nature. Moreover, basic design of the nervous system of mammals is of somewhat similar scale like ours and their neurotransmitters also perform identical functions. It all points out to the path of evolutionary adaptations.

But what really distinguishes us is the size of our brain. As compared to average mammals, our brain is six to seven times larger in size. Elephants and dolphins have bigger brains but their body-brain ratio is just that of average mammals. Most of the nervous system of the elephant goes into service of its huge body. Mike, new areas of your brain are mainly meant for creating the mind, which is the most wonderful invention of nature. Next to humans, chimpanzees claim pride of place for its brain size.

M: *But I don't have either infrared vision or the capacity for echolocation. Nor can I fly away to distant continents in winter with a neural map to guide my tour. Tell me, even with the gift of the best brain size, why am I so poorly equipped with selective sensitivity?*

P: You are also not given the handicaps of a fish or a bat. With your mind, you invented devices to take you everywhere on earth and even to the moon. What more can you expect to achieve from just three pounds of biological butter? The tools you created have capacities for infrared vision and echolocation. It is better to inherit infinite mental capabilities rather than some limited add-ons like infrared vision. It is the choice of nature that precluded certain ornamental capabilities from our property list.

Now, let us not digress from awareness. All our mental structures have deep imprints of the evolutionary expeditions of ancestral species. We also retain in the brain and body certain vestiges to remind us of family roots. The remains of the tail and propriospinal tracts are legacies that recall our colourful past. They are also solid evidences for the fact that the mind and the body are products of evolution, not exclusive gifts from any benign entity.

M: I understand that evolution is a very slow process. Then, how would you explain the sudden and inexplicable developments in the human nervous system, in a very short span of time?

P: Radical changes like terrestrial shift in a basic structure normally happen very rarely. When aquatic life invaded land, they had to restructure their entire body including neural capabilities. The blueprint of our brain was created some 200,000 years ago. We inherited it from the apes who had highly evolved cognitive centers like neocortex and cerebellum in their brain. The expanded frontal cortex and improved wirings in neural network are our latest acquisitions. But we still carry in the brain most of the sensory and motor mechanisms of the great apes. The rapid growth of tertiary cortex and mental abilities probably belong to a different mechanism of evolution triggered by cultural and linguistic catalysts.

M: *I accept that I am an improved or updated version of an advanced ape. I can't question your scientific evidences of evolution. But that is not giving me a clear idea about the emergence of my mental faculties. Tell me, why is my awareness so acute as compared to that of my monkey cousins. Why did the poor creatures fall by the wayside?*

P: That is because most of the improvements in our brain were in the regions associated with consciousness. Higher conscious capacity that distinguishes us from animals is mainly related to monitoring and supervising of mental functions. We create symbols of the external world; own self, thoughts and even emotions. Our thoughts are conveyed through language that gives us the ability to communicate with symbolic representations. But, it all happens only when we are conscious.

M: *How do we become conscious? Is it through activities in the brain modules or some input from external sources? Do we have a biological switch to turn it on and off?*

P: Well, that is a difficult question. Consciousness is a state in which we are awake and alert. Unlike in sleep, dream or coma, our mental faculties become active in awareness. In the waking state of animals, we find conscious activities related only to their basic needs. Anesthetic and such other drugs that affect our consciousness can also produce similar effects on animals. In our consciousness, faculties like self-awareness, linguistic abilities and the wisdom for right choices arise, as if they were always present elsewhere. But, latest scientific studies tell us a different story.

Recent laboratory experiments reveal that consciousness is an awfully inadequate mechanism to achieve such unique cerebral qualities. The evidences indicate that the window of consciousness opens for a very brief period, only fifteen seconds. Our short-term memory can hold perceptual experiences only for a fleeting short span of time. We create an illusion of continuous consciousness by cleverly adding up several short-term memory episodes. Without such skilful deceptions, we would have been mindless morons.

When we come to spatial dimension of consciousness, the findings are more shocking. William James demonstrated convincingly that a single perception could hold only seven distinct things. The golden rule of seven plus or minus two applies to all our cognitive faculties. Even our imagination is a slave to this spatial dictator. We cannot escape from the cruel constraints of the fifteen seconds in which only seven dwarfs can be held. That is the way we are created.

The ignominy of limitations is endless. Our awareness is vulnerable to all kinds of distractions. Any sudden change in sensory signals can interrupt our conscious efforts to hold on to a particular mental task. The mind can be easily enslaved, at least temporarily, by a strong environmental challenge. If stressful circumstances persist, it may even break down with fatigue. Unable to cope up with the multitude of challenging tasks, it might even run away from the field of awareness like a fugitive.

M: You make me feel sad. Am I all that badly endowed? The great civilizations, the vast treasure of knowledge, and the magnificent achievements in science and technology, are they all from the fifteen seconds awareness? It is difficult to believe, but you say that the proof is formidable.

P: Don't lose heart. We are magicians capable of creating continuity even from an incoherent stream of discreet awareness. We can assume, presume and edit the inputs in some unknown regions of the brain. But all the same, we cannot alter the physical fact that we have a very limited conscious capacity. What we create out of it is another story. We will come to that later.

M: *Tell me about the other depressing findings of mind-breakers? Did their myopic vision show only a vacuum? I am now fully prepared to hear the worst. Maybe you are going to prove that I don't even exist!*

P: Exactly, that is what Danniel Dennet said. The modern mind-watchers refuse to accept existence of the mind or its conscious capacities. They are willing to concede that some kind of cognitive demons exist in the unconscious brain. These demons conceive, execute and even control external events. Consciousness is a helpless witness compulsorily watching the intelligent output of the automated demons.

The assumptions of conscious capacities of the mind including self-awareness are all just illusions with no physical basis or relevance. According to them, the complex neural network is capable of becoming aware of itself, solely by virtue of its biological functions. The conscious state is a by-product of neural activity and nothing else. You are right; Mike, you don't exist; a few atoms and molecules in the brain are the real heroes. You are probably the beneficiary of continuous cognitive fireworks in the neural network. At best, you are a biological robot capable of achieving consciousness autonomously. Science cannot find any higher pedestal for you.

M: *If I am only an advanced robot, how did I get all my cognitive abilities? Do the demons in the brain invent them or did an external agency like IBM or Microsoft supply the software to be installed after rebooting?*

P: Well, it is like this. Consciousness has no hand, even in creating our thoughts. They are projected to the conscious state by sensory tools in association with memory. Some scientists concede consciousness to the status of an internal mirror that simply reflects external reality. It is devoid of any meaning or significance. The reflection shows qualities of the mirror and not the viewer.

M: *Okay, if consciousness is only a mirror, tell me who is the viewer? A mirror is useless without a viewer.*

P: The mirror and the viewer cannot be one and the same. But can science accept an external viewer for the cerebral show. It is prepared to assume language as the interpreter of our conscious thoughts. The self-conscious mind is a product of culture without any neural basis. It is pointed out that before the acquisition of linguistic abilities, no mind could have emerged in the brain.

Noam Chomsky has a major role in propagating the idea of the modular mind. His school of thought grants it only the status of a central processing unit (CPU). It has just enough computing abilities to access simultaneously end products of the processes in other modules. We integrate sensory and emotional inputs in conscious state but it has no control over other processors and their independently evolved software.

M: *You are trying to reveal the source of mental software. Has it evolved automatically during the past twenty million odd years? The unconscious mental modules of speech and grammar are not gifts of atoms and molecules, are they?*

P: What else do you expect from the apostles of scientific wisdom? They are not willing to give any credit to the conscious mind. We think, talk and feel in unconscious modules. Dennet has hard evidence to prove it. The neurosurgeon, Benjamin Libet, drove the last nail into the coffin of consciousness. He found that we become aware of a sensory impulse much after its arrival in the cortex. Similarly, our decisions and actions reach consciousness, after they are concluded in unconscious processes of the brain. We do not feel the time lag and that gives us the false impression of having a powerful mind.

The cultural and linguistic aids that convey symbolically the external world to the conscious mind conceal this truth. Are we not easily fooled by the number of frames in a film? We thoroughly enjoy the experience of watching a motion picture, without knowing that actually nothing moves in it. The projector creates an illusion of motion and we are suckers, caught lock, stock and barrel. The dumb show gives Hollywood billions of dollars and intelligent apes enjoy the sensation created by fast moving frames of some still shadows. They can make us laugh or cry! What a humiliating spectacle!

Donald Hebb, proposed an electrical model of awareness based on local activity in a specific group of neurons. Karl Pribram suggested that awareness might also involve slow electro chemical activities in the brain. The stable features of consciousness could be attributed to slow and steady electrical activities in the microstructures. Another method used is called "averaged evoked brain potential", which tries to trace the origin of consciousness. It followed the ionic disturbances created in the brain by sensory inputs. They revealed a close relationship between the brain's electrical activity and conscious processing particularly in temporal dimension.

It is now well established that the source of our awareness is spread over several brain areas simultaneously. Our conscious experiences emerge from the functions of several brain systems in different areas. Every new task creates a fresh program that changes some of the existing functional and structural layouts.

The funny thing is that our awareness can penetrate anything except its own backyard. Scientists have no answer to this riddle. They do not want to concede that our capacities are far beyond the limited span of awareness. All that they wish to establish is that the process and the processor are one and the same. But it just doesn't click, like a mirror sans the viewer makes no sense.

M: *So, we are arch fools claiming credit for everything created by atoms and molecules. We have no mind of our own, no consciousness to rely on. Poor humans! Even apes are luckier. They don't have the consciousness to conjure up an exclusive identity with an eerie mind, to find fault with amorous adventures and selfish acts, don't you agree?*

P: Mike, don't rush to such depressing conclusions. We have to walk a little more to reach the mind. What is served here is just an appetizer; the main meal is yet to follow. Our discussion so far has been on the latest discoveries on the conundrum of brain and consciousness. Mind has much wider space and capabilities. It is much more than consciousness. We can have a clear idea only when the brain and consciousness are put together to create the wonderland of the mind.

The tricky question is, whether we can accept the fact that personal experiences of emotion, pleasure, pain and so on are only the by-products of trillions of atoms and molecules working in the brain. If not, how do we experience and what is the origin of such wonderful feelings? Undoubtedly, ordinary matter is incapable of experiencing our kind of awareness and emotions. We cannot credit them with the intelligence to perform autonomous functions involving the intervention of 'free will'.

Mike, I think this is the greatest riddle of life. Just imagine, who tastes the supper, I mean, life? Is it I, an illusion, experiencing the existence of an independent mind or the collective capabilities of trillions of mindless molecules in the body? Engaged with all these doubts, let us try to unravel the ultimate enigma, the mind.

M: I hope it is not another heavy dose of scientific materialism.

P: We cannot wish away basic science. It may be unpalatable but the bitter pill of truth is unavoidable. Don't forget the fact that our insight to ask these ultimate questions, comes from a scientific mindset.

CHAPTER EIGHT
MIND - MIRAGE OR REALITY

"The seed of the mind is 'I' ness that experiences thoughts and emotions. The mental impressions created by it give us the intelligence to learn all about existence."

[Yogavaasishtha]

"All I know is that I know nothing."

[Socrates]

"Those who know don't say.   Those who say don't know."

[Tao Teh Ching]

"The mind is at its best about the age of forty nine."

[Aristotle]

P: Isn't it interesting that in spite of scientific discoveries that revealed most of the physical features of the brain, even some Nobel laureates support the dualistic model of the mind. Although the modern dualists do not give the mind any spiritual credits, they do consider that it is entirely different from ordinary biological matter that makes up life. In the preceding two chapters, we have seen the close link between brain and consciousness. Let us now put together all our knowledge, on a single platform to create a harmonious model of the mind. I will try to keep it short without missing out on the essential features of this fascinating illusion.

An easy way to understand the mind is to see what happens in its total or substantial absence? Mindless existence is evident in serious mental disorders, drug abuse, and brain damages. Some unfortunate victims of such deprivations may be conscious, but not coherent enough for purposive action and thoughtful behavior. Like less evolved animals, they are driven by instincts rather than intelligence. The clinical studies of brain damage cases and the behavior of certain less evolved forms of life, give us certain clues on the travails of defective minds. We get a comprehensive conceptual frame of the mind from the massive data collected by psychologists, neuroscientists and cognitive and artificial intelligence scholars.

Apart from performing the basic function of facilitating survival, the mind has many interesting qualities, like artistic and spiritual aspirations, caring and compassion, moral and ethical compulsions, and so on. They all emerge from the neural network of a conscious brain. It creates a unique identity and capability to experience the physical world, emotions and thoughts in an intelligible manner. All such emergent qualities of a conscious brain are compositely called 'the mind'.

M: *But you promised to put the mind in a nutshell before
we go on to the Upanishads. Tell me in very simple terms,
what exactly is this mind, where is it located and why does
it come alive only in consciousness, with many cognitive
capacities.*

P: In the hardware of the brain, we do not find
anything other than biological matter and a continuous
torrent of electro-chemical signals. The intriguing question
is, whether consciousness and an intelligent mind can
emerge out of electrical and chemical activities in some
special brain cells. The brain has only atoms and molecules
that perform innumerable functions in an inexplicably
coordinated manner. It has no place for ghosts who can
supervise or monitor any work. The brain functions are
mostly performed in an automatic mode.

Moreover, electrical activities of the brain indicate that
consciousness does not arise from any one area or system,
as many systems are involved in activating it. Some brain
areas perform different functions simultaneously, owing
to the quality of super plasticity. The interchangeability
and coherent performance of brain systems make the task
of locating the mind, a formidable challenge even with
latest scanning devices.

There is no evidence to support the assumption that
the mind and the brain are made up of the same
substance. We cannot rule out the possibility that the
emergence of the mind might be related to some
uncommon qualities of matter like quantum coherence.
Maybe, the mind is some kind of unknown energy
accessible only in awareness.

Scientific studies have now reliably identified some of
the systems and sub-systems of the brain that deal with
different qualities of the mind, like memory, free will,
attention, language, and so on. But the surprising fact is

that such independent systems cannot create an integrated mental experience, on their own. Simple consciousness in lower forms of life cannot give them all the exquisite experiences that we get in our enhanced awareness.

M: *All right, but tell me if the mind is only a receiver of the outcome of the brain processes in a conscious person, can't the brain continue to work without its mediation or interference? Why do we need a mind at all?*

P: That is a good question. The brain can definitely perform several functions autonomously. It has to simply follow instructions of inherited intelligence, which sometimes get modified by relevant experiences of the past. But the brain can, after all project only processed information like images on a computer monitor. A more appropriate comparison is; the television screen that processes incoming signals to intelligible images for the viewer. The signals are integrated and projected for viewing on a screen, but the screen is not the viewer. The map needs a map-reader to create sense out of a multitude of lines.

The fact is that tools like screens, monitors and maps are incapable of experiencing qualities and properties of images processed by them. The brain is just a tool made out of a multitude of biological cells. Even if it becomes conscious without the mind, we cannot experience life of the same kind and quality. We cannot simply write off the mind as an unknown, non-physical entity. That is why I try to converge all the latest scientific knowledge on the brain and consciousness to find out more about its non-physical qualities and ethereal existence.

M: *Tell me, since this wonderful faculty cannot be located in any particular part of the brain, can it be just an assumption or a structural reality in the neural network? Does it include both the conscious and unconscious compartments of the brain?*

P: It is true that we do not know the exact physical location of the mind or consciousness in the brain. Mind arises mainly from activities in the cortical regions of the brain of a conscious person. The mental faculties we possess now are probably acquired during billions of years of evolutionary ascent. We have seen that many animals also have cerebral cortex but they do not have an intelligent mind of our kind. The size of the brain is a very crucial factor in creating a complex neural network, from which the mind emerges with all its glorious qualities. But size alone is not sufficient to create mental capacities; they also depend on connectivity of the basic units with each other.

The first step in understanding conscious capacities of the mind is to figure out how the brain creates an integrated image of the world, out of billions of sensory inputs bombarding it simultaneously. The capacity to bind objects and events into coherent, identifiable images may not be available to all forms of life. It requires extraordinary capacity to detect patterns and similarities in the perceptual field, which contains a vast multitude of unrelated energy vibrations.

Binding process is essential to create an identifiable image for initiating more complex mental activities. Attention is an essential requirement even for the elementary form of automatic and unconscious binding that we find in certain lower forms of life. Integration of images in the perceptual field is definitely driven by the process of attention. We do not remember making any effort, as it is done instantaneously by instinct-driven brain processes.

Some scientists attribute high gamma range oscillations called "40-Hertz rhythms" for binding innumerable neural activities into intelligible features for our perception. These rhythms appear only when an object is in our field of awareness. It creates coherence in the neural circuits, while processing the signals from a particular object. Some others believe that mental abilities are evolved out of the basic capacity of the brain to bind the perceptual field coherently, by focusing attention. The question is that how do electrical waves in some neural circuits create awareness and conscious capacities like the mind? We cannot assume that neurons are capable of anticipating perceptual needs of an organism. The tools cannot read the message. They can only hold it for us to read.

M: *Yes, I wanted you to bring up this vital question. How can the unconscious activities of some molecules in cortical columns achieve the coherence that makes us self- conscious? And tell me, is it the neurons, the brain or the mind, which is becoming conscious? By the way, who am I? An awareness of self or the aggregation of atoms and molecules in the brain?*

P: The evolutionary explanation of the binding process suggests that it all began with selective attention focused on some features of the world relevant to a particular organism. But the mind is much more complicated than the simple process of attention. It requires not only a perceptual binding, but an active memory stick to carry the bound experiences for the current as well as future use.

The capacity to direct attention only to relevant objects and events in a multitude of vibrations in the perceptual field is yet another step required to understand the mind. Controlling of attention is a conscious process to keep out irrelevant features of the perceptual field. Thalamus, prefrontal and sensory cortices are all key brain structures associated with this process. They are supposed to rein in molecular urges to leave the perceptual field for greener pastures. The short span of consciousness makes it difficult to hold attention on some aspect of the environment.

According to Bernard Baars and colleagues, gateway to the mind is an elaborate neural network called ERTAS. The acronym stands for Extended Reticulo-Thalamic Activating System. It consists mostly of neocortical areas and works like a black board on which other brain systems project their messages. This neural device resembles a TV monitor on which the message becomes visible only when we are conscious. Baars considers that effective projection is possible only if there is continuity in self-image and the physical world is represented in relation to it. These studies indicate possible location for the mind without revealing its source or capabilities.

M: *So, they assume that the projector or monitor has also the capacity for reading and understanding. The process itself should monitor the output. But some time back, you said that our awareness couldn't understand even the automatic processes going on in the brain. How then can you suddenly give a contradictory view?*

P: Don't forget that we are still considering some tentative ideas on the mind. The latest model of the mind is based on brain structures supporting short-term working memory, perceptual binding capabilities and automatic skills. In addition to these structures, which are common to most of the mammals, apes and humans have highly developed tertiary cortex areas. We may be creating in ordinary awareness, an image of the self, which is sustained with the help of supporting structures.

It means that we create a much bigger mental space from the minimal awareness, consisting of fifteen seconds and seven objects. Action areas like vocal cords must have assisted the gradual evolution of the mind. The 'perceptual ego center', which is scientific jargon for the mind, can control actions, thoughts, and even emotions. According to scientific explanation, our self-consciousness has evolved out of rudimentary awareness of the first live cell that brought biological existence to the biosphere. It is a model made solely of atoms and molecules. We have managed to demolish phantoms in the brain and replaced them with something like molecular motivation. Of course, no explanation is offered on the unknown force that motivates the molecules for more exciting evolutionary adventures.

M: *Okay, we redeem the non-physical mind by calling it the ego center, located in the entire neocortex. The perceiving self is accepted as a reality, no more illusion. It has the respectability of an exquisite wine of billions of years of vintage. The ego center uses all brain areas, sees projections emanating from each segment, evaluates, and suggests modifications and, in short, gives us back a respectable mind of our own, doesn't it?*

P: I don't want to dissect the mind further. Whatever we assume, it is definitely a self-referential point comprising of perceptual awareness, various kinds of memories and many more conscious capacities. The subjective representations of the external and internal world are projected in mental space in a sustainable loop. Our linguistic abilities extend its faculties further by creating an exclusive world based on symbolic representations that can be transmitted to future generations. In this process, more complex and abstract thoughts are created to unravel mysteries of the material world.

It is intimately related to the cultural environment as brain structures get continuously rewired by fresh external and internal inputs. In fact, super plasticity of the brain changes neural connections with every new experience. If the connections are strengthened by repeating the physical experience or its related thoughts, they become stable memory. The ego center can retrieve the changes in the neural network at any time just like its older acquisitions.

No doubt, the conscious mind is not only a perceiver of the external world, but it also enjoys a unique and meaningful existential experience. The accumulated mental impressions create the distinct identity of an individual, which is fused with the image of a physical body. The conscious mind is capable of categorizing its experiences of various objects and events. But the effects of hypnotic suggestions indicate the possibility of unconscious brain processes automatically registering sensory inputs and storing them for future action. It shows that the mind can be conditioned in a substantive manner by environmental inputs, without any active attention or conscious effort.

Normally people prefer choices that enhance sensations of pleasure. Continuous exposure to benevolent thoughts and experiences creates the highest mental quality of compassionate wisdom. It enables the mind to transcend the narrow band of body related interests and inclinations. Persons endowed with compassion devote more time and resources in the service of humanity, like helping the poor and the needy, preserving the environment, and so on. Mike, that is your mind in a nutshell.

M: I must admit that you described the latest position on the mind without dragging me into a muddle of scientific jargon. Now, I am fully aware of what I am; certainly not an irrational assumption but a substantive piece of existence.

P: It is an impossible task to describe the mind more clearly although we all enjoy its amazing qualities. Our language is inadequate to describe its non-physical existence in the realm of personal experiences. The perceptual experiences that the mind receives from processes carried out by brain cells, create a unique world of mental imagery. We cannot communicate effectively, all the nuances of the imagery and the feelings they invoke on various occasions.

This is in spite of the fact that the external inputs, which the brain receives, are mostly in the form of energy vibrations in different frequencies. How such vibrations are converted into meaningful experiences of reality is still a mystery that we tried to unravel with inputs from modern science. I am happy that you got some clear ideas on it, before we try to understand the Upanishads.

The mind experiences its own existence as a composite entity inseparable from the body. It gives us an integrated self-image called identity, in spite of the fact that the body contains trillions of different kinds of semi autonomous cells and cell clusters, performing specialized functions. The mind is also capable of controlling certain brain processes like attention and memory through conscious efforts. But many of the common attributes of the mind are derived from unconscious activities of the brain and the mind is not aware of what is going on in its own domain. It relishes supper without knowing anything on the source of food or identity of the chef. What is really astonishing is that the mind claims everything cooked up by the unknown source as its own creation.

We can understand the mind better, by tracing its development from early childhood. In infancy, we have a very low level of consciousness, which is not capable of giving us an identity or separateness from the external world. It is true that the child is born with a brain structure fully equipped for establishing trillions of connections. All brain cells are active within a few months of birth and the brain reaches its full weight of about 1.4 kilograms in about 6 years. But, it cannot recognize objects and events or take any meaningful representation of the world in early infancy. The first stage in the emergence of the mind is an increase in the level and quality of awareness. It enables the brain to carry forward memories of experiences for recognizing various objects and situations. In highly evolved primates like chimpanzees, we find similar enhanced levels of awareness. They can also identify situations that enhance the feeling of pleasure. Chimpanzees are only one step behind humans in the matter of brain size and conscious capacities.

M: *You mean to say that we are born without a full-blown mind but brought forth all necessary tools to create one, according to our tastes and preferences?*

P: Exactly, in the undifferentiated awareness of early childhood, no distinction exists between the body and the outside world. The mind with a separate identity from external reality develops with addition of more and more neural connections at synaptic junctions. They are fortified by sustained inputs of experiences received from outside. A full-blown mind is developed only during early teens.

By that time, all connections in the neural network are more or less complete, and the idea of a unique identity gets firmly attached to the image of the physical body. It is something like encrypting an image on the memory mechanism of the brain. As I told you, plasticity of the brain permits changes in synaptic connections with every new experience. And the mind goes on extending and enlarging its capacities exponentially.

In adolescence, it gains more maturity by acquiring new capabilities to make intelligent decisions in response to various kinds of environmental challenges. The continuous clash of interests, created by reproductive urges, family and social bonds gives rise to a mature mind. By about eighteen, it is fully developed to take on the travails of adult life. In response to the innumerable challenges, it takes appropriate decisions and learns from experiences to avoid pain and enhance pleasure. Particularly, it takes great care to remain within the barriers set up by a watchful family and society. While learning new experiences, the brain continuously upgrades wiring in the neural network. If lessons are contextual and repetitive, they are stored in long-term memory, from which it can be easily retrieved.

M: *Can you explain, how parental and social influences affect quality of the mind?*

P: Evolution of the mind involves several complex processes influenced by genetic and cultural factors. The important point is that about 0.2 per cent of genetic differences causes all individual variations in the mental faculties. The average brain is capable of processing all sensory inputs with the help of memory to project a fairly adequate image to the mind. The neural pathways that conduct such brain activities are more or less common to all individuals. It is also a fact that we are all born with the same neural capabilities, but some persons are gifted with the faculty to maximize certain selected aptitudes.

The unfolding of creative abilities in a particular field may not be entirely attributable to genetic variations. It is influenced more by encouraging cultural factors. The cultural environment, in which the child grows, can even cause early or late emergence of the mind. Certain behavioral peculiarities like extreme aggressiveness, lack of compassion, intolerance and so on can be traced to some traumatic experiences of early childhood. Parental attitudes and social influences can also induce such bizarre behaviour. No one is a born criminal; violent tendencies are actually evolved in a cultural cauldron. With sustained effort, we can slowly create a more compassionate and caring mind. It is a kind of reverse brainwashing.

M: *We come across many reports of spiritual visions, hearing of heavenly voices, seeing UFO's and so on. Some people attribute them to a kind of spiritual spot or divine domain in the brain. Do you see any scientific basis for such extraordinary qualities?*

P: From MRI and PET scans on brain activities, scientists find increased temporal lobe activity during such strange occurrences. But the same spot is also active in mental disorders like schizophrenia and manic depression. Strangely, it is also associated with creativity. This area of the brain is critical for the emergence of an intelligent mind. But no definite evidence is available about any specific area of the brain associated with spiritual activities. The so called 'God spot', is probably yet another invention of some over active brains.

M: *All right, now please tell me, what happens when I dream. Am I not conscious while dreaming, and what is mind doing in dream space?*

P: The role of the mind, in dreaming is yet another puzzle. According to latest scientific discoveries, sleep is induced when activities of two neurotransmitters are reduced. Sporadic electrical waves are responsible for the loss of sequence and absence of causal links in dream events. Since external sensory and motor inputs are not available in sleep, the stored imagery in memory activates the brain for no particular purpose or sequence. Several interesting interpretations are available on the significance of dreams. Some people claim that it is necessary to refresh the brain while some others consider it only as an evolutionary hangover. Even divine intervention is claimed for dreams containing some directions for action.

But it is beyond doubt that dreams are caused by a purely physical process, originating in the brainstem. The electrical impulses that create dream imagery are of random nature. It explains the weirdness and irrationality of dream events. The conscious capacities of the mind are weak in dreams because of the absence of external sensory inputs and the lack of volition to create physical responses. It is present in dream space only as a witness and not as an active participant.

But in lucid dreams, the mind is more dominant as body awareness persists at a higher level. The mind can be partially detached from body awareness using psychotropic drugs or by pursuing intense meditation. In such situations it becomes a passive witness devoid of any emotional involvement in body-related events. Physical relaxation methods and yogic meditations seek to create mental detachment of this kind. Some people claim to have reached extreme state of self-realization through transcendental meditation. For them, transcendence is a temporary detachment of body awareness. It doesn't mean liberation from ignorance.

M: *So, what is your final solution to the puzzle of a non-physical mind in a conscious brain?*

P: Undoubtedly, the mind emerges only in a conscious brain. The brain consists of only organic matter and forces that we find in the physical world. But the question is, how can they give rise to a non-physical quality capable of performing intelligent functions. Some people consider that the mind comes out of an unknown quality of matter called 'proto consciousness'. This assumption gives a causal link between the brain and the mind, which is essential for a rational explanation. It also takes care of binding abilities that integrate fragmented reality into coherent images. The tentative conclusion is that, the mind is a state of energy pervading all over the cerebral cortex.

This finding may not be acceptable to reductionists

and defenders of artificial intelligence. They compare the brain to a computer and the mind to the software or the algorithm that operates it. Patrons of artificial intelligence claim immediate prospects of creating consciousness, even in a robot. It is true that mechanical operations like memorizing of data or performing repetitive tasks are much faster on a computer. But, it cannot perform any conscious task outside the boundary of the software created by an intelligent mind.

M: *Aren't we some kind of biological computers created out of ordinary matter with enhanced capabilities?*

P: It is in fact illogical to compare computer with the human brain. The computer works only within limited space of its program invented by a human brain. All structural and functional features of the brain are evolutionary acquisitions of millions of years of struggle for survival. Whatever we have achieved in the field of Computer Technology are results of the ingenuity of human efforts in creating hardware and software. It is like comparing a tool with the toolmaker, as the mind is the mother of all modern equipments. Even an advanced computer cannot add on more capabilities without some initial software to start the process.

It is indeed difficult for scientists to explain rationally the emergence of non-physical qualities of the mind from a biological organism containing nothing other than atoms and molecules. Even the closest scrutiny of the brain using latest sophisticated tools does not reveal any controlling mechanism for the computing processes or any receiver of experiences of pleasure and pain.

But the irrefutable fact remains that there is a mind that is fully conscious of its own identity in the material world. It acts as an observer, a receiver of the outcome of brain processes and has the capability to think and act wisely. Sometimes it can reflect upon the rightness of its own decisions. It experiences unique emotions, which are unrelated to unconscious processing of sensory information in the brain. They are also customized to each individual, in spite of the fact that the perceptual mechanism involved is common to all humans.

M: *What about the concept of "quantum mind"?*

P: Some scientists suggest that a quantum mechanical approach might solve the problem of the mind amicably for all concerned. If we attribute certain quantum qualities of matter to the brain, the mind can be explained in a somewhat rational format, by accepting non-physical behavior of matter at the elementary level. Our thoughts are like fluctuations in primordial vacuum that created the universe. The ion channels in the neural membrane are an ideal location for the occurrence of quantum phenomena, which could be due to neural oscillations, in the range of 40 Hz. It is difficult to conceive that consciousness and the mind are created by such oscillations. All that we can accept now, is that quantum coherence of the brain contributes substantially to emergence of the mind. But, it does not reveal the whole story of the mind.

The discovery of 40 Hz oscillations and application of quantum coherence to the mind are great milestones in our expedition into the unknown space of the mind. Now, we have machines capable of imitating various human qualities. Synthetic enzymes, can bypass billions of years of evolutionary time and processes. If the present trend in the development of evolvable hardware (EHW) continues, we may ultimately get the algorithm that can improve its own original configuration through trial and error methods and from past experiences.

The inventors of EHW already claim that end products

surpass capabilities envisaged in the initial design. It means that what is evolved is far more superior to what the human mind had initially conceived. In this scenario, it is quite possible that the mind that conceived the program may also get bypassed and marvelous new products with greater capabilities may emerge unexpectedly. An exciting future awaits mind watchers, who will find new conscious capacities like extrasensory perception, thought reading, extended awareness, and so on arising from ordinary matter.

Lastly, let us take a closer view of the evolutionary explanation of the emergence of the mind. According to protagonists of the evolutionary model like Steven Pinker and Daniel Dennet, all our actions, thoughts and emotions are evolved in relation to the needs of natural selection. They have identified several universal traits in human culture like promiscuity, male aggressiveness and female coyness as examples of such evolutionary acquisitions. It is pointed out that, the brain consists of several modules of evolutionary solutions to specific problems, like finding a mate, learning a language or behaving differently to changing situations.

They find in the mind, only a mechanical expression of the brain that holds all possible range of behavior patterns. It is considered analogous to the language we use to express thoughts. The fact that the massive cultural evolution of humans was dictated by the requirements for survival is undeniable. The mind is the critical capacity that shaped our destiny on the planet. Admittedly, it emerges from close interaction between the inherited characteristics, cultural inputs and acquired capabilities of an individual. Evolutionary assumptions alone cannot explain a composite quality like the mind that arises from activities of the brain. From the information available so far, we can only say that both nature and nurture contribute to development of the mind. In modern times, nurture gets more credit than nature, in creating a proper mindset.

M: After reviewing tremendous volumes of literature on the mind, you must have reached some tentative personal views. Can I have the benefit of your thoughts on consciousness and the mind?

P: Throughout our discussions, I avoided taking any definite position in this controversy. My idea was to give you all ingredients necessary to create a rational insight on the enigma of mind. Frankly speaking, I still do not know many things, but I do admit that brain activities including emergence of the mind begins with excitation or inhibition in action potentials of the neuron. We are not aware of the causal links in such activities. Neuro-modulations performed by transmitter chemicals are inexplicable purposive actions of inanimate matter. How does the brainstem know in advance, what effects a particular chemical can create in the brain? Such advance knowledge cannot come from evolutionary refinements in biological matter.

Then we find neurons behaving autonomously, creating their own connections guiding glial cells to reach target areas and associating with like-minded neurons. Do they have separate minds? How do they change synaptic connections based on past experiences? And can they create consciousness? These are questions that get no convincing answers from any quarter.

We do not know the physical origin of consciousness. But without consciousness, where is the mind? The mechanism that creates, stores and retrieves memory is still unknown. Mind is an evolved state of brain activity but consciousness is the light that shows all these things to our perception.

In my view, the mind is not as crucial as consciousness. We have to find the nature of consciousness that brings a personalized frame of thoughts, emotions, preferences and self-image to our perception. It gives us memories of the past and plans for the future. The mind that comprises of unconscious brain activities and conscious capacities has a definite origin in consciousness. Its qualities become visible only when the lamp of consciousness is lit.

As a last resort, let us go back to the metaphor of the mirror. Assume that at the time of birth, we have consciousness like a transparent piece of glass. It gives undifferentiated perception without distinguishing the self from the external world. As we grow, the mirror gets coated with more and more experiences that reflect the world; a composite image of the body and mind. The quality of coating given by experiences eventually decides clarity of the reflection. The mirror of consciousness can reflect the world, the body, the mind and all assumptions on personal attributes and achievements. The neural connections, memory and the entire brain process contribute to the coating, but the mirror that reveals them all is consciousness. The brain is real, our conscious capacities are definitely developed in its kitchen, but without the mirror, the whole world is lost.

The unpredictable breakthroughs in science and technology might unveil the origin and reach of all our conscious capacities. We can hope that the mind will eventually be guided by the kind of wisdom propounded by the Upanishads. When we complete our voyage through the Upanishads, we will be convinced that it reveals the eternal truth of existence and the rationale for accepting compassion as the ultimate wisdom.

CHAPTER NINE
INTELLIGENT VACUUM
INCREDIBLE CREATION

"The cosmic vacuum was the original cause of creation of the universe, life and our thoughts. Our achievements are only reflections of its infinite wisdom. Can any human subsisting in the endless ocean of consciousness claim originality or individuality?"

[Mandukya Upanishad]

"Tao is the mother of the universe. It is changeless and indescribable and pervades equally in all beings."

[Tao Teh Ching]

"My equation was smarter than I was."

[Paul Dirac]

"Imagination is more important than knowledge."

[Albert Einstein]

P: We have already seen that the stories of the Upanishads give a logical explanation of existence. In ancient times, different styles of narration and contexts were used to convey the core message to disciples. Here, I present the essence of the insights of the Upanishads that explain the process of creation and evolution.

Let us begin with the cause of creation, which is still an unsolved enigma to the scientific fraternity. They claim that the universe was created in a big bang about thirteen billion years ago. Immediately after the bang, the elementary particles appeared and the forces got separated. It was a kind of divergence from an unknown state of absolute convergence.

Science gives us no definite cause for the explosion or for the extremely dense and indefinable nature of the initial entity. But they do not tell us how a universe obeying physical laws could emerge from a big explosion. Could it be created by some Providence or by sheer coincidence? If the odds for creating such a wonderful entity from a vacuum is one followed by 229 zeroes, who could have accomplished the marvelous task? Who could have guessed the right number to win the biggest lottery ever? What an attractive price - a universe with so many glittering galaxies and stars!

We now know that the chances of emergence of a universe with all the necessary parameters for creation of stable structures like galaxies and stars are an astounding impossibility. It is simply beyond any cause conceivable by humans. But the very fact that we are here contemplating creation gives ample proof of the immense intelligence embedded in the initial entity.

Martin Rees, an international leader in cosmology, points out certain basic constants and values, which were essential for creation of the universe. They were not originally conceived by any intelligent physicist or a great mathematician. All ingredients necessary for creating the universe could be envisaged only by the initial entity that existed before the big bang. An explosion would not have conceived the accurate combination of numbers for making matter and forces, unless they were earlier imprinted in the primordial vacuum. From huge galaxies to the lowest form of life, everything contains matter and forces that were created in the big bang with great mathematical precision.

The enigma is what kind of a genius could have created the blueprint of a complex universe in which we are privileged to live? It is the most complex riddle that science is currently trying to unravel. The six magic numbers Martin Rees points out, as the recipe for our universe, are so crucial that if any one of them were not chosen correctly, we would not have emerged here to speculate on it.

The first number is 10^{36}, which shows how much feebler gravity is as compared to electrical forces that hold atoms together. If it were less than 10^{36}, the force of gravity would have been supreme. No evolution, no human kind and no irritating enquiries on origins, would have ever emerged. Gravity would have simply crushed everything. The reality is that we are here to enjoy life because some entity made so many accurate choices on creation of a universe containing matter and forces.

M: Has he not given an explanation for these magic numbers?

P: I will come to that later. First let us see some more basic numbers.

The second number is 0.007. It is the bonding strength of atomic nuclei. All 92 atoms starting from hydrogen and ending with uranium exist on the strength of the force that holds protons and neutrons together in the nucleus. This number also decides life span of stars. Compared to other forces, it has negligible strength that can act effectively only at very short ranges. But in the micro world, it is a dominant force that keeps stars burning to give us precious heat and light.

Value of Omega is the all-important third number that depends on the total amount of matter in the universe. It is the ratio of actual density to critical density and the ultimate fate of universe depends on the fact whether it is above or below one. The density of all known kinds of matter in the universe makes up to an omega of 0.04, which means we will go on a course of infinite expansion. But we do not know how much dark matter exists in the universe. It is definitely there, but we cannot detect it, as it does not emit any light.

The fourth is the value of Lambda, which is also related to cosmic expansion. Since it is a very small antigravity force, it helped the formation of stars and galaxies. The idea of lambda was conceived by Einstein, who later confessed it as the biggest blunder in his life. Although it is a very weak force, it offers stiff competition to gravity in the intergalactic space.

The Fifth number is also a small one (1/100,000) that represents the ratio of two energies. It is the ripple amplitude of microwave background radiation. The correct choice of this ratio was responsible for the condensation of structures in an expanding universe. The seeds of the diverse structures of the universe were sown in the form of ripples in the big bang. The original cause perhaps knew that the ratio should have the value of exactly 1/100,000. Any deviation would have been fatal for existence that evolved in the perfect universe.

The last of the numbers is three, which stands for

spatial dimensions. We assume time as the fourth dimension with a forward arrow. If spatial dimensions were less than 3, no life or structures could have existed in our universe. So it shows that all these calculations were done much before the big bang by primal intelligence that worked like a super fast computer.

M: *If everything, including numbers, the thermal contexts and physical laws came out of emptiness, only a magician could have performed such mind boggling feats, don't you agree?*

P: Martin Rees considers all such options. No scientist can accept the first and the most obvious possibility. The role of divine grace or intelligent vacuum is anathema to rational wisdom underlying scientific enquiries. That leaves us with the proposition of a strange string of coincidences. In fact, it is just a meaningless argument that leads us nowhere. At best, it gives only a honourable exit from a puzzle, which precludes solution.

Assigning everything to coincidence, is as irrational as accepting the grace of providence. Both explanations lack experimental evidences, except the fact that the emergence of the final product is inexplicable without one of them. They do not obey any physical law that supports material science and its worldview. The root cause of an intriguing phenomenon like creation cannot be found by substituting one impossibility with an equally inexplicable one. Anyway assumption of a supercomputer as creator is unthinkable.

M: *I read somewhere that Martin Rees proposed a 'multiverse' instead of coincidence to explain the cause of creation. What was that all about?*

P: The concept of 'multiverse' is as good as coincidence. Go on creating billions of big bangs and in one of them, all correct parameters to evolve a habitable universe, may be found. It is like an interesting observation of a scientist that if a monkey strikes at random on the keyboard of a typewriter, it may eventually create a Shakespearian classic. It may take billions of years, but we cannot rule out the possibility of the emergence of an outstanding piece of literature one day. 'Mutiverse' is also like winning a great lotto with very heavy odds. Don't forget the fact that the six magic numbers were fixed much before our great scientists identified the physical laws and patterns that evolved the universe. It is a fact that we discovered them but no human can claim credit for the original invention.

M: So you want to go for the providence option. You mean all these came from the wisdom of the greatest scientist.

P: I am not suggesting either providence or coincidence. But I would like to remind you of one thing. All our knowledge on the six magic numbers and the fact that the stars empower us through fusion reaction and so on came to our knowledge only in the last one hundred years. At this rate, we may get at all ultimate answers, may be in another one or two hundred years.

Till then, let us assume that an intelligent vacuum was the cause of creation. It is an undeniable fact that the greatest intelligence must have been working overtime to create a viable universe. The breakthrough in the year 2003, according to the journal "Science" was the discovery of an unknown force opposing gravity called dark energy, existing and pushing the universe on an inexplicable course of expansion. Don Kennedy, the Editor-in-Chief of the Journal says, "It stirs our imagination even though it challenges our ability to understand". Let us leave it at that. We have no option; there are many more coincidences like the six numbers. No one has any idea on such cosmic conundrums.

We can now explore the Upanishads to arrive at some

acceptable solution to the mystery of creation.

M: I agree with you. The insights of the Upanishads could probably give us some clue on the cause of creation and the various processes that culminated in the emergence of life and the mind.

P: We will begin with the Aiteriya Upanishad. It envisages the eternal existence of the Supreme Self or the Brahman, which was presumably an unmanifested entity. Any attempt to name or describe such an entity could only reveal our abject ignorance on its real identity. The Upanishads speculate that the worlds emerged out of its intractable thoughts. In other words, the intelligence of the initial entity was the real cause of creation. Scientific explanations like symmetry breaking, bubbles of uncertainty popping out of quantum vacuum, and so on, are much less convincing than the concept of supreme intelligence of the initial entity. Maybe, it was the thoughts of Brahman that appeared like bubbles or virtual particles in the primordial vacuum.

Such profound speculations may not give us any accurate description on the sequence of evolution of the universe. Modern science derived physical laws and basic numbers by observing the regularities and patterns in nature with sophisticated tools and accumulated wealth of inherited information. The relentless process of testing and verification now gives us the models that truly explain nature. But they do not tell us who envisaged the blueprint on creation of the universe and life in the first instance.

Nevertheless, let us see how Vedic scholars explain the process of creation and evolution of the universe and life. It may not have the mathematical precision and symmetry of the standard model or the Grand Unified Theory. But it will definitely make us wonder how ancient thinkers made such accurate observations without the support of scientific tools like the computer and telescope.

According to the Upanishads, the highest world created by primordial intelligence of the Self was 'ambhas', which is above the sky and the earth; the mortal world is at the middle point. Beneath the earth, there is yet another world called 'apa', which is in the region of water.

After creating the three worlds, the Supreme Self started thinking, 'What are these worlds without their guardians?' Out of its thoughts 'Purusha' emerged with no clear features or form. When 'The Supreme Self' brooded over the entity of 'Purusha'. It then spontaneously developed a mouth capable of speech, eyes for sight, nostrils for breathing in the air, ears for hearing, and so on. The sex organs emerged to contain the water of life to create off springs.

The guardians who emerged from the thoughts of the Supreme Self sought a definite form to live in, eat and procreate. The form of a cow was brought which they did not like nor did they accept a horse.

When the human form was presented, it immensely pleased their aesthetics. Then the guardians of the elements were asked to get into the body and function from appropriate places. Fire entered the mouth and became speech. Air became smell, the sun moved into sight, the plants, herbs and trees turned into hair, the moon became the mind, and the god of death entered the navel. The god of living water became the sperm and got into the sex organ. Hunger and thirst could find no particular place, so they were asked to live in all organs. They shared all organs, creating thoughts and actions to fulfill the energy needs of biological existence.

M: I feel a bit uneasy on the fast pace of your description of creation and evolution. You mean to say that after creation of the worlds, that might be referring to stars, galaxies and all that, the earth was chosen for life to begin. Humans were given the privilege to reach the highest level of intelligence by design and not by evolutionary forces alone. Evolutionists are not going to like all this mythical stuff.

P: Here, we are only trying to describe the process of creation as given in an Upanishad. The most important feature is the basic cause of creation, which is attributed to the thoughts of the Supreme Self. Once the cosmic intelligence installed in various forms of life began to interact, evolutionary variations might have modified the original blueprint, maybe to maximize the chances of survival of each species. Two essential requirements of evolution are acute competition with other species and intelligent adaptations to innumerable environmental challenges. The collective wisdom of the bacterial kingdom is the best example of sharing and communicating evolutionary information and collaborating with other species for survival. It reveals the guiding hand of the original intelligence in the evolutionary ascend of all species. That apart, let us continue with the Upanishads.

The Supreme Self knew that man could not survive simply on faculties like sight, sound and smell. He had to get energy from some source to make all organs function. So food was created for the children of its thoughts. It was brought out of water and when man tried to catch it with sight, he did not get it. The smell and sound of food also failed to satisfy his hunger. Finally, it was caught in the stomach and got digested. It empowered all internal organs to function effectively. They shared the flow of bio-energy generated by the digestion of food.

The most precious gift to humans came last. It is the astounding intelligence that enables us to understand life. When the Supreme Self reviewed its creations, they were found imperfect without its own presence in the guardians.

The words that are uttered, the breath that is drawn, the eyes that see and the mind that thinks and even the sex organs that propagate the species are simple tools to perform certain functions.

The tools are, after all, like the instruments of the clockmaker to indicate time, but not the knowledge of the correct time of day. They cannot perform the role of the perceiver who experiences the emotions aroused or can they think and act in a cogent manner. The creator found that the whole exercise was futile without its presence in the body. Then it entered the guardians by opening the skull. The entry point of the Supreme Self is called "bliss".

M: *Well, so you mean to say that is how the brain became the seat of consciousness.*

P: According to Aiteriya Upanishad, in all forms of life, the creator is present as the core element. It means that the intelligent energy is the essence of our existence. In different physical states like waking, dreaming and sleeping, we find its presence in varying degrees of intensity.

It is transmitted to the new generation through genetic instructions. The foetus has its intelligence kept in a dormant state. It undergoes transformations through various evolutionary stages to reach the human level. Finally, guided by the presence of the Supreme Self, it emerges from the womb with a brain having neural foundations capable of thinking and experiencing its existence in terms of pleasure and pain. Even neurons know how to establish the correct connectivity in target areas. We don't know who guides them in performing such delicate tasks.

While we are awake, the Supreme Self is in the mind, which is inseparable from personal identity. For convenience, we call it the individualized self. In dreams, it witnesses the dream events and in dreamless sleep, it becomes the potential for reaching awareness when woken up.

Our mortal life as separate individuals ceases when it is understood that we are just a spoke in a giant wheel of existence controlled by consciousness. The culmination of the process of evolution is the ultimate acceptance that the Supreme Self dwells in the mind as eternal and intelligent energy. We can experience this true knowledge of existence only when the level of awareness is enhanced to transcend body-related thoughts. It enables us to recognize the presence of the Supreme Self shining in all beings. It is not the undifferentiated awareness of early infancy in which physical and mental boundaries are merged. Both infantile ignorance and extreme enlightenment lead to the same state of mind.

M: *But the intriguing question is, what exactly is this Supreme Self or Brahman or universal consciousness or whatever you call it? What is it made of and what qualities and properties does it contain to create this vast diversity of existence? Is it the great creative genius that invented the magic numbers, physical laws and all that? What is its objective in making short-span human existence with immense intelligence?*

P: Many people speculate about this wonderful entity that created the universe. Some worship it as the almighty God or by whatever name or form in which it is known. Simply stated, it gives us our capacity to perceive the world through various sensory organs. The discriminating mind that can think, remember and perform various intelligent functions is its subtle expression that sustains our exquisite existence. Maybe, less evolved animals get only a smaller share of its presence. That probably explains their instinct driven life as compared to our intelligent thoughts and deeds. The difference may be intentional, not entirely accidental.

According to Aiteriya Upanishad, senses, mind and all kinds of matter are manifestations of different qualities of the Supreme Self. The animals are not given evolvable hardware or software to think and feel on the quality of life. They simply subsist within the boundaries created by genetic algorithm. We have an additional dimension of culture, the space containing the inherited and acquired wisdom of humanity.

The Supreme Self, according to Upanishads, is pure consciousness or a kind of unknown energy. It is the creator of all matter, forces and in short, all existence. From its eternal intelligence, emerges reality that is seen and heard through our sensory organs. Even after one particular physical form perishes, it continues existence in new creations.

It is pure consciousness that guides the material world in its pursuit of chosen functions. The world is visible and cognizable only when we are conscious. Death and decay are the inescapable destiny of biological life but consciousness is beyond all such eventualities. The enlightened one, who understands the Supreme Self, also knows the true meaning of existence. He reaches immortality even before death and enjoys the thrill of eternal existence in the mortal world. That is how he gets liberated from the chain of rebirths.

M: Before you proceed further, kindly let me recapitulate the scene of creation. We find highly improbable stories of creation in the Holy Scriptures of various faiths. Conflicting speculations create confusing scenarios on the process of creation even in scientific literature. Of course, what existed before the universe came into being is totally unknown. The western concept of universe before invention of the telescope followed the geocentric model proposed by Aristotle in 340 B.C. For several centuries, his ideas were accepted as the true description of existence.

In fact, we can find the seeds of reductionism in the explanations of relations suggested by Aristotle. It was only in A.D.1514 that Copernicus suggested, for the first time, that the sun is the center of the universe with planets orbiting it. In 1609, Galileo confirmed the proposition of Copernicus by actual astronomical observation of the movement of planets. The differential equations invented by Isaac Newton were used for explaining the movements and position of celestial bodies.

The astronomical equations falsified many fanciful accounts of creation in theological literature. Aristotle assumed that humanity existed forever without any evolutionary changes. Christianity and Islam approved the idea of creation at a definitive point in time. Until 1929, in spite of the knowledge about gravitational force, the theory of static universe was in vogue. But now, there is ample proof to support the big bang theory that explains Universe, time and space. Didn't I get the picture right?

P: Yes, I agree. Science gives us more accurate information about what happened after the big bang. For almost a million years after the big bang, there was no spectacular creative activity in the universe. It simply went on expanding exponentially and cooling down from billions of degrees Celsius to a few thousands. It was only when the temperature reached a comfortable level of a couple of thousands of degrees that electrons and nuclei overcame the electro magnetic attraction to create complete atoms.

Huge galaxies were formed out of tiny ripples released from the big bang. In computer simulations on the process of creation, we can verify theoretical predictions. It is seen that the cluster of proto-galactic fragments got merged over millions of years to create structures like galaxies in the real universe. The slower rate of expansion that caused re-collapse of the galaxies could have created rotating galaxies that we presently observe in the universe.

Stars were formed by the collapse of thick clouds of hydrogen and helium under their own gravitational attraction. Their internal temperature would have reached the high levels required for initiating and sustaining nuclear fusion reactions. The tremendous pressure developed by fusion reaction prevented further collapse of stars and sustained high levels of radiation, heat and light. The bigger stars might have used up their nuclear fuel at a faster rate and re-collapsed giving out more heat and light. The additional heat converted helium into heavier elements like carbon and oxygen.

Actually, life would not have originated in the universe without the formation of carbon in the core of bigger stars. When big stars exploded as supernova, heavy elements like carbon were thrown out into interstellar space. The stardust in interstellar space later on, re-collapsed into new stars. Planets like earth were created out of re-processed dust from explosion of the stars. In our planet, most probably, life began in a single organic cell about 3.5 billion years ago. Evolutionary changes over time diversified life that finally culminated into intelligent species called humans.

From the process of creation described in scientific literature, we find that some kind of energy would have existed in the initial conditions before the big bang. That unknown intelligent energy must have contained all known and unknown absolute qualities. But presently we cannot comprehend the secret of its great convergence. It could have been something like a neutron star or a point of infinite singularity or even a quantum vacuum. Or was it the dark energy that still goes on accelerating the infinite expansion in spite of the pull of gravity. Whatever it was, the universe undoubtedly emerged from that original seed.

The primordial energy, according to science, is the substratum of all kinds of matter and forces in the universe. All forces were united firmly in its infinite hold. The diversity of structures that we now find in the universe is derived from its ancient wisdom. Without its inherent intelligence, correct values for physical constants could not have emerged for creating a working universe. It implies that some kind of basic design was embedded in the original energy that exploded to evolve the universe, matter, and life. Otherwise, all particles created should have been destroyed by equivalent quantity of anti particles. It was the accidental leftovers of particles that gave rise to our universe. Actually, some scientists jokingly say that we are the meal made out of the original leftovers.

From primordial energy, our universe came into being in a sequential manner. Theologians attribute the creation to God's wisdom, while rationalists assume that the universe was brought into being by changes in the original state of energy in different thermal contexts. It is not possible to discover the qualities of initial energy or the cause of separation of forces and emergence of elementary particles. Of course, we can attribute many things to the thermal state of the early universe, but not the leftover quarks and electrons. Nor could such coincidental contexts conceive the six magic numbers and all other values that were essential for creation. We have to find a more convincing excuse for avoiding the hand of Providence in allowing leftovers to enjoy existence.

That is where Upanishads indicate the missing link. They hold that an unknown kind of energy created our universe. They called it the Supreme Self or Brahman, which is present in all beings. Now we accept it in scientific jargon as infinite singularity. Even the possibility of a kind of dark energy working against gravity is postulated in the latest scientific literature based on astronomical observations. And the process of evolution that definitely required a benign push to start could also have derived guidance from that energy through intelligent exchange of information.

M: Creation is the most fascinating event that engaged the inquisitive mind of humans from time immemorial. Now, tell me more on the contribution of the Upanishads to this interesting field of inquiry.

P: Mundaka Upanishad gives further insights into the enigma of creation. It says that with higher knowledge, we understand the unchanging and unborn reality of Brahman or pure consciousness. With lower knowledge that deals with the physical and biological sciences, arts, linguistics, etymology, astronomy, and so on, we get a clearer idea of our material world. They are derived from the sensory perception of a conscious person assisted by the memory of his past. The inherited intelligence makes our observations more or less perfect for enabling us to live comfortably in the physical world.

But the higher level of knowledge reveals what is beyond ordinary perceptions. Our inherited intelligence or memories of the past cannot create the awareness required to reach out to Brahman. Since Brahman or the Supreme Self is indefinable and inaccessible to the senses, it can be realized only by the kind of knowledge that is far beyond the physical laws of nature. Such higher levels of comprehension are outside the scope of the conditioned perception conveyed by sensory organs.

In scientific materialism, we look at the causality of all phenomena that occur in the universe. If something cannot be defined or understood in terms of its cause, we categorize it as an inexplicable coincidence. Brahman is such a concept, which contains both the cause and the effect in the same entity. It is the cause of all creations and all kinds of existence including space and time. They all came out of its primordial thoughts. And it also exists in all creations.

Mundaka Upanishad traces the sequence of creation, beginning with the emergence of evolutionary energy called 'Prana' from the Supreme Self. The mind, sensory organs and all elements arose from it. The chain of cause and effect began only after the creation of elements and their subsequent evolution into matter and forces in the universe. That is why it is said that the Supreme Self alone knows everything, as it is the basic intelligence underlying all creations. It is also the embodiment of the concepts of time and space and the interactive intelligence that directs evolutionary changes.

M: *That probably explains the correct choice of physical constants like magic numbers and thermal contexts for the creation of matter, forces and structures of all kinds. It was no chance or accident. We don't need any bizarre concepts like 'multiverse' to explain creation.*

P: Yes, that is why some people say that God is omniscient. In quantum physics, they admit that elementary particles can act autonomously and events like the big bang are some sort of cosmic accidents, which are inexplicable at present. Nature is nothing but the kind of intelligent energy envisaged in the Upanishads. We have to admit that it is intelligent and interactive, as every object carries the stamp of ingenuity. A little bit more extrapolation can take us to the cause of creation, which is the intelligent thought of nature or the Supreme Self. It is difficult to deny the obvious.

It appears that the primordial energy had all the knowledge required to create equations for relativity, Grand Unified Theory and Super strings. What we still miss is the equation for a Theory Of Everything. Our scientists will soon stumble upon that also, but they may not admit that it was all written by the one who knew everything. We may not know the purpose of creation, but we can read the clear writing on every form of life. The undeniable signature of a creative energy is evident all over the universe.

Those who pursue lower levels of knowledge remain uninformed about the unknown Supreme Self. They are bound to the cycle of birth and death every day and get totally involved in activities performed to succeed in the struggle for survival. They learn only to enhance the capabilities of sensory perception and memory. The basic biological instincts for fighting, fleeing, feeding and reproduction are the major activities that engage their attention at all times.

The concept of consciousness does not appeal to them as the heavy agenda dictated by biological instincts keeps them fully occupied. Finding out the causal links of natural phenomena is another interesting pastime for some intellectuals. They conveniently forget the fact that it is only in consciousness that they can pursue such intelligent activities. Awareness is simply taken for granted.

But truly wise men strive to understand the imperishable nature of existence. They know that Brahman is action, knowledge and goodness, and so on, in the supreme state. It is both the cause of creation as well as its effect manifested in various forms. Everything exists only in its ambit of interactive intelligence. Conversely, it also exists in all forms of life as innermost vital energy. The concepts of heaven, earth, hell and whatever the human mind can think of emanates from inherent intelligence that we have inherited.

The metaphor of two birds perched on the same tree is used in the Upanishad, to illuminate the concept of Brahman. The individual self and the immortal Supreme Self or Brahman, are two birds sitting on the same tree of life. While the individual self or ego takes both the bitter and the sweet fruits of life and suffers from the consequences, the Supreme Self simply observes the ongoing action. It does not participate in any event or tastes the fruits of labor. The individual self is totally involved in his daily activities to realize that its identity is not different from that of the Supreme Self. The separate identity is only an illusion created by the memory of past experiences stored in the brain.

By following the path of simple, truthful and ego-less existence, one could attain higher level of intelligence required for understanding the Supreme Self. The undeniable truth is that individual differences and dualities exist only in our conscious perception. Universal consciousness does not contain divisions and polarities, and once this truth is internalized, total tranquility should prevail in the mind. The mind will be set free from all cravings for sensory pleasures when it has realized that the world of Brahman is in your own consciousness.

When death occurs, all the vital energy that makes up the biological body goes back to the cosmic pool. The senses, karma, all symbols and objects that created the separate identity of an individual are all lost in the vastness of universal consciousness. Actually, a person who realizes himself, as Brahman while he is alive, is no longer worried about the destruction of physical form. He becomes as immortal as Brahman or the Supreme Self. Infinite consciousness becomes his abode or paradise in this life itself.

M: *In brief, the insights on the Upanishads are really consistent with the latest knowledge on genesis. The DNA is not solely responsible for the creation of an organism. Different kinds of life share the same basic material. What matters is the development of the fertilized egg in a suitable interactive context. The environment is the main guiding factor that directs the course of development of the brain even after birth.*

Similarly, the thoughts or intelligence of the primordial energy would have created the universe and life by providing basic parameters like magic numbers and ratios. Further developments were guided by interactive intelligence of both the environment and the organism. The super plasticity of the human brain must have given us the edge to surpass capabilities of all other species. Or as they say, Brahman must have specifically chosen humans by putting more conscious capacities like a magnificent mind in an evolvable brain. What more can we say on existence? It is written clearly all over nature. Let us read it and be wise to understand the underlying unity of life.

CHAPTER TEN
EXISTENCE EXPLAINED

"What is the use of water for the well, which is full and overflowing? What is the use of Vedas and Mantras to the mind that is already enlightened by God?"

[Bhagavad Gita]

"In the beginning was the word".

[John 11,14]

"Utter darkness prevailed before the beginning with no existence of any kind. The primordial void created the universe from its benevolent thoughts."

[Rig Veda]

"I am still an atheist, thank God."

[Luis Bunuel]

P: Now that we have completed our knowledge expedition on creation, let us try to find an acceptable explanation of our existence. We can try to construct a modern worldview by eliminating inconsistencies and inadequacies in existing ones, by taking into account acceptable scientific evidences on universe, matter, life and the mind. We may also consider how inexplicable coincidences can be resolved by applying the mystic wisdom of the Upanishads.

M: *Many scholars have given such explanations in the past. Are we trying to converge all available wisdom to create a secular worldview for the benefit of people belonging to different faiths and cultures?*

P: We now know that objective reality in all its splendour and complexity is projected to the mind in a virtual and condensed version by computing processes of the brain. Unfortunately, the modified version of reality conveyed by the sensory organs and memory, do not give us a correct and complete worldview. We do not know all the causal relations of natural phenomena nor can we explain cogently the cosmic coincidences that created the universe. All that we have are some assumptions about the unknown.

The deficiencies in our perception are partly attributable to the inability of our sensory organs to comprehend nature beyond or below certain frequencies of energy vibrations. In the Upanishads, we find several ideas, which are consistent with scientific knowledge on existence. In fact, the harmonious fusion of science and mystic thoughts gives us a complete model of existence that explains causal connections in a convincing manner.

Our quest for the ultimate answers should take us to the origin of the universe and evolution of life. The worldview that we try to create should yield verifiable predictions and propositions. It should also correspond closely to all commonly perceived features of nature that is known as objective reality. The fact is undeniable that presently we have a fairly accurate description of various natural phenomena both at microscopic as well as macroscopic levels. The great discoveries of science particularly in the last hundred years, have given us tremendous knowledge and power, even to modify creations of nature.

But we still do not have satisfactory answers to the amazing puzzle of coincidences that culminated in the creation of the universe, the diversity of life and emergence of the mind. If we consolidate our inherited knowledge and acquired wisdom into a consistent model, it can probably explain the causal links underlying creation and organization of the universe.

The basic premise of the model is that before creation, an unknown form of intelligent energy subsisted with absolute qualities. In scientific literature we call it infinite singularity or quantum vacuum. Everything we find in the universe was united in that entity, in a manner unknown to our current comprehension.

In the Upanishads, this state of energy is described as Brahman or the Supreme Self. We have seen in the previous chapter that it is from the thoughts of Brahman that the universe came into being. Since thoughts are the expressions of intelligence, the big bang itself was probably conceived by the wisdom inherent in the initial conditions. It would have knowingly left out a few excess quarks and electrons to begin the process of building the material universe. Even thermal contexts required for creation of matter and separation of forces could have emerged from its thoughts.

The initial vacuum would have been empty of matter

but full of potentials for their creation. Even when the universe was at 10^{-35} seconds, it must have been a small speck compared to its present gigantic size that spans about ten billion light years across. Can such a huge structure arise out of total emptiness, quantum vacuum, or whatever? Einstein actually found that vacuum could have a warped structure. The condensed vacuum presumably consists of latent capacities to create matter and forces. If that is so, we have to admit that it can create things according to its own inherent intelligence. What we find in the universe could have come only from primal vacuum. The primal intelligence may not correspond to our current ideas, but it can be described as an unknown ability to take correct decisions.

Presently, we have lot of scientific information on the concept of energy. It is generally described as the capacity to do work. Energy is also the broadest measure of the state of a physical system. In spite of any change in the form of energy, in an isolated system, the total energy remains constant. It gives a clear idea on all changes in a system like money flow that indicates transactions in an economy.

The fact is that the primordial energy is, undoubtedly, the basis of all existence. The greatest attribute of energy is that it can neither be created nor destroyed. Several forms of energy are known, some of which are very familiar to us like kinetic, thermal, chemical and nuclear energy. When energy is in the process of transferring from one system to another, we find heat and work, as emerging manifestations.

The equivalence of matter and energy is established in Albert Einstein's Theory of Relativity. However, in spite of all our knowledge on energy, it is only a useful scientific concept to understand the physical world. The concept of energy does not give it a concrete entity like matter, as it cannot be described or defined in physical terms. Its presence and effect are felt when a system undergoes some change.

The changes in manifestations of energy do not affect the totality, as a balancing effect is always felt in some state or the other. The qualities of this abstract concept are beyond causality and constraints of time and space. Even space and time become interchangeable in a certain state of energy. James Hartle and Stephan Hawking proposed that quantum uncertainties could even affect the identities of space and time. They conceived the big bang as the continuous emergence of time from space in an inexplicable explosion of energy.

Our present level of scientific knowledge cannot answer questions like why the primordial energy existed in an infinite state and how it held the present universe. It could have been a huge black hole that suddenly exploded to bring out a universe, which was squeezed by some force into an atom of compressed energy. We can only speculate that the physical qualities known to us at present might have existed in some manner in that state of energy. It can be taken as the potential energy that created matter, forces and all kinds of structures that we find in the Universe. The latest confirmation of the presence of a dark energy is a definite pointer to its existence even in the initial conditions.

The primal vacuum might have contained all intelligence required for estimating and fixing the correct parameters necessary for creation. The evolvable hardware of life could have also been conceived by that entity. All that the big bang brought about was a transformation of the potential state of energy. According to the law of conservation of energy, the total quantum of primordial-energy should be equivalent to all matter, forces and various kinds of energy including dark energy present in the universe. The initial scenario must have been totally opaque, as no photon could have existed independently outside its ambit.

M: You are not giving me any clear idea on the strange concept of primal energy. How do you know that it was some kind of energy? It could have been some other unknown entity, not necessarily the kind of energy, as told by science. And how can you be so sure that it was intelligent enough to conceive the correct configurations for all cosmic coincidences? You cannot answer one puzzle by creating a more complex one. Then the game of guessing will go on and on.

P: Your questions are well founded. Let us see what kind of answers emerge from our explorations. Out of an infinite state of energy, a great transformation through the big bang brought about the present universe and its innumerable structures. But creation in such an enormous scale is possible only if we assume that the original infinite energy contained the intelligence to fix accurately all basic parameters required for the gigantic task. From scientific evidences like the 'red shift', 'background microwave radiation' and the quantity of hydrogen and helium in the universe, it is now confirmed that the big bang was the starting point of creation.

It is a fact that all manifestations of existence in the universe are derived entirely from the original state of energy and whatever. We have no means at present to understand the nature of the transition of energy and the thermal contexts created for separation of forces and creation of elementary particles. From the available facts, we can only surmise that an energy transition of tremendous magnitude took place at the time of the big bang. In a series of consequential interactions involving various parameters of temperature, gravity, and so on, it gave rise to our universe.

If it were a simple physical process, it would have accurately maintained the ratio of particles to anti particles. Then there would have been no matter in the universe. It is from the leftover quarks and electrons that the present universe emerged in all its pomp and glory. But all that makes up only ten per cent of the matter actually required for an expanding universe. We are unaware of the force that made this wonderful world inflate incredibly. And more intriguing is its sedate but accelerating rate of expansion. It is neither going to collapse soon nor is it likely to go at a much faster course of eternal expansion. Only one conclusion emerges that the primal vacuum contained much more intelligence than we can even speculate. But still our scientists refuse to admit the obvious.

What is surprising is that both scientific knowledge and the Upanishads correctly identify the initial conditions, as a kind of intelligent energy. Extending the same premise, we can infer that the primal energy could have known basic values required for creation of matter and forces. We find that its intelligence became interactive only in certain suitable contexts conducive for the transformation of energy. If the universe had remained for some more time at a billion degrees than the actual duration it took to cool down, all atoms would have become iron. Similarly, if nuclear reactions were faster, we would have had only iron in the universe. Everything seems to have colluded to create a universe, in which some small creatures like us emerged to speculate on big questions.

The initial conditions were like a seed with all genetic information encoded for the growth of a plant. It resembles an embryonic cell that develops into a body with a mind. We know that a plant or the mind cannot emerge from a vacuum. Most of the genetic instructions are also common to all forms of life and what determines the variety is the interaction between genes and the medium of growth. The conclusion that the primordial energy had the intelligence, at least in some rudimentary form to initiate the process of creation, is unavoidable.

The origin of life on our planet is analogous to the origin of the universe. Life on earth probably began in a single cell organism, which went on evolving into vast varieties of new species. The genes in the cell contain all information necessary for creating energy for existence and also for replicating itself to perpetuate the species. The first organic cell has undergone several evolutionary transformations utilizing its inherent capacity for intelligent interaction with the environment. But we have to accept the fact that the first live cell could have been conceived by cosmic intelligence, may be using information stored in its eternal memory bank.

It is quite possible that at certain higher levels of complexity, the phenomenon of consciousness and the mind could have emerged from our neural network. Conscious capacities enable us to perceive the external world intelligently and enjoy existence with all the advantages of knowledge and its applications. But the origin of all our capabilities is in the primordial energy that gave rise to the wonderful universe and precious life. In our extended conscious capacities, we have definitely discovered many things, but it all started with the intelligence borrowed from an unknown source. There is no shame in admitting our origin, or indebtedness to the creator, whatever it maybe.

Even the end of the universe will only be yet another

change in the state of energy. Assuming that the universe will ultimately end up in a big crunch or in an infinite saga of expansion, all matter and forces will then return to the initial state. In that state, all basic designs required for another creation may lie dormant. Several billions of years later, a new explosion may probably initiate another cycle of creation and destruction. It may go on eternally with the guidance of the self-sustaining loops of intelligence.

The most interesting feature of cosmic intelligence is that like the genes it gets activated only in appropriate contexts. All scientific evidences of the big bang, the inflation of the universe, the cosmic coincidences, the magic numbers and so on, indicate that an intelligent energy was essential for creation. Even if the universe is set on a course of infinite expansion for hundred billion years, some other mode of creation might make a new universe. The Upanishads also attribute creation and evolution to the same kind of energy that it calls Brahman or the Supreme Self. Brahman is an all- inclusive entity that becomes manifest only in suitable contexts. May be, thermal contexts are required to trigger massive changes in the state of energy to create matter and forces.

This view is further strengthened by the observation that everywhere in the universe, matter interacts intelligently at the elementary level. All structures in the universe, like galaxies, stars, and planets emerged from the interaction of elementary particles and forces. Even at the molecular level, exchange of information is absolutely necessary for the existence of biological organisms. Although classical physics does not admit such possibilities, the quantum theory supports them with the necessary conceptual framework.

Quantum non-locality means no mediation by a local

force or even any kind of signals is required to exchange information. The particles can relate instantaneously without the intervention of any intermediaries. We can see such phenomena in the spin of photons. It is also confirmed by Aspect's experiments applying Bell's theorem that the intelligence exchanged between particles has indeterminate potentialities. Simply stated, at the level of elementary particles, there is something like telepathic communication.

M: Would you equate quantum qualities of elementary particles to the intelligence of primordial energy? How did it possess the level of intelligence required to initiate creation? Or is it that the primordial energy is what we call intelligence?

P: In the absence of matter and forces, the initial state could have contained all the energy of the universe, including the aggregate of all intelligence and capacity for interaction in material manifestations. It is true that we do not know how intelligence is encoded in a state of energy and transmitted instantly across the barriers of space and time. We now know that the dual existence of particles collapse into a single state when they are observed or measured. Do we know how our thoughts originate or where they terminate? Some such mechanism must have existed even before the beginning; it is a fair assumption that intelligence is also a kind of energy. Anyway, a vacuum devoid of any substance or activity cannot create a universe.

The cosmic intelligence must have created matter in appropriate contexts by collapsing the super imposed designs derived from its past experience. The new forms of matter could have evolved into more complex varieties by modifying the original design with some kind of self-organizing software. Environmental feedback must have guided the process of evolution. But I admit, they are all in the realm of speculation. The question is whether we can find a better way to assemble the pieces in the puzzle of existence?

Wolf Singer, a noted neuro-physiologist, found undeniable proof of intelligent interaction at the elementary level. When we see familiar objects, all the neurons receptive to the qualities of that object, start firing together indicating instant recognition of a known quality in the visual field. It clearly establishes that there is an exchange of intelligence between photons of the object and molecules in the neurons. Our scientific knowledge has no rational explanation for such coherent firings of neurons, even before the entire visual information is processed by the brain.

It shows that neurons are sensitive and perpetually connected to some features of the outside world. We differentiate objects only when they are broken down to elementary level and then put together to create identifiable images. The processing of information in the brain takes about one-tenth of a second. During this period, all discrete data on colour, motion, shape and so on gets integrated into an intelligible image. It means that the brain is in constant communication with the interactive intelligence in the external world through sensory organs. Classical physics, which is based on causal relationship and mediation by local forces, cannot accept such weird ideas on intelligent interaction. But quantum mechanics supports such possibilities as many strange things happen only in the world of elementary particles. Order, predictability, and physical laws are probably the qualities found in higher levels of organization.

Our scientific knowledge of matter shows that at the elementary level, up quark and down quark are held together by gluons, to create protons and neutrons.

Electrons are held to this nucleus by photons to make a complete atom. Atoms combine in different ways to create molecules of a variety of matter. The elementary particles do not have any definite size or structure but they are indisputably, the basic building blocks of matter. Our model of the universe is essentially based on the process of self-organization beginning at the level of fundamental particles and building up to the order of gigantic galaxies.

In this process, new patterns of different sizes and scales appear on a complex and indeterminate substratum. Examples of such products can be seen in Bose-Einstein condensates, living organisms and even in crystals. All biological organisms grow according to basic self-organizing pattern initially encrypted in a fertilized egg. Similarly, the universe could have evolved using intelligent patterns inherent in the original state of energy. They were indeed the seeds of existence. Mike, there is no way to dispute our origin.

Cellular chemistry gives, another proof that the cell can switch on or off some genes, depending on its actual requirement. The embryo does not develop, simply by expanding an inherent design or pattern. Intercellular communication in the human embryo is essential for its proper growth. It is mostly based on the location of the cell. The diversity of life depends on subtle differences in the genes, but the mechanism of growth and genetic instructions are common to all forms of life. The mouse, the monkey and man came through the same developmental process, using the same genetic vehicle.

In the computerized model on the behaviour of genes developed by Kaufman, it is seen that the components remained inactive when connections were sparse. With the addition of more connections, new patterns began to emerge through the process of self-organizing software, which is embedded in the program.

The evolutionary advances could have been motivated by original intelligence that probably wanted its creations to survive through fitter and better varieties. It may explain the exclusive choice of benign mutations in genes for creating evolutionary upgrades. The self- organizing pattern is also evident in the emergence of galaxies and stars and also in the growth of a fertilized egg. The very fact that only random mutations of the benign kind are passed on to future generations shows that original intelligence could have had advance knowledge of the likely consequences of its choice. Our current knowledge cannot fathom the exact motive for self-organization or how particles exchange information at the elementary level. However, we cannot deny the fact that they do exist.

Another supporting evidence on intelligent exchange of information is the phenomenon of unconscious perception, found in cases of blind sight. Persons, who have become blind following brain damage, sometimes spontaneously respond to objects in their visual field without becoming aware of seeing any object. Similarly, the 'EEG' of patients suffering from hysterical deafness shows brain response to sounds even when they are not conscious of hearing any sound. The fact is that all inputs received and processed by sensory organs, do not reach our awareness. But the processes go on as if they were designed specifically for our survival albeit for a short duration.

It confirms our assumption that there is a clear possibility of exchange of information at elementary level without any need for intervention by our awareness. Some people think that such unconscious perception is intuition or insight. It is the capacity to arrive at right solutions without consciously receiving or processing any information relating to that matter. If we want to avoid invoking providence, we can accept the view that all processes in the universe are based on constant exchange of information at some elementary level. The only problem is that we have to attribute immense intelligence to the lowest entities, which means a drastic down grading of our self-esteem.

M: I am with you in all these assumptions and extrapolations. Rather, I admit I have no alternatives to offer. Your explanations made it so convincing and scientific that it must be the true state of affairs. But, tell me, how can your model solve the mystery of the mind that emerges in the brain.

P: The model that we discuss here can also accommodate the concept of a non-physical mind. The mind arises probably only from intelligent interaction of the molecules in the conscious brain with energy vibrations in the environment. That is why we cannot physically locate it anywhere in the brain. It is an emergent quality existing only in consciousness. The brain processes open a window of consciousness to perceive integrated images of the world including the self-image. The perceiver is pure awareness without which we do not understand the world or our own conscious capacities. We are simply slaves of consciousness.

This model would not permit any body-mind dichotomy. The brain is the reality and the mind is a capacity, emerging in consciousness. Actually what exists is only the brain. Many theories like self-organization, non-linearity, chaos, complexity, feedback loops, bifurcation points, and so on, help us in understanding the mechanics of existence. All scientific enquiries are based on Hegel's dialectical process with the focus on becoming. The distinction between being and becoming, as we understand today, is irrelevant in our model as the being that emerges in the complex and an inexplicable process of self-organization is an evolutionary manifestation of the original intelligence, in the undifferentiated primordial energy. We should be on hot pursuit of the original being, rather than running after the knowledge of becoming.

Our model is in consonance with the wisdom of the Upanishads that attributed the creation of universe to the intelligence of the primordial energy. The idea of an undifferentiated non-being having all the information essential for creation and continuation of evolutionary processes is an admirable deduction. We find that modern science has also reached the same viewpoint. Our preoccupation with the physical features of evolution underlying present manifestations, only conceals inadequate knowledge on the enormity of origins. Becoming is, more or less, an automatic process guided by intelligent exchange of information but without the original being can there be any beginning? A part of that being exists in all its creations.

We find that every individual manifestation of the original Being tries to achieve an optimum level of existence. Consciousness is fully utilized as a medium of interaction for evolution to higher levels of awareness. It also helps humans to control the environment in the most effective manner.

The outstanding difference between organisms is that the highly evolved ones are capable of having an intelligent mind that helps them to extend conscious capacities. The lesser varieties are just conscious enough to exist and perpetuate the species, in accordance with the genetic algorithm. Maybe, they are spared the burden of thoughts that urge to seek their roots of existence. In our case, intelligent speculation has become a glorious occupation, as well as an entertaining pastime.

The lowest possible state of energy like quantum vacuum may also be active in terms of uncertainty principle. Since all possible frequencies of vibrations are aggregated in that state, an inexplicable infinity may emerge, which is far superior to individual vibrations. The infinite energy of vacuum in one cubic centimeter is supposed to be more than the energy of the entire universe. That is why we can safely state that quantum vacuum that might have existed before the big bang, contained supreme intelligence and unlimited energy for the creation of all existence. No harm in assuming that intelligence is also some kind of energy vibration.

The concept of quantum vacuum is something like transcendent reality, in which our existence appears as waves in the ocean. Virtual particles can probably appear and disappear in quantum vacuum although it is totally devoid of any kind of known matter. The virtual particles have very short life as they cancel each other with opposite charges. We now know that the universe emerged with matter because of an imbalance in the ratio of particles and anti-particles.

We can assume that synchronized oscillations in the neural network may be extending our ordinary awareness, to comprehend the energy of consciousness, pervading the universe. The mind and its qualities enable us to keep in touch with the interactive intelligence of universal energy, which can be called God or Brahman or consciousness or whatever. The simple truth is that the mind is a rare gift given to us to experience the ecstasy of existence and enable us to ask such profound questions. Our quantum coherent perception may be the faculty that collapses the dual existence of particles to gain access to the external reality.

All our knowledge leads to the common thread that unites the existence of all forms of matter. It is the undeniable fact that all of us are evolved from the same original state of energy and we return to it after the physical body perishes. This understanding should liberate us from fear and worries on woes of the present and uncertainties of the future. As nothing can perish in the universe, including life, all such events are only transformation of energy from one state to another. The primordial energy exists eternally with all creative intelligence, while forms of matter or force may change depending on environmental conditions.

The supreme reality envisioned in the Upanishads is probably the primordial state of energy, now accepted as the initial condition, by our scientific wisdom. The Upanishads compare death, to the process of a lump of salt dissolving in the sea. It is neither lost nor destroyed; only a change in form occurs, by merging individual identity with a larger entity. In short, it becomes one with the supreme state of existence in yet another form. This is the sum and substance of the explanation that emerges when we converge scientific knowledge and mystic contemplations on existence. It is the truth of reality that is evident in all manifestations of the primordial energy that exists eternally in this universe and may be even after its destruction.

M: It is an excellent model, cogently presented with lot of convincing proof. But can we test it empirically, without which no scientist will accept it as a theory?

P: I am not equipped to follow the empirical part. Nor am I interested in collecting more evidences. My own life is sufficient proof of the irrefutable origin of existence.

The body contains atoms created several billions of years ago. I am the highly evolved outcome of intelligent interaction conceived by an unknown form of energy. That knowledge is good enough to keep me happy, active, and satisfied. It gives me a vision with a mission. I have found a noble purpose for my mundane existence, a purpose beyond mere reproduction. What more can I aspire for?

M: *I hope to reach your level of happiness. After all, you spent several decades of contemplation on existence when compared to my few years of spiritual pursuits.*

P: But with the early acquisition of true knowledge, you can go farther. I am a late starter. I reached it at the fag end of my life and I don't have much time left to propagate its wisdom. I am on an extended bonus period, after an inexplicable escape from near death. You have an entire lifetime before you. Go ahead with full conviction. Tell people, young and old, all about the truth of existence, the concept of Brahman, the Supreme Self or consciousness or whatever you would like to call it. It is out there; choose the right path to reach enlightenment, no matter whatever faith you follow, as all of them lead to the same entity that initiated existence and terminates everything eventually. This is the message of the Upanishads to the militant youth misguided by sectarian interests. It can also empower HIV positive persons, condemned to death by a cunning virus. You have more time to tell all of them that life is a more meaningful and enjoyable experience. Let them not miss this golden opportunity to celebrate existence.

CHAPTER ELEVEN
UPGRADED AWARENESS

"As the fire hidden in a stick is not seen until it is rubbed on a rough strip, God lies dormant in the mind until awakened by enhanced awareness."

[Shevetaswatara Upanishad]

"In Tauria, the fourth stage of awareness, the mind is neither turned inward nor outward. Beyond all emotions and thoughts, it beholds infinite peace and unity of all beings."

[Mandukya Upanishad]

"There is no time or space, no life or death, for the one who realized the Self and dissolved all ignorance. The enlightened mind knows no distinctions, conflicts and desires. It encompasses all polarities and existence."

[Ashtavakra Gita]

"Minds are like parachutes - They only work when open."

[Thomas Dewar]

P: With clearer ideas on creation, you can now consider the use of true knowledge for removing ignorance that leads to unhappiness in the world. To understand all about life, we have to explore deeper into the interesting phenomenon of awareness. Mandukya Upanishad describes three states of awareness that are experienced by all human beings. They are waking awareness, dreaming awareness and sleeping awareness. Beyond the three states of ordinary awareness is the fourth state, which is called super consciousness or oneness with Brahman or the Supreme Self. At that level, one gets undifferentiated perception and the sensation of bliss. It is symbolically represented by the syllable 'OM' which empowers ordinary awareness to transcend to a higher state.

Different states of awareness can be described in relation to the concept of Brahman. Whatever we see is created by consciousness and the mind also arises only in that state. Consciousness probably is the reflection of the Supreme Self or a kind of infinite energy that empowers our perception. The syllable 'OM' may be vibration of the energy that creates awareness to make the world perceptible.

The Supreme Self exists in all four states of awareness. When we are awake, it makes us aware of the external world of objects and events. We comprehend the world mainly through signals received by the five sensory organs. The mind and body are fully integrated to create and sustain the illusion of a separate identity. The body, functions using both the organs of action and thought.

In waking awareness, thoughts arise and actions are initiated. The mind experiences pleasure and pain created by sensory inputs and memory. Without waking awareness, human life, as we know it, has no meaning or purpose. It is the most important state in which we develop mental faculties to pursue various goals in life. Our creativity blossoms only when we are awake and alert.

In the second state of awareness, the conscious mind is only a witness to dream events. In the absence of inputs from outside, it is confined within the boundaries of dream space, which are mostly created by memories of past events. While dreaming, some unfulfilled wishes and action plan for the future may appear, in the borderline of consciousness. The dreamer in a subtle way experiences some of the past deeds, once again. Some mechanism of memory recall brings dream experience to the conscious mind, after the dreamer is woken up suddenly by an interruption in sleep cycle.

The Self lies dormant in dreamless sleep in the third state of awareness. In this state called 'Prajna' there is no desire, action or enjoyment. A veil of unconsciousness covers all intellectual and physical capabilities of the person. There is no conflict or anxiety in this state and we are in perfect peace and harmony with nature and all other beings. It is the supreme state of existence that we go through in a routine manner in the sleep cycles. Our conscious capacities remain in a potential state in the brain.

The Upanishads hold that the supreme awareness of the unknown kind is the cause of all existence. If we cannot regain consciousness lost for any reason, it invariably leads to death. If life is continued even after brain death, it has no quality but simple vegetation. Devoid of intelligent support from awareness, sooner or later, the agony of existence will be over for the clinically alive body.

In the fourth state of supreme awareness, we are fully conscious without any specific subjective experience. It is not a negative state of mind that obliterates memory. The information received through the senses is used only for limited existential purposes. The speculative wisdom we achieve from inferred knowledge cannot take us to this supreme state of awareness. It is beyond our normal perceptual capacities and contains only pure, undifferentiated consciousness, which do not contain the polarities that exist in the world. When we reach the fourth state of awareness, total peace and happiness prevails in the mind. It gives a feeling of unity with universal consciousness, which is the blissful state of self-realization.

M: *The description of different kinds of awareness in the Upanishads seems to conform to the latest scientific discoveries about the phenomenon of consciousness. Can you relate it with the stages of evolution of consciousness discussed by Ken Wilber and other modern philosophers and psychologists?*

P: As you know, the origin of consciousness and its multifarious qualities are fascinating subjects that still elude scientific enquiries. We have discussed the current scientific ideas about consciousness in an exclusive chapter. I will give here a brief comment on Ken Wilber's path-breaking work on the evolution of consciousness. We will confine our discussions to the context of the state of supreme consciousness described in the Upanishads and its parallels in modern literature.

M: *It should be really brief. I am getting overloaded with this heavy stuff of consciousness about which none of us seems to have any definite idea.*

P: Well, let us see the beginning of human consciousness and the evolutionary stages it passes through to reach the so-called supreme Self. As you know, in early infancy, only undifferentiated awareness exists in which the physical body is not differentiated from the external world. It responds to various environmental stimuli instinctively like an automated toy.

M: *Is it not the ultimate state of spiritual wisdom? You said undifferentiated awareness is the supreme goal of all spiritual quests.*

P: This is a misapprehension. The spiritual quest takes you through all stages of evolution of consciousness to eventually reach the goal of unity. It has nothing to do with infantile non-differentiation that arises from total ignorance of reality. The undifferentiated awareness of the mystics emerges from the supreme knowledge that all existence has its origin in consciousness. It arises when we accept the truth that the Supreme Self or Brahman exists in all beings and our perceived polarities disappear in the light of knowledge. As Ken Wilber points out, it is a mature and stable state of mind that engenders compassionate wisdom and not complete indifference to the world. In fact, it should give stronger motivation to help the less endowed persons by extending material and spiritual assistance.

M: *That is clear. Tell me when do we become self-conscious and start differentiating the external world and its objects and events?*

P: The undifferentiated awareness of the infant normally ends in about 12 months. By that time, the child gets all the neurons that it will have for its entire lifetime. Anyway, by about 24 months, the physical and emotional fusion of the infant with the environment gradually ceases and a rudimentary form of self-consciousness appears in the horizon. It is not the loss of paradise or primal happiness; but a kind of mental phase transition required for growth. The physical separation from the environment begins with the formation of the ego, which is attached to the self-image. The strong emotional bond with the mother also gets slackened at this time. Symbolically, it means the withering away of the vestiges of the umbilical cord. Conscious capacities are enhanced by the ability to form images and make symbolic representation of objects and events of the external world. The brain reaches its full size by about 6 years.

M: You mean the acquisition of linguistic abilities also enlarge the mental space of the infant.

P: Exactly. Language opens up new avenues for the self to develop and diversify. Impulsive acts are controlled by thoughts of rewards and punishments and the child enters a new world of experiences. The effect of parental influence is imprinted deeply and permanently at this stage. The child slowly evolves an egocentric worldview, which is conditioned mostly by cultural and parental controls. By about 14-15 years, the egocentric self-concept is complete and the child becomes mature enough to take on the world without parental support. Maybe, nature completes the groundwork for conscious capacities to emerge and lead him towards the chosen direction.

M: But psychologists describe the early developments in the infant in elaborate details of sequential acquisition of conscious capacities. You are condensing the whole evolutionary drama on a small canvas.

P: There are some common stages in the development of human psyche, like the emergence of ego, self-consciousness and enhanced conscious capacities. They generally fall into patterns indicating sequential differentiation from physical environment, liberation from parental dependence, emergence of an independent ego and so on, which are essential for survival. The pace of growth is set by the social and family conditions and the neural equipment at the starting point. In some exceptional cases we find precocious children possessing mature qualities and perception.

M: *In these amazing developmental patterns of consciousness, which are unique for each individual, how do some reach the supreme level that transcends ordinary perceptions? The mystics claim to get a direct and undifferentiated perception of reality through meditation and introspection. Is it possible to extend conscious capacities to such exalted super human levels? Most of us get stuck with the egocentric worldview, isn't it?*

P: Ken Wilber and many others point out several paradigm shifts that take place in adult humans before they get a global or undifferentiated worldview. It is the fourth level of consciousness described in the Upanishads as 'Tauria'. We cannot delineate every stage of growth and find out how a person achieves transcendence or paradigm shifts. It is difficult to find the exact cause for such profound mental changes in a few persons, but intense introspection and true knowledge are essential for achieving the state of super consciousness. Those who are capable of developing a global perception act with compassionate wisdom, but the key to unlock the conscious capacities is the seed· of awareness that remains dormant in us so long as we are alive.

M: *You mean the awareness in dreamless sleep is the seat of all conscious capacities. The Upanishads say that the energy that created the universe lies dormant in all of us in that state of awareness. Modern science has discovered that our experience in the phenomenal world arises from the inputs of tiny packets of energy that bombard sense organs. They are integrated in consciousness to create a faithful replica of the universe in our brain. For all these processes to occur, body-awareness is an essential condition, isn't it? How do we transcend them to reach the fourth level or global worldview? Can transcendence be achieved without leaving behind the all important body-*

awareness and memory data?

P: We have about twelve perceptual senses including the five major ones for seeing, hearing, touching, tasting and smelling. There are many minor senses like balance, feeling of fullness and muscular tension. The sensory organs collect information from the vibrations of energy in the environment. They are processed in association with memory and projected for mental experience. The brain is only a tool processing the sensory and memory data for correct perception that is essential for our smooth existence in the world. As you know, our perception is not capable of receiving some inputs like Radio waves, Infra-red rays, X-rays and so on that are probably not relevant to our existence.

In waking awareness, all our sensory organs are active and whatever is perceived is comprehended to the extent that it falls within the domains known to our memory. While ascending to the highest level of perception, body awareness is not totally wiped out. It remains at a much-reduced level adequate for the functional necessities. Egocentric thoughts and excessive emotional attachments to body-related needs and relationships are minimized by true knowledge of reality.

One who reaches this state of super awareness can be a very ordinary looking man of the world, but with a different vision based on compassionate wisdom. He may not be eager to spread his enlightenment by establishing institutions giving instructions on transcendental meditation or showing the way to achieve spiritual excellence. Self-realization leads to a dream like existence that does not require any intelligent support for sustenance.

M: *You mean the mystic is a dreamer and transcendence is an ethereal experience?*

P: Not exactly. He can be a common man with clearer perception. Dreams are not mystic visions of the unity of existence. Experiments with Ketamine show some experiences similar to lucid dreams. I explained dreams in detail elsewhere to dispel the popular misconception that mystic awareness is a dream like vision. It has certain qualities of detachment like the self in the dreams but basically the mystic is awake and alert. But for his transcendental perception, he is a very practical man of the world.

M: So extended awareness is no dream. It arises when the mind is liberated by true knowledge of the Supreme Self.

P: To sum up, the Upanishads clearly distinguish different levels of awareness. In the waking state, we have the highest level of alertness. While dreaming, it is much reduced and in dreamless sleep it becomes the potential to create consciousness. The fourth state of awareness is an acquired capacity for undifferentiated perception even when one is wide-awake. It is called 'Tauria' in which the perceiver transcends to a higher level with full awareness but undisturbed by associated memories.

In that state, sensory inputs are deliberately ignored or passed over without focusing attention on any external reality. There is no interference from memories of past or expectations of future events. The mental imagery is independent of the constraints of space and time. Children before the age of two are said to be experiencing such undifferentiated kind of perception, which arises out of lack of awareness and not any self-realization. That is probably the reason for our long-term memory getting a late start as the events in the early years are blacked out for want of differentiation. In fact, the concept of self and individuality begins only after achieving differentiation from the external world.

In ancient times, the mystics would have reached the fourth state of awareness through meditation, or other mind-altering means. They must have discovered in that state that the Self in dreamless sleep is the ultimate seed of all existence. The individual self in this state is fully identified with the eternal reality of universal consciousness. Accepting mortal life as a temporary manifestation of the mother of all matter, they probably conceived that the body was only the physical guardian of the potential to become conscious. In the waking state, the mind and body get together to ensure that the organism functions as an undivided person to perpetuate survival of the species.

M: *Have you ever experienced the fourth state of awareness called 'Tauria'?*

P: It is difficult to say whether the experiences that I sometimes get can be called "enhanced awareness". Occasionally I do slip into a state of mind in which awareness is very much undifferentiated. It gives an experience of oneness with the whole universe, a feeling of tranquility and imperturbability. A kind of close connectivity with the entire spectrum of existence enters the mind even when I am physically lonely. No bitterness towards anything exists in that state. It may not be sustained throughout the waking period, but it remains as the substratum of my thoughts and actions. You may call it "mystic awareness of the modern kind". But it is not a continuous state of existence; frequent interruptions compel the mind to come back to normal mode.

M: *You didn't tell me how you reached it. Was it through meditation or by any mind-altering means?*

P: Well, I could reach it by reading over and over an interesting book called "Ashtavakra Gita". It is all about consciousness and like the Upanishads, it does not preach any faith or religious practice for self-realization. I have given a gist of this book in an epilogue. It gives many interesting ideas on consciousness, which will take you to a higher level of contemplation.

In my case, an unexpected cardiac arrest was another contributory factor. It is what you call a near death experience and I survived on account of several inexplicable coincidences. I don't want you to take that risky route to reach spiritual awareness. You are too young for such dangerous experiments to understand existential wisdom. Better achieve it with a healthy body and mind. In that way, you can enjoy life better for a longer period. It is truly a stress buster that can alleviate the anxieties of modern life.

CHAPTER TWELVE
TRIUMPH OF TOLERANCE

"Anger begins in folly, and ends in repentance."

[Pythagoras]

"Anybody can become angry. That is easy; but to be angry with the right person, and to the right degree, and at the right time, and for the right purpose, and in the right way, that is not within everybody's power, and is not easy."

[Aristotle]

"Let the divine fire of wisdom burn in me to remove all ignorance and fear. Let it fill my life with the light of compassion to love and serve entire humanity."

[Atharva Veda]

"Trust the unknown future to a known God."

[A proverb]

P: Having created a rational worldview with the wisdom of scientific knowledge and insights of the Upanishads, let us now close our session with some practical suggestions for moderating the mindset, that leads to avoidable violence. Well, the most challenging part of the learning process is to unlearn the innate and acquired attitudes of aggressiveness and substitute them with tolerance and compassion.

All noble intentions and right worldviews tend to remain cerebral if they do not modify our behavior. The teacher may be the best, the disciple may be receptive, but true knowledge imparted does not necessarily transform, the well-settled psyche of the recipient. Our thoughts and actions are mainly driven by genetic agenda and attitudes imbibed in the formative years. To wean a person away from violence, fear or anxieties by using rational knowledge is an uphill task even for great visionaries.

The Upanishads point out that self-realization gives true knowledge to the mind. Sensory pleasures and material possessions cannot give us the enduring feeling of tranquility, that comes from the experience of oneness with Brahman, the all pervading intelligent energy. Only in that state of mind can we get rid of aggressive urges created by perceptions based on ignorance and fear. But the militant youth is immune to such pious exhortations for sanity. To make him listen to reason is a gigantic task.

M: Can you first tell me briefly, how we get angry and how fear causes stress and outbursts of violence?

P: I will explain the process in detail, in the epilogue on the brain. Here, we can see briefly the physical changes that lead one to a fit of rage. To begin with, a real or imaginary threat perception has to enter the brain mainly through sensory gateways.

In rage and fear, Amygdala, the rapid response mechanism of the brain, becomes overactive. The threat perception received directly from the thalamus and amygdala activates hypothalamus and pituitary to produce cortisol and adrenaline. They make the muscles tense; the heart beat faster, and raises the pulse rate and body temperature. The net effect is to make the body and mind focus on the subject of anger by temporarily relegating all other functions.

Actually, the body and mind gets into an emergency mode for a "fight or flight" response. The fight response gives rise to aggressive behaviour, which was conceived originally for ensuring survival. It is an essential response mechanism originally created to procure food, secure shelter and sex partner in a highly competitive habitat. The uncertainties and fierce challenges of nature made it imperative for humans in the foraging era to evolve such aggressive postures. It is a marvelous achievement of adaptation to meet effectively all emergencies of existence. The body has also invented its own exit route to relax, after a bout of stress response. The parasympathetic system slows down the heartbeat and a normal pace is set for all bodily functions. Once again, let me remind you that the Supreme Self or nature knew all about stress response needed for survival and a subsequent cooling down phase to bring the body and mind back to normal mode.

M: *Tell me; is it true that the responses to fear, violence, anxieties and phobias are all identical?*

P: Stress response emerges in threat perception. But it is only a short-lived one. Amygdala is the main brain center involved in fear situation and it triggers the sequential secretion of stress boosters. Anxiety is a long-term response to unspecified threats. It is activated by the bed nucleus of stria terminalis, a structure close to amygdala. Unlike fear, which arises on a real threat perception, phobias creating chronic anxiety are not based on any specific challenge. In chronic anxiety, the prefrontal cortex of the brain that sorts out real threats fails to control amygdala. It goes on creating stress responses that last on a long-term basis, but with reduced intensity. Stress becomes an uncontrollable and sustained way of life. Persons suffering from chronic anxieties think that they perform better when stressed. Some authors also suggest that stress is good for creativity. They believe that its impact on the body and mind gives an extra punch.

M: Is it not eventually injurious to the body and mind?

P:. Yes, very much. Unlike fear, chronic stress and anxiety do not generate intense feelings in our awareness but they cause immense damage. The stress hormones like adrenaline, cortisol and norepinephrine flood the bloodstream to temporarily suspend many essential bodily functions. Consequently, digestion and immunity are · overlooked for mobilizing resources necessary for stress response. Prolonged and low-grade stress damages the heart and shrinks the hippocampus. High blood pressure, stomach disorders and impaired memory are the major disasters that follow phobias.

M: What is the way out of over stress, unfounded fears and chronic anxieties?

P: Many readymade remedies are now available in the stress market. You have medicines, counseling and psychiatric treatments aimed at removing phobias, chronic stress and fear. They are based on scientific studies and temporary relief is guaranteed.

M: What about Yoga, Pranayama, Kriyas and Vedic counseling?

P: Yoga and Pranayama are effective in diverting attention from stress perception to a chosen physical exercise. The stress level immediately comes down with such efforts. But the recurring basic cause of stress becomes active again after the initial euphoria is over which puts the patient back into the cauldron of misery.

M: Lot of people offer exotic alternative therapies like color therapy, aromatherapy, gem therapy, Ayurveda and so on? Are they effective?

P: There is no scientific basis or proof for their unverifiable claims. Stimulating a particular part of the prefrontal cortex can improve the fear busting ability of the mind. Some electro magnetic devices can also achieve good results in stress control. But they are not yet standardized and certified by a competent authority.

The most scientific way of managing stress and anger is by taking care of its origin. The amygdala, which is the fear perception center of the brain, has to be trained to accept only real and specified threats. Cognitive stress therapy is the only effective tool that can remove the root cause of misconceived fears and phobias. Meditation on the true knowledge of life can lead the mind to identify the source of stress. The idea is to create a new worldview based on a rational vision of existence. It can convince the mind that the fear perception is totally misconceived.

After initiation, unfounded fears can be evaluated by the patient in the background of rational worldview. When distorted memory that leads to threat perception is removed by the right knowledge, the anxieties and phobias slowly vanish. This therapy can be given to a group of persons who can share experiences to derive maximum benefits. Along with the cognitive approach, massage, breath-control, meditation and Yoga can help in improving general health. The combined effect of the physical and psychological approach may reduce depression and anxieties in course of time.

M: *So you want to apply cognitive therapy to remove fear and terror from the world. Have you packaged your proposal to propagate it?*

P: I am on the way. We have seen how the stories of the Upanishads can help in creating a rational worldview. We can use its wisdom in cognitive therapy to transform pessimists who wallow in self-doubt and depressive thoughts.

M: *Well, tell me how an ordinary person can achieve the blissful state of mind that shuns violence. Your cognitive therapy is not available to everyone. At least here you can give an outline on the methodology.*

P: There is no easy way out of the woods. First, the mind has to accept the logical and flawless perception of the wisdom of consciousness as the ultimate answer. It is a secular vision as followers of all faiths can consider their God as universal consciousness. Then, its undeniable presence in all other beings has to be acknowledged. To reach that state, you have to keep away from misleading sensory inputs and the mind has to avoid misconceptions created by memory and desires. The expectations emanating from the mind on past deeds or future actions should be replaced by the benign presence of the Supreme Being in the mental space cleared of all egocentric thoughts.

In the complete silence of the mind, attention can be focused on the unmanifested cause of all creations. In that stillness, an experience of unity with Brahman or the Supreme Self begins to fill the vacuum. It is the yogic state of extreme bliss beyond all feelings of ego and body-related desires. Once we reach that state logically with full conviction that it is the only reality, we will remain in that frame of mind forever. This is the bliss that Nachiketa experienced after his initiation into the domain of the Supreme Self. We can create a cognitive worldview with the vision of the Upanishads to remove all fears and anxieties. Maybe, Nachiketa was the first beneficiary of cognitive therapy, given by none other than the god of death.

M: *You mean to say that by emptying the mind of all emotions, thoughts and even perceptions, one can experience what lies beyond all of them? The pure consciousness that makes things visible and intelligible to the mind is your focus, isn't it?*

P: Yes, it is the closest elucidation on the concept of the Supreme Self or Brahman in the Upanishads. Although many faiths assume it as the creator, they do not know what consciousness or universal consciousness is and how it remains dormant in a sleeping body. We know fairly well what is life in its absence. Only in consciousness, do we have existence, knowledge, emotions, desires, cognition and all that we consider as the basic attributes of existence. That is why we equate the Supreme Self to the core of existence.

Precisely for the same reason, we should celebrate the gift of life every moment until it is taken away. True understanding comes only with the firm conviction that death can only temporarily remove consciousness from a biological body. Consciousness will continue to enlighten other live bodies. It means consciousness is a universal energy that goes on making the world visible and intelligible, to all its present and future abodes. Can you find any flaw in the logical explanation that consciousness is supreme?

M: *I get your point. You put all faith on consciousness. I admit it is difficult to find a different explanation for life. I accept that all sensory organs, the mind thoughts and actions emanating from it are unquestionably the conscious capacities gifted by awareness. In fact, the whole human body functions only as a tool to carry out the commands of consciousness. I fully agree with you on this point, but tell me how can this knowledge give me unlimited bliss and take me beyond terror and fear.*

P: Chandogya Upanishad gives an interesting account on the city of Brahman in the inner mind space of everyone. It is as infinite as space beyond the body. Everything in the universe is also found in inner space, which contains all conceivable qualities and configurations of matter and forces. This is the temporary abode of consciousness or the Supreme Self that resides in a body for a limited time. It is free from all body related feelings, desires, passions and death.

Thoughts arising in the inner space of the mind are symbolic representations of all existence in the external world. In that magic space of thoughts, desires can be fulfilled; the dead can be seen and heard. But clouds of bodily thoughts hide the Supreme Self. They·go on creating innumerable desires, pleasures, pains and unlimited ambitions. In the medley of thoughts, we forget the fact that it is consciousness that keeps illusions to appear and disappear in different states. If true knowledge that consciousness alone is eternal is accepted as the guiding principle of life, all misconceptions and miseries are automatically removed from the mind. Those who succeed in reaching that level of awareness achieve blissful existence in consciousness. It is limitless ecstasy found only in infinity.

M: That is what you said on the Supreme Self in dreamless sleep, isn't it?

P: Very true. Every night we enter the blissful world

of oneness with the Supreme Self. All beings exist together in total harmony in deep sleep. Even the Supreme Self or Brahman might have been fast asleep in infinite singularity, before it woke up with a big bang. And then the process of creation might have begun with a lot of heat and dust! The consequential activity produced all of us like a seed growing into a plant with plenty of leaves and flowers."

M: *So, we do have two spaces; the cosmic space of Brahman, which is the creative substratum of intelligent energy and the mind space, which is an extension counter specially made as a niche only for human kind. While we are asleep, we are in the cosmic space; the children of God in total peace and harmony. When we wake up, all miseries created by misapprehensions in the mind arise with us in the limited space of thoughts.*

But the one who knows the intimate link between the two spaces is in the blissful state of enlightenment. The mortal body, with all its frailties and desire-based distractions, is the barrier between the two spaces. Once that barrier is mentally removed, the state of unity or bliss begins in this lifetime itself. We can say that death erases the physical barrier to unite the two spaces. Hope I did get the picture right!

P: You understood it much better than many modern preachers of spirituality. Now you can see how all that I have explained earlier makes sense. It is the rational wisdom of existence and one who realizes it goes to eternity with universal consciousness. What more can I say on the ecstasy of knowledge? You are now in that seamless space and blissful state of undifferentiated awareness, far beyond the reach of any fear of death. No terrorist can ever upset your absolute tranquility.

M: *Yes, I do feel some kind of serenity entering my mind conquering my ego, fear and frailties. The true knowledge of the Self has cut down most of my fetters on attachment. I feel like a bird flying towards far horizons. In my mind I can feel the presence of primal energy, illuminating my days and sleeping with me in the night. I don't know what more I can ask for. But do you think same medicine can moderate misguided youth?*

P: Well, I am happy to be helpful and I hope the same effects will be felt by all readers of the Upanishads. But before we part, let me take you through the great vision of two Vedic scholars who transformed the concept of Brahman into a practical way of life. Take it as a parting gift. They give invaluable insights to seekers of knowledge. Then you have an exhaustive note on the brain and the mind, that you can read leisurely and brood over.

All this material can be used to teach the values of life to youth. If we practice tolerance, all of us can live happily in this world with compassion and wisdom. But if you do not allow the mind to ponder over ideas other than the inherited ones or the acquired ignorance, our level of tolerance would continue to remain low. On the slightest provocation, we let loose a reign of terror and inflict pain and destruction on innocent people. That is how the militants are made to react. No one is born as a merchant of death. They are converted to killing machines by the uncontrolled amygdala. The phobia of hatred continuously bathes their bloodstream with cortisol and adrenaline.

M: I accept that family and society are definitely responsible for the development of an aggressive mindset. It is very easy to indoctrinate youth brought up in highly restrictive societies. They are told to obey only the commands of religious institutions. There is also a scheme of rewards and punishments. If you serve the cause of the chosen faith, which is the only truth, you will reach the glorious world of the Lord. Failure means punishment with eternal sufferings. I think once you become a victim of indoctrination, the phobia reigns supreme.

P: Agreed. But fortunately the super plasticity of our brain comes to the rescue of the misguided mind. The conceptual framework created in the neural network in the formative years may not remain effective forever if new learning situations change the synaptic connections. Every new experience is recorded in the neural connections and if they are further strengthened by sustained thoughts, they can control the misconceived urges from earlier indoctrinations. That is how cognitive approach to fear management comes to the rescue of the misguided. And I feel that is the only way to overcome fear and terror.

When I told you to empty the mind to focus on consciousness, I was trying to rewire your neural net with new thoughts. The concept of consciousness is so self-evident and convincing that if we think about it in a sustained manner, the mind automatically accepts it as a rational paradigm. It can remove from the memory, prejudices learnt in early childhood. Long-term memories are erasable only when the rationality of new ideas strikes at the very root of misconception. Educational institutions would have to make intense efforts to inculcate rationality in the brain, trained to worship violence.

M: You want to hold the mirror of wisdom before misguided youth. If they cared to look, they would find the truth. All kinds of terror and fear would then vanish if they sustain that vision of reality. You mean to say that continuous contemplation can rewire the neural connections. But, is it an achievable objective in the current reign of terror?

P: It is not an easy task; but we can try. After all, the benefits are immense for the society if we can convert at least some people to a new worldview based on tolerance and compassion.

You have been patiently pursuing the lessons of the

Upanishads. I hope all readers are like you and that they would enjoy the kingdom of heaven; I mean, a mindset capable of appreciating the true knowledge of existence.

CONCLUSIONS
PROVIDENCE OR COINCIDENCE?
[THE ULTIMATE ANSWER]

"For me, abiding in the grandeur of the Supreme Self, where is the individual self or the non-self, where is the past, present or future. There is no need for any wisdom, discourse or goal of life for me, as I always exist in the glory of the immortal Self."

[Ashtavakra Gita]

"You grope in the darkness of ignorance seeking the elusive goal of your spiritual quest. But it lies deep in your own mind and becomes visible only to those who care to look inward."

[Yajur Veda]

"The evolutionary energy of the Supreme Self created the universe, life, and the mind. Its infinite intelligence has enchained us in the endless conundrum of cause and effect."

[Mundaka Upanishad]

"If God didn't exist, man would have to invent him."

[Voltaire]

M: I have carefully followed your lucid presentation on the wisdom of Upanishads in the context of the latest scientific discoveries. Although I am not a scientist, I could appreciate the spirit of systematic enquiries that revealed most of the secrets of the visible world. Since the discussions on various topics are scattered, I wish you could converge all of them in a simple worldview in the concluding part of our intellectual expedition.

P: I am happy that you mentioned about converging our thoughts in a structured conclusion. In fact, I suggest that you ask questions for seeking explanations to remove any doubts still lingering in your mind.

M: I would like to begin with what existed before the beginning.

P: Scientists speculate that a primordial kind of energy existed in infinite state before the beginning. They like to call it a state of quantum vacuum or quantum gravity. It must have contained the potential for all possible vibrations and frequencies of energy. We can assume that it was that primal energy that created matter, forces, and all kinds of structures in the Universe.

The Upanishads also assume the existence of an immense kind of energy before the beginning. They attribute creation to the infinite intelligence of a primal energy. Possibly, it might have chosen the physical constants and basic design necessary for the creation of the Universe. Scientists are not likely to confer any intelligence to the primordial energy that initiated the process of creation. But without such intelligence, they cannot explain how the correct parameters necessary for making the universe and life could be fixed. All religions assume that before creation, a divine entity existed and that it guided the subsequent evolutionary events.

M: Can we substitute the scientific explanations of creation for the religious worldviews that give misleading interpretations?

P: There is no doubt whatsoever that the universe was created in a cosmic explosion. The astronomical evidences of red shift and the presence of the remnants of background microwave radiation give us acceptable proof of the big bang. The presence of huge quantities of hydrogen and helium in the universe in a definite ratio also supports the big bang theory.

On the other hand, theological explanations of creation do not conform to the physical features of universe and its innumerable structures. It is interesting to note that the Upanishads give the closest approximation that the primordial energy created Universe from its thoughts. All that we find missing is the exact process of conversion of thoughts into concrete physical entities like matter and forces. But science also fails to give us any specific cause for the big bang and consequential conversion of energy.

M: Can the convergence of the vision of the Upanishads with the big bang theory explain cosmic coincidences and the evolution of matter in the Universe?

P: Cosmic coincidences mean the choice of correct parameters like the mass of elementary particles and relative strength of various forces. If their numerical values were not correctly fixed, no stable universe or structures would have emerged. Science has no explanation for the magic numbers that enabled the creation of the universe.

Unless the big bang produced some excess matter in the initial stage, no structures would have come up anywhere. Compressing the initial entity into the size of an atom or pinhead is unthinkable unless a big crunch preceded it. Until science finds out the cause of cosmic coincidences, we cannot avoid the presence of providence. But the concept of an intelligent primordial energy should be an acceptable solution for all concerned.

Vedic thoughts also attribute all cosmic coincidences to the intelligence of the primordial energy. Since there is no scientific explanation so far, the acceptable alternative is the assumption that the primordial energy contained some kind of memory of its past existence, which created a blueprint for the new universe. The dormant memory would have become active at the time of the big bang that unleashed favourable physical conditions for energy conversion.

M: How did life originate in the Universe? Was it created out of the interaction of ordinary matter without any divine intervention?

P: Scientific discoveries clearly establish that there is undeniable continuity between the creation of matter after the big bang and the appearance of life on earth. All biological organisms are made of atoms and molecules, which are also constituents of ordinary matter. Life is distinguished only by certain capabilities for achieving reproduction, metabolism, coding genetic messages in the DNA and so on. They are probably the acquired qualities of inanimate matter, which got organized into a biological configuration. We cannot rule out even the possibility of some innate quality of matter like proto-consciousness contributing to the evolution of life on earth.

M: Could evolution create a wide variety of complex organisms without any design or motivation?

P: It is true that several coincidences must have occurred simultaneously, which created conditions for the appearance and sustenance of life on our planet. Evolution is the capacity of self-organizing matter to reach higher levels of complexity through the process of interactive intelligence. In the absence of any protective cover of the atmosphere, the basic ingredients of biological life could have reached early earth through meteors or some similar means. The bacterial kingdom that constituted life for more than two billion years has contributed to the creation of suitable context for nucleated cells, to appear and diversify in a life-supporting biosphere.

The evolutionary explanation of life misses the point that it can work only from the starting point of a live cell capable of undergoing random mutations. The minimum requirement is a single cell organism, like bacteria, that can evolve into more complex forms of life. But the basic question is; how did the first organic cell come into being with the propensity for further complexity. Before the giraffe could extend its neck, a short-necked one in need of a long neck was the essential requirement. The same logic applies to the story of the flinches in Galapagos, as explained by Charles Darwin.

Evolution cannot begin its benign work in a vacuum. You need some evolvable material to work on and the assumption of a starting point would not suffice. Molecular biology now reveals that proteins follow some predictable course to achieve a specific goal. At the molecular level, the activities are so intricately organized to make them move purposively towards a predetermined goal. It is difficult to accept that evolutionary changes would promote only beneficial mutations. That is why we find lot of wisdom in the Upanishads that attributes the motivation for evolution to an intelligent form of energy. Although it is difficult to give an accurate description of the infinite entity, it is definitely interactive at the basic level.

M: *I accept the view that some kind of original intelligence was essential for creation and evolution of life. Now, tell me how did the biological organisms get awareness?*

P: We have seen that consciousness is some kind of an

innate ability of life to reach higher levels of perception. The brain creates a massive neural network of about hundred quadrillion connections that can perform serial and parallel processing of information received through various sensory organs. Consciousness arises probably when the brain functions based on coherent electrical and chemical activities cross an awareness threshold. The neurons start firing in a synchronized manner when they come across familiar signals.

Some people assume that consciousness may be the emergent quality of quantum coherent neural processes that create orderly patterns in the chaotic electric fields of the brain. The structural and functional complexities of the human brain can probably contribute to the creation of an appropriate context for its appearance. All these are only surmises based on some clinical evidences and observations. It is not known how the appearance and disappearance of consciousness are related to some body rhythms.

M: *How do we create a separate identity?*

P: Self-awareness is absent in early infancy and also in lower level animals. A conscious self emerges only when body awareness reaches some stable state capable of differentiating itself from the external world. It is closely connected to the memory of self-images created continuously from early childhood. Just like memory, self-awareness is also kept at abeyance in sleep. It is another emergent quality of the brain supported and fortified by the wonderful faculty of memory.

M: *What is free will? Can it control the genetic urges that motivate the brain?*

P: The concept of freewill indicates that the mind can act independently in spite of the compulsions of genetic instructions that conduct the normal bodily functions.

Experimental evidences now point out that the brain is capable of doing computations necessary for taking decisions much before the mind becomes aware of them. Several routine activities that we perform are totally automated. An assumption of freewill is perhaps helpful for creating an illusion that all actions emanate from the considered wisdom of the mind.

M: *Do you agree with the Upanishads that the individual self is a reflection of the Supreme Self?*

P: In the conscious state, what we actually experience is a virtual reality created by the processing of sensory information by the neural network of the brain. Memory and emotions can marginally modify the inputs to create a true prototype of the external world. But all neural activities are of no use unless we are in a state of consciousness in which trillions of inputs are integrated for a coherent experience of existence. The capacity to become conscious and correctly perceive the world is not a unique human quality. Many animals are also capable of reaching conscious states quickly to survive in a hostile habitat.

In spite of all our enhanced abilities, without the medium of consciousness, we cannot experience existence. It is consciousness that culminates all brain activities into a meaningful perception, which gives us individual identities to enjoy unlimited experiences of thoughts and feelings. The assumption that our consciousness is a localized reflection of a universal phenomenon called Brahman or the Supreme Self seems to be an acceptable explanation.

M: *Is the dualistic nature of the mind and the body an illusion or reality?*

P: I think the dualistic nature of the mind and body is just an illusion. There is no place for the mind in the brain. The brain contains only physical matter like atoms and molecules. But it is the brain that does all the processing of sensory inputs received both from the outside and the inside. Without consciousness, we cannot experience the outcome of the brain processes. It is evident that consciousness and the mind that emerges with it are the qualities of some unknown form of energy that exists universally. The physical processes of the brain become cogent and intelligible only when they are seen by the conscious mind. It consolidates the information received by perceptive faculties to experience emotions and thoughts. No other acceptable explanation is available for the enigma of consciousness and the mind.

M: *What is objective reality, and how does it become visible to us only in consciousness?*

P: There is constant interaction between the brain and the external world, may be at some basic level of electron, photon, and so on. They interchange intelligence through the vibration of energy at different frequencies or by some other means. All such exchanges become meaningful only in the context of consciousness, which gives us the conscious capacities of the mind like memory and thoughts. The mind itself is probably an experience created in consciousness.

M: *From what you described so far, can you infer the true meaning of our existence?*

P: Biological existence is a phenomenon common to all forms of life. The genetic instructions for creating and maintaining life, which are coded in the genes, reflect billions of years of evolutionary changes for enhancing capabilities. The only purpose of biological existence appears to be the perpetuation of species. Their capabilities are attuned to achieve higher level of reproductive fitness. The adaptations of the flinches in Galapagos confirm this universal truth.

But for humans, existence particularly in modern times is driven more by cultural influences rather than genetic instructions. In fact, human genetic algorithm has acquired a lot of cultural inputs from social interactions. The original genetic compulsions contain the basic instincts to seek food, sex, safety, parenthood and so on. The new items in our agenda are the quest for understanding the unknown, more power, and socially important positions. They are the modern contributions of cultural evolution that has replaced most of the original genetic agenda.

It is true that we also have a strong tendency to move towards pleasure promoting environment and objects. Our existence is an incessant search for pleasure enhancing activities, which now include cultural goals like social acceptability and achievements. For some of us, intellectual pursuits have become an absorbing activity. Probably, a lot of re-engineering is going on in our neural network that makes profound changes in the instinct driven pleasure circuits to include intangible social and academic objectives.

M: What is the ultimate purpose of human life?

P: The genetic goals are fixed by nature taking into consideration basic requirements of the organism for food, sex and security. Since in modern days, service providers take care of many of the essential needs of life, we are left with plenty of leisure to pursue pleasure-enhancing activities. The purpose of life has now switched over to new intellectual pastimes, altruistic and adventurous activities. In fact, achieving social recognition and acceptance has become the main motivating force. Briefly stated, the existence now seeks culturally determined goals that give us a sustainable sense of satisfaction. They vary depending upon social contexts and conscious capacities of an individual.

M: Do you accept the view that God or the creator initiated the process of existence?

P: As we have seen earlier, there is an undeniable presence of an intelligent energy underlying all existence in the Universe. We do not know what kind of qualities it has, except the fact that it is highly interactive at the micro level. It does not even require the support of any medium for exchanging information. Like our thoughts, it can go beyond all barriers of time and space.

You may like to call such an intelligent energy by names like God, consciousness, Brahman, Supreme Self, destiny or nature. All that it conveys is the same conclusion. The fact is that without its interactive intelligence, the creation and maintenance of the universe could not have occurred. We have to acknowledge the reality that all of us are its biological manifestations in different shapes and sizes. The unity of existence becomes spontaneously evident when we consolidate all kinds of knowledge in search of the ultimate answer.

M: Is there any hidden purpose in the creative activities of the intelligent energy?

P: We are normally conditioned to see the causal connections in all material things. Action has to be purposive; otherwise it has no meaning or utility. Such relationships are based on our perceptions and the intelligent energy that created us may not require the support of causal connections.

The external reality must have evolved from some basic intelligence through the process of exchange of information in different conducive contexts. The main objective of the evolutionary activities of primordial energy is probably to create conditions suitable for coexistence. It simply provides room for all kinds of matter to exist in a symbiotic manner without intervening to favour any particular species. All that it gives is an opportunity for existence, which is available equally to its creations. No one is exclusive, nor is there any niche created for man or beast.

We indulge in senseless conflicts presumably to perpetuate survival at any cost. Undoubtedly, we are the most well equipped creation of nature with the capability to understand even the complexities of our origin. Our physical attributes like agile hands, big brain and improved vocal cords are no longer considered exclusive; but the quest for understanding the unknown is definitely a unique human trait. It enables us to perceive the basic unity of all kinds of matter in the cosmos. The energy in the initial conditions created the universe and paved the way for emergence of the first cell of life on planet earth. God has no time to write the horoscope of every form of life. It is our restless pursuit of knowledge that gives us different destinies.

All that it does is to facilitate evolution to create a variety of life, in which we are undoubtedly placed at the top. We should humbly accept the fact, that whatever we know is just an insignificant fraction of the original intelligence that pervades the entire universe in an inexplicable manner. It should also make us compassionate to all manifestations of the Supreme Being irrespective of their capabilities. We are expected to use our intelligence to understand the complexities of existence and also to extend a helping hand to less fortunate brethren.

That is the worldview we arrive at when we combine the vision of the Upanishads with the essence of scientific knowledge derived from the latest discoveries. Now I hope that you understand all about existence and the means to convert it into an enjoyable experience.

M: *Thanks; I have no more ultimate questions to ask. When you put all the pieces in proper places, the puzzle of existence has simply vanished. The benign presence of intelligent energy is self-evident in all beings. I am grateful to you for connecting my modern mind to the essence of ancient wisdom.*

EPILOGUE - I
THE VISION OF ASHTAVAKRA

"In the boundless ocean of consciousness, waves of phenomenal worlds appear and disappear. Eternal consciousness, which is the cause of all perceptions is unaffected by the rise and fall of a universe at the end of its allotted time."

"Knowledge, knower, and the object of knowledge are useless to the one who has realized his existence in the Supreme Self. He is free from all desires and has no need for any 'nirvana'."

"You are neither earth, nor air nor sky but you live happily in all these things. You are pure intelligence that creates and witnesses the drama of existence."

[Ashtavakra Gita]

"Only the wisest and stupidest of men never change."

[Confucius]

M: I am eager to know more about the vision of Ashtavakra. You mentioned elsewhere that it has changed the course of your life. How did it influence you so deeply in spite of your considerable exposure to all kinds of Vedic thoughts?

P: Well, it is like this. About twenty-three years ago, a friend of mine gave me a copy of "Ashtavakra Gita". He cautioned me on the possibility of its explosive impact on the mind. I did not heed the forewarning, but when I read it, more out of curiosity than any genuine interest in the philosophy of life it propounded, I felt some perceptible changes in my attitudes. That was the beginning of my romance with this revolutionary worldview, based entirely on the concept of consciousness. Every time I read it, I found a new meaning that gave me immense happiness. In all the difficult phases of my life, I sought solace in its wisdom. I was never disappointed.

M: Does it improve upon the insights in the Upanishads? I thought that it gave all the ultimate answers.

P: The wisdom of the Upanishads gives us supreme knowledge on existence. It contains ultimate solutions to the puzzle of creation, origin and evolution of life and the enigma of non-physical qualities of the mind. But Ashtavakra goes farther. He converts the philosophy of the Upanishads into a practical way of life. Both the common man and the king can practice it, without giving up on worldly possessions and pleasures. It gives an attractive alternative to the rigorous practices of austerity and denial of materialistic desires. That is why I feel it is much easier to install its algorithm in the modern mind. Even after enlightenment, you can lead a normal life consistent with the true knowledge of existence.

To begin with, let us see the socio-economic milieu in which Ashtavakra began to propagate his thoughts. We find in the Upanishads that the individual self is an integral part of Brahman or universal consciousness. Deep meditation and sustained speculation led sages to the insight that existence began from an intelligent kind of primal energy. They envisioned the basic unity of all life in consciousness. To reach that higher level of perception, they advised disciples to live an austere life with minimum bodily awareness. But as you know, ascetic way of life is not everyone's cup of tea. It is too harsh on the youth.

Surprisingly, in spite of all the irrefutable insights in the Upanishads that created a secular worldview, no institution was founded to popularize it. Not only that, new religious practices that claimed heritage of Vedic thoughts overlooked the concept of the unity of all life. Hinduism began to promote blind faith in a multitude of rituals and practices and no one bothered to enlighten people on the basic idea of Brahman. The priestly caste indulged in expensive rituals to propitiate deities, which was beyond the means of the common man.

A new social order known as 'caste' came into being to discriminate people on the basis of inherited vocations. Instead of creating unity, Vedic thoughts gave convenient excuses for vested interests to divide and control the society. The practice of apartheid was developed into a fine art; for keeping the working class oppressed as untouchables. The priests deified the rulers as incarnation of one god or the other, and the lower classes were kept in perpetual poverty and ignorance.

Ashtavakra, a great scholar of Vedic thoughts, resented the travesty of the true vision of the Upanishads by self-seeking individuals and bogus institutions. He strived to explain the concept of consciousness both as the cause and effect of existence. His verses presented a secular and logical worldview founded on the concept of universal consciousness. Using the medium of dialogues with a royal disciple called Janaka, he conveyed the ideas of unity convincingly, to the common man. The universal energy that pervades in all living beings was the central theme of his vision on life. He argued that all mental activities, like thoughts, emotional experiences, and even unconscious tendencies become perceptible to us only in the space of awareness. Once it is removed, our existence comes to an end.

Accepting the wisdom of the Upanishads, Ashtavakra also conceived that the essence of consciousness is embedded in the core of the human mind. The true nature of consciousness becomes evident to us only when illusion or "maya" is removed from the mind by the right perception. Self-realization or understanding the meaning of life can remove fear of death and all other miseries from the mind forever. It requires a higher state of awareness to understand the logic of universal consciousness.

M: What is the path he suggested to achieve the goal of true knowledge?

P: Instead of following the path of meditation prescribed by Vedic scholars, Ashtavakra suggested that the self could be realized only by internalization of true knowledge. It is a kind of self-enquiry to seek the real 'I', beyond the ego-bound thoughts. The enquiring mind eventually accepts the fact that the individual self is only an infinitesimal part of universal consciousness. The basic paradigm of existence should be the principle that the same Supreme Self is present in all beings irrespective of any perceived differences in capabilities. Rituals and meditation may give us occasional glimpses of the Supreme Self, but only the abiding knowledge that existence has no separateness, can remove mental agonies arising out of ignorance. It can't be achieved without sustained self-enquiry.

The unwavering adherence to the concept of consciousness as the sole cause and effect of existence is the landmark of Ashtavakra's thoughts. The Upanishads conceived the Supreme Self as an entity beyond all physical attributes and qualities of the phenomenal world. The individual self exists in biological matter for a limited period of time. On expiry of the allotted span, it merges with the great ocean of universal consciousness.

The conclusion is inevitable that universal consciousness is the only eternal existence and the essence of all reality in the world. In other words, the inner self is only an extension of cosmic consciousness, which temporally abides in a biological form. All notions of dualities and individual differences disappear when we internalize the fact that existence of any kind is invariably bound with the common thread of consciousness.

We now accept the fact that our perceptions are based on the projections made by the brain to the conscious mind. The brain processes convey the external reality in the form of trillions of sensory inputs, which are bound in consciousness as symbolic representations of reality. The mind is actually an interface between the physical and non-physical dimensions. Our sensory organs cannot give a true reflection of the reality without consciousness.

In fact, the conscious mind that receives the experiences of reality projected by the brain is beyond all the qualities applicable to biological or other forms of matter. The comprehensive nature of consciousness can be understood only when we transcend our limited understanding of the nature of reality. This is the explanation of existence proposed by the Upanishads and subsequently elaborated by Ashtavakra in his treatise on consciousness.

M: *It is easy to accept this logic, but isn't it difficult to implement it in every day life. I don't understand how it can transform my attitude all of a sudden.*

P: Yes, I agree. The great contribution of Ashtavakra is that he gives practical guidance for a spiritual way of life. At the very outset, he advises the disciples to avoid excessive dependence on sense-related objects and to be straightforward, compassionate and truthful. It is pertinent to note here that to follow his worldview, one need not run away from moral and social responsibilities.

The knowledge that the individual is just a derivative of consciousness does not give us the license to indulge in whatever the body demands. A truly enlightened person spontaneously detaches himself from pleasure enhancing activities. Greed for material wealth automatically vanishes from the mind when consciousness is accepted as the truth of existence. The physical body simply becomes a transient medium created for purposes unknown to us.

The indisputable assumption that all intelligence emanates from the eternal wisdom of an intriguing form of energy removes our misconceptions about a personal identity and achievements. The mind liberated from ignorance is then spontaneously drawn towards the ocean of universal consciousness. True knowledge extends our ordinary awareness to a higher level so as to perceive unity in the external world. Then the realization takes root that all sorts of existence is an integral part of universal consciousness. It also becomes clear that consciousness cannot be tied down to a physical body, which is only a temporary abode of consciousness. This thought liberates us from the fear of death and desire for rebirth.

It also removes our confusion about the mind-body dichotomy. Being the expressions of the transient states of the body, polarities like happiness and sorrow, love and hate, and so on, slowly leave the mind. The true knowledge gives us the awareness that the Supreme Self exists in all beings and that all beings exist within its ambit. Life is seen as a bubble in the vast ocean of consciousness and when the bubble bursts, it simply merges with the ocean. If it assumes a separate identity that lasts for a short span of time, it only shows the abject ignorance of reality.

After reaching the higher level of awareness, an enlightened person acquires a new perspective. Worldly objects that used to give him sensory gratification become less appealing. His body-related desires and the tendency to acquire wealth, slowly reduce to the minimum required for the continuation of life. The urge to enhance sensory pleasures of a particular kind and the need for the close proximity of some persons becomes less persistent.

True knowledge releases the mind from such bondages and disturbances created by self-centered thoughts and emotions. The new worldview makes us fearless and compassionate. Fear of death is replaced by the awareness that it means only the destruction of the physical body and not the end of consciousness.

Before self-realization, the mind is driven by ignorance to pursue many impossible goals. The intense greed for worldly possessions and close attachment to family and friends creates severe mental agony and chronic stress. Since the mind is firmly attached to awareness of the body and its needs, whatever affects it adversely makes the mind also miserable. Meditation can give a temporary respite from such tribulations without removing the root cause of the discomfort. When the mind finds enduring peace in the Supreme Being, compassion becomes its dominant expression. Freedom from attachments gives us less worries about future prospects and serious set backs in the present life.

M: *Don't you think the same things are discussed in the Upanishads?*

P: There are parallel thoughts in both because they try to answer the same basic questions. Both identify the Supreme reality or universal consciousness as the pure intelligence that encompasses all identities, ideas, and actions. It also brings the phenomenal world to our perception through the interaction of sensory inputs and accumulated images of past experiences. Since supreme intelligence is neutral and its attributes are unknown, the descriptions about such an amazing, all-inclusive entity may have many common ideas. Hence we find the same view even in scientific enquiries.

With the acceptance of the supreme reality of consciousness, a sense of benign detachment prevails in the mind. Ashtavakra compares consciousness to infinite space and the individual body to a pot of clay. The space inside the pot does not have an identity separate from that on the outside. The individual self is just the space enclosed in a pot for a limited time. Similarly, the supreme reality of consciousness can be taken as the ocean in which innumerable waves of different shapes and sizes appear and disappear. Can any wave claim a separate identity when it doesn't exist even for a short while outside the space of the ocean?

In this new worldview, even the concept of a God is redundant. When the entire universe is the manifestation of consciousness, the idea of any entity like God is a conceptual anomaly. With self-realization, all thoughts and actions like worship, rejection, acceptance, love, and hate become expressions of ignorance. According to Ashtavakra, even the physical body attains perfect calm and serenity, as it is no more perturbed by any disturbing thoughts. The knowledge, that nothing more remains to be achieved, calms down even an agitated mind. At that level, even knowledge becomes a burden, which is no more required in the life of unity with consciousness. For the liberated mind, all thoughts and actions are simply illusions created by ignorance.

M: *Does it not entail total indifference to normal life?*

P: It does not mean indifference, but gives the correct perspective to have equal attachment towards all persons. The enlightened one does not show eagerness to enjoy life nor does he reject the pleasant experiences that the nature offers spontaneously. He does not differentiate between objects of pleasure and pain. For him, everything in the world has the same value and appeal, as his awareness is detached from the qualities of any particular object. The knowledge that our experiences are felt only in consciousness makes the mind indifferent to the gains and losses in the material world.

The mind that transcends all temporal and spatial dimensions achieves perfect tranquility. Such persons keep away from arguments and disputes, as they very well know the futility of verbal exchanges. No spiritual training or meditation is necessary for the one who is already united with universal consciousness.

In the material world, we find changes occurring in various objects in course of time. The fluctuations in matter of the primary or secondary forms, like atoms and molecules, are not applicable to the basic nature of the Supreme Self that is pure consciousness. Since, it is unborn and unattached; changes do not affect it in any manner.

M: *Tell me the easiest way to reach such a higher level of awareness.*

P: It is easy to say that one can attain self-realization by understanding and accepting the supremacy of consciousness. What is really difficult is to reach the state of mind that transcends all illusory perceptions prompted by body awareness. Many teachers and spiritual gurus suggest meditation as the most effective method to reach the goal. In one form of meditation, attention is focused on a particular thought or object to bring about a kind of transcendence. It means that we concentrate attention in one direction to exclude all other thoughts and objects.

But the fact is that the tremendous effort required in directing the mind becomes a major source of distraction. It is difficult to achieve detachment from body-related thoughts through any taxing physical activity like concentration. Even if we manage to focus attention for sometime, when the mind returns to the normal state, all the excluded thoughts suddenly rush in. Forcing the mind towards a particular thought or object is of no use unless it spontaneously fixes attention on the chosen goal.

In the second mode of meditation, the mind is deliberately withdrawn from all sense objects and thoughts. A conscious attempt is made to keep it blank without any activity. Since it is difficult to empty the mind, all the fleeting thoughts have to pass through it without focusing attention on any one. But such intentional inaction is also a cause for the distraction of the mind, as tremendous effort is involved to exclude unwanted thoughts.

According to Ashtavakra, the mind can be liberated from attractions and distractions only when it accepts the rational wisdom that consciousness is the only reality. All our physical efforts and mental labor cannot take us to this correct conclusion. Sustained self-enquiry and reflections on the qualities of consciousness can lead us to a stable state of the mind. Evidently, there is no shortcut to 'Nirvana'. You have to work hard to reach the truth but the fruits of the relentless quest are the sweetest. The teacher can only open the door, the student has to enter on his own.

True knowledge will reveal that universal consciousness had existed even before the beginning of the universe. The indisputable fact, that the intelligent energy that pervades the universe and is inherent in all objects, becomes the basis of an unshakeable new faith. We see in nature only limited manifestations of the capabilities of the original energy. Our cocooned consciousness may not be equipped to receive the full details of reality. Universal consciousness has no such restrictions, as its existence is seamless.

The egocentric worldview that we acquire in the normal course of life gets erased when consciousness gives a new perspective. All unwanted memories get automatically obliterated and perception becomes sharper with a hitherto unknown kind of clarity. The miseries of life slowly melt away as one gets detached from the awareness related to the body, wealth, relations and even the family.

They are now replaced by a spontaneous experience of ecstasy. Even in the waking state, an enlightened person enjoys a dreamlike life without any desire even for liberation from the material world. The detached mind does not see any meaning even in the denial of worldly bonds. It simply becomes neutral to all objects, attributes and attitudes. The greatest happiness is found in neutrality, which the Supreme Self enjoys in abundance.

M: Isn't it dangerous to keep the mind in the neutral gear all the time? Don't you think others will exploit your liberal and lenient attitude for their selfish purposes?

P: This kind of ultimate knowledge is definitely dangerous for immature minds. It may tempt them to withdraw from all kinds of activities. Young people with family responsibilities should avoid knowledge that leads to total detachment. It is desirable to reach this mental state only after discharging worldly obligations. Otherwise, the very survival of human species will be threatened. If the separate identity is lost, normal life will be impossible within the parameters of the relationships evolved for our orderly social existence. But it has the positive impact of reducing stress that create mental torture.

M: *Knowing about such unpleasant consequences, why do you recommend it?*

P: In our rich heritage of knowledge, consciousness is a unique concept. It is an undeniable fact that the entire world of existence becomes perceptible only when we are conscious. We have to accept the reality that only in consciousness all our ideas, opinions and concepts are created and acted upon. The fact that nothing exists before consciousness emerges in the brain, conclusively proves the correctness of Ashtavakra's claim that every individual is a reflection of cosmic consciousness. It is true that the exact nature of consciousness is beyond the capabilities of our current comprehension, may be because our intelligence is derived from it. All pursuit of knowledge, therefore, ends with the ultimate realization that universal consciousness is the Supreme Self that creates and maintains manifestations of matter in the universe.

The true knowledge of existence is a unique experience of enlightenment enjoyed by great mystics like Buddha and more recently by Shri Ramana Maharshi through meditative reflections. It is now scientifically proved that the information processed in the brain is experienced only in consciousness. Scientists call it 'the perceptual ego center' or 'the self-referential point'.

The mystics enjoyed harmony with nature in an

elevated state of existence in universal consciousness. The chronic stress that leads to physical and mental disorders can be controlled effectively with the knowledge of consciousness.

What we learn from the worldview of consciousness is the practical wisdom of compassion, straightforwardness and simple mindedness. It should make one enjoy every moment of existence without indulging in aggressive activities that create agonies.

Ashtavakra reveals that seeking early deliverance from life is meaningless as eventually we all return to universal consciousness after death. A spontaneous and natural life is all that is required for achieving peace and happiness. In fact, enjoying legitimate acquisitions is the natural way of reaching 'Nirvana' or deliverance. By denying this world, you don't reach a better one. Heaven and hell are very much here, and you can choose the one you want by controlling thoughts and actions. Detachment is the key to an enjoyable worldly existence.

Let us see whether the mystic vision of consciousness is consistent with the latest scientific knowledge about the brain and the mind. We know that every newborn child is equipped with all the essential tools for creating a neural network in the brain. The brain gets fully programmed in a few years to learn almost everything about the material world. Individual differences, particularly in the matter of intelligence, arise from less than one per cent genetic variations.

It is now established that every important additional capacity of the brain is built upon the original equipment inherited from several ancestral species. We still have remnants of even bacteria and reptiles in our cells. Our primary instincts are carefully preserved to respond automatically to the known challenges of the external world. Let us not forget the fact that we have about ninety eight per cent of our genes common with our simian ancestors.

Another interesting scientific breakthrough is the revelation that most of the cellular and molecular activities appear predetermined. It shows that the evolutionary explanation of the diversity of life is not entirely true. Several specialized systems of the human body, like the neural network in the brain, the circulatory system, the immune system and metabolic pathways, involve interconnected organs and predetermined molecular activities. The basic question is how the exact function and location of each organ was known to the molecules involved in the genetic transmission of intelligence.

The protein molecules seem to follow a perfectly designed flow chart of activities assigned to achieve a common objective. They work within certain chosen parameters for achieving a common objective. Our immune system reveals a foolproof defence mechanism that can detect the presence of disease causing alien microbes and destroy them in the most ingenuous manner. First, an appropriate molecular response is chosen to deal with the invading microbes, and then consequential processes to mass-produce accurate antibodies is unleashed. It shows a highly organized system, which ensures a trouble-free existence for the organism. The question is whether it is possible to evolve such an excellent design for defence out of a series of genetic accidents? In my opinion, it is an impossible task.

A more interesting story is the evolution of the brain. It contains several common systems that can perform different functions. Its plasticity and redundancy are designed for the effective survival of the organism. But the amazing fact is that, several systems of the brain perform functions, which are not even remotely concerned with survival. It is difficult to imagine how mathematics and music are related to the reproductive fitness of an organism. Great musicians and scientists are not reputed for their enhanced reproductive abilities.

We cannot explain why the brain is saddled with all these additional capabilities, which are not even remotely concerned with any activity for achieving evolutionary objectives. We may have to accept the explanation that such faculties are developed probably for the purpose of spending the spare time more usefully and creatively. No such comparable systems for arithmetical abilities or music appreciation are found in animal brains. They are driven by the instinct for survival and not for enjoying recreational activities. We are given the exclusive gift of enhanced conscious capacities by a benign nature. It enables us even to unravel the puzzle of the purpose of creation.

M: How will you relate the scientific knowledge of the functioning of the brain and the mind with the concept of universal consciousness?

P: According to Upanishads and Ashtavakra, the mind is only a reflection of universal consciousness. The astonishing fact now revealed by scientific studies is that neural processing of information is concluded in the brain much before the mind experiences the result of its computation. Whatever is presented to the conscious mind is normally accepted without further addition or subtraction. It is well known that our autonomous nervous system is fully equipped to perform various physical functions independently without the intervention of the mind.

Blind sight experiments establish the fact that our conscious perception at times can be faulty. We know that more than 98 per cent of our brain activities are beyond the reach of consciousness. All sensory and motor activities are initiated and executed without the knowledge of the mind. There is a perceptible time lag between the completion of the brain processes and the mental experience of its outcome.

It shows that the mind is indulging in the worst kind of self-deception. The products of strenuous processing in the brain system are claimed as its own creation. It has very little option to reject or even modify the decisions taken by the brain. All that the mind does at times is to add an explanation or justification for a particular act of commission or omission.

But the indelible impression remains that the brain processes are solely designed and determined by the mind. The masterly imposter conceals the fact that it is the brain containing only ordinary biological matter that creates all thoughts and emotions. The mind can read the poetry written by the brain only when we are conscious.

M: *If that is the fact, what is the role of the mind and consciousness in existence? Can't we live spontaneously, like other animals without entering into endless debates on our origin and existence? Simply enjoy the activities of eating, mating, and sleeping. Why should we make all the fuss about knowledge and achievements?*

P: We cannot deny the fact that the brain is a dynamic, rule driven computing device designed and developed by genetic instructions and environmental influences. It is well known that 'axons' in neurons can even pass through unfamiliar and un-chartered areas to reach their ultimate destinations. Maybe, some molecular sensory device or signals coming from the final destination, guide them to proper positions.

We know that the basic connections for the neural

network are established much before the birth. The sensory signals go through certain designated pathways to the cortical targets. But the question is, what kind of intelligence could design the massive system that anticipates all the functions to be performed well in advance of its physical arrival in the world? The mind is not at all aware of the programs laid down in the brain by genetic instructions. And who could have done the entire spade work for a universe even before our existence.

The amazing truth is that the mind simply assumes that everything belongs to it even though it does not even have a decent shelter in any part of the brain. It is nowhere in the picture until the dinner is ready and all the dishes are laid out on the table.

When misleading memories confuse our perceptions and creates misapprehension, it simply goes back to the past to choose a favourite position. Memory keeps alive the deeply imprinted messages that the mind and body belong to the same identity. In addition, the impression is sustained that the mind controls all thoughts and actions emerging from the body.

Mike, as you suggested, ordinary awareness available even to animals is sufficient to keep us alive in a competitive world. Survival surely does not require intimate knowledge of consciousness or the complexities of the arrow of time. The higher knowledge of the causal connections of natural phenomena does not improve the capabilities for performing the simple functions of eating and mating.

In the early days of our evolutionary history, we would have started off with a rudimentary form of the mind. An exclusive identity of the physical body must have emerged when the cerebral cortex began to expand for creating more conscious capacities. Our acquired additional capabilities probably helped us in understanding the universe and seeking the rules and patterns inherent in nature. That would have enabled us here to reassemble the puzzle of existence using the conscious capacity for symbolic representation.

The contribution of modern science is in the realm of unraveling the mystery of brain functions and revealing the fact that consciousness creates the mind. Ashtavakra correctly focused on consciousness and interpreted the mind as an illusion, which is now confirmed by modern science.

We now know that the contribution of the conscious mind is to experience the events coherently in relation to time. In addition, it gives us some justification for the weird choices we make from the available alternatives. Science also accepts the possibility that consciousness may be the reflection of a kind of energy. The mind is now established as an emergent quality of consciousness and not a physical reality in the brain.

In the absence of self-awareness, our perception becomes the simple reflection of external reality. It is not tainted by the memory of any self-related thought or experience. Pure awareness is like a dream, but with no separateness between the body and the external reality. The perception becomes a continuous flow of information uncontaminated by memories of the past or expectations of the future. It is the final outcome of reaching the highest level of knowledge, not the instant reaction arising out of infantile ignorance.

M: So Ashtavakra demystified the mind much before the scientists dismissed it as an evolutionary appendage.

P: In our scientific pursuit of consciousness, we have not yet come across that quality in any inanimate matter. Philosophers like Russel and Huxley assumed the presence of some kind of proto-consciousness even in ordinary matter. They disagreed with the idea of assigning intelligence to an unknown entity like consciousness. According to their view, nature should be explained by its own laws and not with reference to any ghost in the human brain. It is now considered possible that elementary particles may have the capability for volitional activity before observation creates an event. But there is no scientific evidence for ordinary matter becoming self-conscious under any circumstances. We have no idea how inanimate matter becomes a biological entity capable of experiencing consciousness.

Our current knowledge indicates that consciousness comes through the activities in the network of specialized cells called neurons. They are the building blocks of intelligence that can simultaneously receive and process billions of sensory inputs. Neurons have the capacity to decide whether to respond or not to any input. Some device in the brain keeps the image of the body probably in its memory sub-systems. But, we cannot rule out the possibility that consciousness may be some kind of energy vibration that is probably beyond our present comprehension.

The missing link to consciousness may be the electrical activities of the brain in the prefrontal lobes, which are more active while attending to specific tasks. The neural network is probably capable of resonating with the frequency of consciousness. Such resonance may occur only during the waking state. It explains the absence of the mind during anesthesia, deep sleep or hypnotic trance. The mind reappears as soon as the subject wakes up from the trance or drug induced amnesia. The coherent firings in the neural network may be the missing link between mind and consciousness. We have no other explanation for the conundrum of consciousness.

When we reach the end of the tunnel, we find that the mind is just an illusion created by our memories of self and related objects and events. The eternal truth of existence is consciousness that makes the reality of the phenomenal world accessible to our perception. It creates a composite image of the self, which is stored in memory to emerge as one of the great capacities of mental faculties. In serious brain damages, when the memory is irretrievably erased, we find that both the mind and identity disappear forever. The brain can function in a coherent manner only in the presence of consciousness. It resurrects the mind from the representations stored in memory.

M: *Now I understand the ideas of Ashtavakra. But tell me, what is the ultimate reality? Is there anything beyond consciousness?*

P: If consciousness is accepted as the ultimate reality, forms, properties, polarities and all other attributes of matter can be explained as its emergent qualities. Consciousness is not an inherent quality of matter, but an eternal reality, beyond the qualities of matter. Some people consider proto-consciousness as a part of matter that survives destruction.

Even if we accept such views, the undeniable fact is that an energy like entity must have existed even before the big bang. Since the universe is perceived only in consciousness, the ultimate question is whether we are only a specific combination of biological matter carrying the illusion of a personal mind. The answer is that we are just a special kind of matter and nothing more. Other attributes of life are the assumptions of our fertile imagination in conscious state. The gift of imagination is not given by atoms and molecules; it comes out of only conscious minds.

Even after consciousness leaves a physical body, other bodies capable of becoming conscious continues existence. The conclusion is that consciousness is an unknown state of energy that exists eternally. How can we deny this obvious fact?

Even before the beginning of the universe, consciousness must have existed as an unknown state of energy or a quantum vacuum. It had the inherent capability to create the universe with all sustainable structures out of self-organizing intelligence. We find no other rational solution to the puzzle of cosmic coincidences and the origin and evolution of life on earth. It is the same energy that still maintains the universe with its interactive intelligence.

Science has now established that elementary particles of matter, like quarks and electrons, are capable of exchanging intelligence. Quantum coherence may be the context required for extending intelligence existing at the primary level to more complex structures. I am sure that in course of time, science will unravel the exact mechanism that conducts such instant exchange of intelligence.

The ultimate explanation to the puzzle of existence may be that the cosmic vacuum containing nothing but pure intelligence in the potential state might have initiated self-organizing cycles of creation and destruction. We have no idea why it indulged in such weird experiments with existence. Since we are created by its intelligence, the intentions of the creator will continue to baffle our feeble minds.

In the wisdom of consciousness, Ashtavakra gives us an acceptable answer to the riddle of existence. Our conscious capacities are unique, which other forms of matter cannot access. When we reach the highest cognitive state that gives undifferentiated awareness, all problems created by divergent thoughts and emotions disappear. We acquire the correct perspective of the unity of all beings in consciousness. Only expressions of love and compassion towards all forms of matter exist in that supreme state of awareness. The persistent fear of death is removed with the realization that it is only a temporary transformation of one form of matter. The essence of life is consciousness that is eternal and imperishable. Ashtavakra puts it in a practical perspective whereas the Upanishads give us the spiritual solution to the riddle of existence. Ashtavakra has transformed the knowledge of consciousness to an enjoyable life-style.

M: One last question. Is it possible for the common man to reach such higher levels of awareness without giving up body awareness?

P: Anyone can reach an enduring state of enhanced awareness with minimum distractions. Our inherited intelligence alone cannot take us to the knowledge of consciousness. It requires acceptance of a worldview based on scientific knowledge, which is supplemented by mystic wisdom of unity of existence. No material possessions can give us the extreme bliss that arises from the true comprehension of the meaning and purpose of life. Ashtavakra tells us that the purpose of our life is to reach unity with consciousness. It will make us more compassionate with no feeling of ill will towards anyone. Nothing more is expected of us, and there is no vision that can give us a better worldview for peaceful existence. I hope you appreciate this version of the vision of consciousness. If not, you can move on to the next epilogue, which is meant for younger minds seeking spiritual enlightenment.

EPILOGUE - II
PATANJALI'S PATHFINDER

"When the mind is detached from memory, perception gets total clarity. It gives correct and complete knowledge beyond which nothing remains to be known."

"The Yogic mind abides in total silence. In supreme silence, the mind is liberated from the world of change to rest in unbounded consciousness."

"The world truly exists only in consciousness. Everything else is illusion."

[Yogasutras]

"Not all of us have to possess earth-shaking talents, just common sense and love will do."

[Myrtle Anvil]

"Silence is frequently misinterpreted, but it is never misquoted."

[Baltasar Gracian]

"Beliefs are what divides people. Doubts unite them"

[Peter Ustinov]

P: Before we conclude, let us have a close look at another yogic vision of existence. Here we find an entirely different approach to self-realization based on deep meditation. Patanjali, the Vedic scholar belonging to the later period of Indo-Aryan civilization, expounded a different approach to achieve the yogic state of mind. We don't know his personal details, but some people believe that he belonged to the 2nd Century BC and authored a comprehensive treatise on Sanskrit grammar. His profound vision known as 'Yogasutras' is one of the six schools of thoughts in Vedic philosophy. It is called "Darsana", which, in Sanskrit, means a mirror that reflects life in its totality. Actually, all the six Vedic Darsanas present worldviews from different perspectives. They attempt to explain existence as understood by the ancient mystics.

Patanjali explains yogic philosophy in the form of sutras, which are characterized by limited use of language. The few chosen words are supposed to convey the full meaning of the intention when one meditates over it. A new vision or worldview, which has universal application, evolves out of the meditation on the words. They may not make a complete sentence, but the competent teacher can construct a clear idea out of the seemingly unconnected words. A well-trained teacher is required to convey the complete meaning of the 'sutras'. First, the disciple has to memorize the sutras following the recitation by the teacher. Then the teacher explains the meaning by expanding the intention of the word in the context of the concept of mind and its qualities.

In Yoga sutras, the word 'yoga' is used in a limited sense. It is actually a pathfinder to direct mental activities towards a chosen object without distraction. The direction is sustained by getting rid of all thoughts and emotions that normally interfere with attentive meditation. Patanjali first analyses the way the mind works and then gives suggestions for directing the mental processes. By successful focusing of mental processes on an object, we can achieve enhanced capacity to comprehend all its characteristics correctly. The idea of God does not arise when it is assumed that the teacher, who helps one to attain the yogic state of the mind, is equivalent to God. Once the ultimate destination is reached, God becomes superfluous as the mind achieves unity with him. This is the basic assumption underlying all Vedic thoughts.

M: What is Patanjali's concept of yogic mind? Nowadays we hear lot of things about yogic exercises to remove stress and achieve longevity. How is it related to mental activities?

P: According to Patanjali, yoga is a comprehensive concept that can be taught only by a competent teacher. The teacher should convey only correct ideas to the disciples. Patanjali defines yoga as a state of the mind that attends exclusively to a chosen object or situation. Once unwavering focusing of the mind is achieved, it should be sustained without any distraction.

The idea is that a stable mind alone can comprehend an object in the correct and complete manner. The preconceived notions created by memory are reduced or eliminated in the process of direction, which makes the mind totally transparent. It achieves the capability to understand even the most complex of subjects with great clarity. This state is somewhat equivalent to undifferentiated awareness described in the Upanishads. It is also comparable to Ashtavakra's idea of unity with universal consciousness.

In ordinary life, the mind is subject to several misconceptions based on the memory of past experiences. Patanjali does not define the mind, but considers it as comprising of about five activities. Some of them are beneficial but others have harmful effects. The five activities described are comprehension, misconception, imagination, deep sleep, and memory.

An object can be comprehended on the basis of direct observation, inference or instruction from learned persons. Ordinary perception that carries the emotional and cognitive contents to the mind is always conditioned by the memory of experiences. In the yogic state of mind, comprehension is complete as attention is exclusively focused on an object. Misconception arises from incorrect comprehension of an object or situation. The mind is misled either by faulty observations or by misinterpretations of memory. In the yogic state, all such misconceptions are removed and comprehension becomes correct and complete in all respects.

While comprehension and misconception are direct consequences of observation of an object through sensory organs, imagination is a mental activity without perception. It is conceptualization of an object through symbolic representations. Poetic descriptions and abstract works of art follow the path of imagination. This kind of mental activity is also seen in dreams and emotional states of the body. Imagination is conceived and controlled by sensations and memory. It is an intuitive extension of mental faculties.

In the state of sleep, the activity level is at the lowest. It is achieved when both the mind and body are thoroughly tired. A biological cycle induces rest, which is essential for refreshing various organs. Another activity of the mind is the making of memory, which contains impressions of all personal experiences. It may not always convey the correct comprehension of reality. Our perceptions and subsequent comprehensions are conditioned by existing memory. If the initial experiences are coloured or conditioned by the state of the mind or the body, memory will always carry an incorrect version of reality.

According to Patanjali, the mind exists in terms of its activities. It can be sequentially described as comprehension following direct perception through the sensory organs. Imagination is another activity of the mind without the help of sensory perception. Misapprehension is comprehension arising out of defective perception, imagination, and memory.

M: *How can we reach the yogic state of mind?*

P: Patanjali prescribes constant practice and total detachment to reach the yogic state of mind. He describes practice as a sustained effort to move away from the ordinary state of mind to the yogic state. Practice is also required to maintain the yogic state that can be disturbed by day-to-day activities and several kinds of body related deficiencies.

It is a time consuming and tiresome process that demands tremendous self-control and a disciplined life style to get rid of the adverse effects of the environment. By gaining perfect knowledge of the visible world and avoiding harmful objects and habits, that create craving for their continuous possession, one can improve physical strength and extend mental capacities.

Continuous practice to reach the yogic state can gradually detach the mind from temptations and relationships. But in real terms, complete neutrality can be achieved only when one understands the nature of the Supreme Self. The true comprehension need not involve sensory perceptions, memory or imagination. It can emerge from prolonged meditative reflection on the cause of the visible world without getting distracted by its attractions. Comprehension becomes deeper and clearer with the correct knowledge of the actual perceiver who experiences the external world. The perception becomes flawless, since it is untainted by memory.

In the yogic state, memory also becomes neutral without causing mental distraction. According to Patanjali, some great people are born with the yogic state of mind, but ordinary persons require constant practice and detachment to achieve it.

An essential requirement to reach the goal of yogic mind is the confidence that one can overcome all worldly distractions. The aspirant need not be distressed by temporary setbacks, and with unshakable faith he can attain the objective in a short period of time. Some people have natural inclination to that state, as they have inherited capabilities and cultural influences.

Faith in God can be of great help. Patanjali describes the qualities of God as correct and complete knowledge, timelessness and total comprehension. To understand them, one has to see what are the defects and deficiencies of mortals. Proper guidance of a teacher can be of great help in understanding the concept of God. Repeated recitation of his name and qualities in a mechanical manner does not bring about any perceptible change in one's mental status. But sustained meditation on the qualities of God can bestow the yogic state of mind even to an ordinary person.

The knowledge of the qualities of God will make one understand the real nature of the mind. Self-realization is the correct appreciation of life without getting distracted by the conditions of the body or the mind. Mental problems can arise out of illness, boredom, self-doubt, fatigue, illusions, and over indulgence. They are debilitating influences that prevent us from understanding God as well as one's own mind. The negative thoughts created by them make the body tense and sick. The reason for physical distraction is our inability to control breathing and other bodily activities.

Sustained positive thinking is possible only when objects and events in our immediate environment do not disturb the mind. If we are well disposed towards people happier than us, and compassionate to those who are less happy, we develop a neutral and peaceful state of mind. Noble persons devoted for the service of the poor and needy keep themselves and the environment pleasant and clean. They deserve our appreciation. Mistakes committed by others should not perturb us and our own misdeeds should not be repeated. The past should never be a guide to future actions; there will always be some scope to improve upon it.

Patanjali prescribes breathing exercises like extensive exhalations for relaxing the body and the mind. The exact manner in which breath control can be practiced should be learnt from a competent teacher. Another way of controlling the mind is to meditate on the role of the senses that give information about the environment as well as the state of the body. Our deep reflection on the cause of existence can also reduce distractions. We can seek the help of enlightened persons to get a correct worldview and the knowledge to avoid mistakes. If a competent teacher is not available, instructions can be taken even from the writings of self-realized persons.

When we probe deep into the enigma of existence, we get to know more about the visible world. Normally, on becoming more knowledgeable, ordinary people erroneously assume total enlightenment. Such presumptions lead to arrogance unless the understanding that what is learnt is not even a fraction of the total reality makes one humble and pious. We can also direct enquiries into our own mental states to get a relaxed mindset. It ultimately leads to the yogic mind in which we understand the simple as well as the profound, the infinite as well as the infinitesimal, the perceptible as also the imperceptible.

Patanjali states that the yogic mind, which is free from distractions, turns the focus of enquiry to deeper mental processes. When the mind is stable, it gets totally involved with the object of perception and begins to comprehend its features more clearly. In this state, one can achieve total comprehension of any object or situation by spontaneous transformation from the ordinary to yogic state. All memories imprinted in the mind about that particular object or situation are gradually erased.

The perception becomes undifferentiated when the perceiver merges with the object of perception. This process will be possible with all kinds of objects and situations. Even in the yogic state, one object that cannot be perceived correctly is the mind. The perceiver is beyond comprehension so long as we assume separateness from it. When the perceiver, the act of perception, and the object of perception are integrated, we achieve the enlightened state of yogic mind.

In the yogic state, one reaches self-realization or the correct comprehension of the meaning of existence. At that level of knowledge, there is no chance of errors creeping in through disturbing thoughts. The newly acquired insight is not based on memory. It is a direct experience of the truth of reality. With continuous exposure to the yogic state, the chances of relapse into the previous restless life get reduced. The mind does not store impressions of experiences and becomes open and transparent to the external world. It is an existence beyond description, which has to be experienced through practice of detachment over a long period of time.

One can reach the yogic state of mind only if all obstacles like misapprehensions are completely removed. Patanjali suggests an eightfold path to reach the yogic state. The first step is a thorough change in our attitude to the environment. It means a feeling of compassion for all kinds of living beings particularly, the weak and the disabled ones. The change should engender right communication, truthful speech and writings. We should not be covetous for things that really do not belong to us. Our actions and ambitions should become moderate. Nature gives us enough according to our needs and actual abilities and one should feel fully satisfied with God's gift of life.

The second step involves the rectification of mistakes that cause serious problems to the environment including one's own body. It means keeping the body and surroundings free from pollution. Good habits such as sound sleep, regular exercises, proper diet, and relaxation can keep the body clean and healthy. We should also respect enlightened persons who acquire higher levels of knowledge and accept the failings of the less learned, with a sense of compassion.

Full faith in God is an excellent means to achieve the yogic state. According to Patanjali, attitudes of violence, aggressiveness, anger and possessiveness are the expressions of the dominance of lower instincts. One can learn honest and effective communication only when the mind is devoid of undesirable inclinations. Such basic changes in attitudes require sublimation of lower instincts to higher moral values.

Patanjali holds moderation as the greatest virtue. In moderation, problems created by excesses like wastage are avoided. Conversely, if something is very inadequate, it may not meet the minimum requirement. Moderation makes us capable of deep and sustained introspection. It is a close examination of one's own thoughts and source of perception without getting distracted by misleading sensory inputs and memory. Deep reflection gives correct knowledge of the Supreme Self, the universe and life. Lasting happiness and peace prevails in the mind that acquires the true knowledge of reality.

Introspection is the means to understand our strong and weak personality traits. It enables us to slowly reduce the weak points and improve the strong ones to the maximum extent. With the full realization of true capabilities, a new sense of confidence and respect for the highest intelligence of the creator emerges in the mind. Patanjali also suggests certain physical exercises like 'asanas' to purify the body and the mind. They can improve alertness and induce a sense of relaxation.

Yogic exercises help us defend against the rigorous attacks of debilitating factors like age, climate, bad food, and stress. They involve the control of breathing patterns and body positions. "Pranayama" is a deep pattern of breathing that can replace the defective rhythms causing serious ailments. It involves prolonged exhalation and inhalation and the holding of the breath. When breath is modulated, a rhythmic breathing pattern can be maintained for long periods of time. During this exercise, the mind is focused only on the process of breath modulation.

Regular practice of Pranayama improves physical strength and removes many mental problems. The mind gets more time to concentrate on the direction of the chosen goal. In the yogic state of consciousness, one enters a new phase of life. In course of time, deep breathing becomes spontaneous without any conscious control of the rhythms.

With a healthy body, the practice of directing the mind towards the chosen goal becomes easier. When the senses are restrained, the mind can steadily focus on the object selected for reflection. Other objects creating distractions get naturally ignored.

The successful culmination of the practice of concentration of the mind is in overcoming all kinds of distractions. The liberated mind can then explore objects and ideas in a new perspective. Objects are perceived with a previously unknown insight. Sometimes even knowledge becomes a source of distraction. At the highest level of freedom, the mind discards all kinds of knowledge.

The choice of the object of attention is immaterial, as what is important is to keep the mind focused on it. Uninterrupted contemplation gives us correct and complete comprehension of an object. In that state, one does not feel separateness from the object of attention, as all its qualities and features merge with the perceiver's existence.

The yogic state can be achieved by adopting appropriate attitude towards the environment, own body, and control of breathing and the senses. It leads one to the ultimate objective of self-realization. The ability to direct the mind to have uninterrupted interaction with the chosen object gives us the true knowledge of its existence. The awareness becomes undifferentiated when it is felt that the vibrations of all kinds of energy emanate from within.

In the yogic state, the capacity for concentration goes far beyond ordinary limits. Normally we live in two states of mind. In the first state, attention is focused on a particular object or situation. In the other, the mind is continuously in distraction. Prolonged practice can keep the mind fixed on a particular object. In the beginning, it may move between several objects but ultimately returns to the object of inquiry. It is possible to control the mind by understanding its qualities.

According to Patanjali, the three qualities shared by the mind, the senses, and the objects of senses are clarity, activity, and heaviness. Different patterns of behaviour can be obtained by changing the sequence of these attributes. We can reach complete comprehension of objects by developing a keen interest to have full knowledge about all its features and qualities.

With undifferentiated awareness and total involvement in the object of enquiry, the perceiver and the perceived undergo profound changes. The mind is spontaneously disconnected from all objects and begins to understand the perceiver. When it acquires correct knowledge, ordinary perceptual abilities get elevated. Continuous practice of 'pranayama' and 'asanas' takes the mind to the yogic state. If the senses that transmit information to the brain are tamed, we can also control the sensory inputs. In the yogic state, the relationship between the body and different objects in the world become transparent.

Normally, memory colours the process of perception. If the mind can control memory, the confusions created by past experiences are considerably reduced. The liberated mind has the extraordinary faculty to understand and access other minds. It can also anticipate the changes that may take place in various objects and their consequences. But such knowledge is not the ultimate goal of yoga. True liberation of the mind lies in getting rid of all desires for more power and material possessions including the quest to understand one's own mind. To reach this goal, one has to merge the self-identity with the infinite existence of the perceiver.

The mind is the master of ignorant persons. But with

constant practice one can make it an obedient servant. It involves changing the mindset from instincts to acquired higher qualities. Even a competent guru cannot bring about any profound change in an ignorant person unless he has the inner motivation to seek more knowledge. An intelligent teacher can give proper instructions to achieve the yogic goal. He can keep the door of knowledge open; but it is up to the disciple to enter and enjoy the bonanza of wisdom.

The mind cannot easily give up the inherent tendencies and the strong desire to enjoy the fruits of action. But the intensity of such instincts will gradually subside if correct knowledge enters the mind.

Finally, we proceed to the more basic issue of the perception of reality. The question is whether it is possible for objects to exist solely for our perception or do they have independent existence? Patanjali holds the view that the existence of objects is not subject to our observation. It depends on the accessibility to the object and the motivation of the observer. We can see the object only if it exists independently and we have the interest to look at it. If that is the case, can the mind be seen by the perceiver? Since the mind is always changing, and the perceiver is beyond any change, we can assume that the perceiver can observe all mental activities. Probably, an observer can see the mind in the same manner, as it perceives any physical object.

Some may argue that the mind itself is the perceiver. It is impossible to imagine that the mind, which presumably processes information, can simultaneously review its own work. The mind cannot play the double role of making as well as monitoring the information at the same time. There is something beyond the mind, which perceives the processed information. The source of perception should be independent of the mind but the state of the mind can always influence the perception. It is also possible for memory to modify the perception. Without our knowledge a lot of adulteration takes place while processing perceptions.

When the mind is disconnected from external objects and reflects only on the perceiver, it assumes the identity of the perceiver. With no sensory inputs and memory to interfere, the mind can get firmly attached to the perceiver. According to Patanjali, the mind serves two purposes. First, it presents the external world to the perceiver. Secondly, it can also reflect on the perceiver for ultimate enlightenment. The perceiver motivates the mind to seek new levels of knowledge.

Patanjali states that a truly enlightened man is one who reaches the highest state of clarity. He totally identifies himself with the perceiver and never asks the question "Who am I?" The main concern, after achieving clarity, is to remain in that state without any distraction. It gives a life of contentment and no errors or selfish interests can cloud the vision of true reality. Everything becomes crystal clear because the mind is now totally free from all distortions. It is the highest level of intelligence that understands life without any doubt or after thought. The achievement of the yogic goal gives complete freedom from miseries. The perceiver makes the mind its life long servant while imparting it the highest level of wisdom to understand everything in the universe.

M: Patanjali gives a lot of ideas for refining our attitudes. But I feel that all of them identify the perceiver as the Supreme Self or Brahman or universal consciousness. They may suggest different paths to reach it, but the vision of the ultimate remains the same.

P: The names and means are immaterial; the substance

is that there is something in us, which is beyond the
physical body. It is not attached to awareness of the body
or sensory organs. We will get more ideas about it in the
Appendix on the mind. I am sure that all this knowledge
will enable you to choose the correct path to reach the
goal of self-realization. What we are about to crack is the
hardest of all nuts. It is a tough task, but the rewards are
really mind-boggling.

APPENDIX
MASTER OF BIO-MATTER

"Mental impressions that create attachment are the basic cause of all worldly worries. The detached mind is devoid of all such illusions of ignorance."

"Memories are the seeds of action embedded deep in the mind. They motivate actions in unknown ways. Wrong actions lead to misery and the right ones give immense happiness."

"The mind reaches the highest level of intelligence when it realizes the supreme state of eternal consciousness or Brahman."

[Yogavaasishtha]

"The real history of consciousness starts with one's first lie."

[Joseph Brodsky]

"The existence of a problem does not necessarily indicate that a solution must follow."

[A proverb]

"Science without religion is lame. Religion without science is blind."

[Albert Einstein]

First, let us see some undisputed facts about the human brain that creates the mind, the ultimate biological wonder.

It is an accepted fact that the mind arises from the activities in the cortical region of the brain. We have a highly enlarged brain mass in this area that must have emerged in the last phase of our evolutionary ascent. Some animals also possess cerebral cortex but its size and properties are probably not good enough to create an intelligent mind. Evidently, the human brain has to be big enough for creating the complex neural network in which consciousness appears accompanied by the mysterious mind.

The fact that we have about seven times more of brain mass as compared to our mammalian brethren clearly shows how different we are from all other forms of life. The big animals like elephants have more brain but it is good enough only to serve the huge body. Our brain-body ratio is much higher than that of whales and elephants.

To the naked eye, the brain looks like a wrinkled jelly like material. It weighs on an average about 1.3 kilograms. A closer look reveals certain distinct regions that are interlocked to function in an integrated manner. Two halves or 'hemispheres' sitting on a stout stick is the striking feature that hits us at first sight of the bare brain. Behind the main brain, is a small protrusion called "cerebellum".

It is difficult to understand the mind without getting some basic ideas about the various structures of the brain and their functions. The brain and the spinal cord constitute the central nervous system containing neurons and different types of supporting cells. The supporting cells assist the neurons in the maintenance and metabolic functions. In the central nervous system, we find two classes of material, the grey and the white matter. The outer part of brain has a grey hue but most of the material inside looks white. The inner material of the spinal cord is white, which is the colour of myelin insulation. The switching area, where the neuron synopsis connects with other neurons, is grey. Most of the mental activities are performed in this area. No wonder 'grey matter' symbolizes intelligence.

The brain has four major regions starting with the 'Cerebral cortex' on the top. The 'midbrain' contains switching areas and passages for the nerves. The brainstem contains most of the basic nervous system controls. The fourth major area called 'cerebellum' is behind the upper part of the brain stem. It is concerned with the control of complex movements. In this note, we focus attention on the cerebral cortex, which is the most recently evolved area of the brain. This wonderful blanket separates us from even our closest evolutionary cousins, the Chimpanzees.

The human brain is also viewed as a showcase of hierarchical evolutionary progress. The reptilian brain consisting of the brain stem is the seat of instinctive behaviour. The structures in the middle brain are called 'Limbic System'. They contain the old mammalian brain controlling emotional behaviour, sex, and aggression. The outermost region is the cortex, which is the area of abstract thoughts. It is the seat of our intelligence.

The frontal cortex is actually a bridge between the sensory and motor circuits of the rest of the cortex. It also coordinates with the older structures of the brain that regulate instincts, emotions, body functions, and so on. The prefrontal cortex creates our complex and abstract thoughts. It also contains a timing device to relate the present with the past and future. If this area is severely damaged, a person becomes aggressive like a wild animal.

Sometimes he may turn indifferent to all that happens in the world.

Behind the frontal cortex, the sensory and motor regions are neatly divided to correspond with specific areas on the opposite side of the body. Audio processing and verbal information occurs in the temporal lobes. Inside the cortex, there is a region called the 'Hippocampus', which coordinates the transmission of information received from the sensory organs to other areas of the brain.

The 'occipital cortex' at the back of the brain, processes the visual information. The seat of emotion and impulsive action is called the 'amygdala'. This structure in the limbic system had evolved much earlier than the cerebral cortex. It is also deeply involved in sexual behaviour, stress response, sleep, and depression. They are all part of our inherited mammalian past.

In the midbrain we have the 'thalamus', which switches on the sensory system and the 'hypothalamus' that controls the body temperature and functions of several organs. The pituitary gland connected to the hypothalamus sends hormones into the blood stream to control body responses.

The brainstem, which connects the upper brain with the spinal cord, controls the autonomous nervous system. The 'axons' of the nerve cells that make amine neurotransmitters like norepinephrine, serotonin, dopamine, and histamine are situated here. These neurotransmitters are essential for maintaining the conscious state and when they are not available in sufficient quantities we fall asleep. This area also controls eye movements, hearing and balance.

The 'cerebellum' is another important structure behind the brain stem. It has the control mechanism for movement and balance. Automated movement responses to external stimuli originate here. It processes the incoming sensory information to produce reflex action. The spinal cord sends motor impulses to muscles to contract in a coordinated manner. They leave the spinal cord as nerve roots at every level of bone segments called 'vertebra'. The spinal cord also has control circuits including the reflexes. The network of nerves throughout the body is controlled by the autonomic nervous system, which takes care of the functioning of organs like the heart, digestive tract, blood vessels and many others.

It is divided into sympathetic and parasympathetic nervous systems. The sympathetic system contains bead like collection of cell bodies that sit along the spine. When we are under stress, it stimulates the glands to release hormones into the blood stream. The parasympathetic system is meant for relaxation. It causes the slow down of heartbeats, salivation, relaxation of sphincters and such other activities. The brain, along with its structures including the spinal cord, functions in a harmonious manner for the growth and maintenance of the body.

We can trace the organization and the functions of the brain from the beginning of life in a single fertilized cell called "zygote". Between the third and fourth week after fertilization, the cell develops neural tubes. They multiply rapidly to form the brain and the central nervous system. After about four weeks, the cells near the neural tubes make a curved structure that develops into the brain.

By the fifth month, all the important features of the brain are laid down and the cells begin to migrate to the designated areas according to some kind of a predetermined schedule. By the seventh month, the synapses between the neurons that exchange the chemical messages begin to appear. Electrical activities in the brain region of the foetus have been recorded in the third month. But distinct, regular waves appear only in the sixth foetal month. Up to the age of ten, the brain generates mainly the slow delta and theta rhythms.

The basic functional unit of the brain is an advanced kind of cell called 'neuron'. There are different varieties of neurons performing specific functions. We have about 100 billion neurons in the brain and they make a vast network with trillions of connections. An average neuron has a nucleus containing the DNA and specific areas for production of energy and other functions. The structure resembling a tree, which moves out of the central body, contains a lot of branches called 'Dendrites'. They receive the basic inputs from other neurons. A fiber like branched out structure called 'Axon' is the output junction for making connectivity with the neighboring neurons. Nerve signals pass on to other neurons in a process combining both chemical and electrical activities.

The signaling device in the neural network consists of emission and reception of special molecules. The membrane of the neuron contains different types of molecules known as "receptors". The outer side of the receptor can accept only a molecule with a specific shape. The receptors are channels allowing atoms of sodium, potassium and calcium to flow in and out of the neurons.

They also function as pumps for removing the atoms from the cells. When the neurons are not sending any signals, the sodium channels remain closed and the potassium channels are kept open. The protein, that works as a molecular pump sends out the sodium ions and lets in the potassium ions. When the neurons are inactive, the axon has a negative charge created by the imbalance of the ions.

When a signal is received by the neurons, a series of

processes begin with the entry of sodium ions until the axon becomes positive. The flow of the charge called 'action potential' allows the sodium ions to spread out in the inside of the membrane. The nerve signal is in fact the result of the process in which the sodium ions get into the axon on the upstream side and the potassium ions move down from the downstream side.

As the action potential reaches the end of the neuron, a chemical agent takes over the messenger service. In this process molecules called neuro transmitters are dumped into the gap between the neurons. They float across the gap and are received by the receptors of the membrane in the downstream neuron. It sets off another chain of complex chemical processes in the message receiving neuron. A single neuron can receive and process several kinds of signals. The neuron can even function autonomously in deciding whether to convey or cancel the message by firing appropriate signals.

The most important chemical functionaries of the brain are the neuro transmitters that carry signals in the neural network. They are capable of triggering different chemical processes in the neurons. Neurotransmitters cause a wide variety of changes in the brain in which different mental states emerge in an inexplicable manner. Several mental disorders are now traced to the excess or deficiency of neurotransmitters. They are sent to the cortex from the brainstem through the projections beginning in the reticular activating system. Each type of projection sends a different neurotransmitter.

The chemical transmitters like dopamine, noradrenalin and acetylcholine are also related to the arousal levels required for sleep and wakefulness. We can say that the activities of the brain are truly controlled by the neurotransmitters. They can affect attention, alertness and create different kinds of emotional states. In addition, they can also achieve neuromodulation, which means controlling the response time of the target cell.

The advanced imaging technology now allows us to see the actual functioning of various areas in the brain. In PET scans, radioactive isotopes of oxygen are used to detect the blood flow in neural areas. MRI can indicate the hot areas that are performing certain tasks. They enable us to trace the major chain of activity such as processing of sensory inputs. They are also useful diagnostic tools for treating mental disorders.

While focusing attention on a particular thought or activity, the brain images show blood flow in a few areas. It indicates a minimum level of distraction from competing stimuli. The nerve cells that release neurotransmitters acetylcholine, dopamine, histamine, norepinephrine and serotonin are collectively active in creating an attentive state of mind.

Acetylcholine is the essential chemical that is present almost everywhere in the brain. It is involved in many functions including the ability to focus attention on a task or thought. Consumption of alcohol, caffeine, nicotine and certain psychedelic drugs initially stimulate attention but addictions eventually cause irreparable damage to the brain cells.

Unlike attention, memory is not highly susceptible to short-term fluctuations in neurotransmitters. A balanced supply of some vital neurotransmitters, like acetylcholine, norepinephrine, serotonin and dopamine is essential for keeping long term and short-term memory circuits intact and fully functional. Chemicals like 'ketamine' can cause temporary amnesia.

Caffeine and nicotine are known agents for short-term memory boosting, but they adversely affect memory in the long run. Addiction to large amounts of alcohol affects the capacity to remember past experiences cogently. Permanent memory loss is also noticed in excessive alcohol consumption that affects the natural thiamine storage. Chronic stress state is also a well-known cause for memory loss.

Neurotransmitters like serotonin, dopamine and histamine receptors also take part in sexual activity. PET scans taken during sexual orgasm indicate the areas of neural activity, particularly in the right side of the brain. It explains how orgasm gets delayed if attention is diverted by any deficiency in the neurotransmitters that keep the mind focused. Serotonin and norepinephrine levels fall during the sleep cycles.

Similarly, decreasing levels of acetylcholine induce drowsiness. In stress situations also we find higher levels of serotonin and norepinephrine, which are necessary for focusing the mind on the object or situation that poses serious challenges. The hypothalamus causes the release of the stress hormone 'Cortisol' into the blood stream to cope with the additional demands of the body. In brief, the brain chemicals decide all our mental and physical state and make a concerted effort to maintain our fitness in a competitive environment.

We have seen the general layout of the brain and its important systems. The specific contributions of the neurotransmitters for creating physical and mental states have also been briefly surveyed. But no explanation is available for the riddle of cellular/molecular changes affecting our mood and mind. Why should we feel happy or depressed just because some chemical in the brain is present in excess or less than adequate quantity? How do we become conscious by the action of a few chemicals? Why do we have neuronal plasticity that allows some brain areas to perform different kinds of functions?

We will explore all these puzzles and more importantly, the emergence of the mind itself in the ensuing parts. But one thing is certain that all our discoveries so far do not find any specific seat for the mind in the brain. Throughout the day and even in the night, the brain is continuously receiving signals both from the external and the internal sources. These vibrations of energy are processed with the help of memory to present a cogent image of reality to the mind. The mind is not at all aware of the kind of processing that goes on in the brain. The autonomic nervous system and the fully automated reflexes take care of most of the functional needs of the body. They manage even stress situations without our conscious intervention.

Stress response is an excellent example of creating a mental phenomenon out of a purely physical reaction. It is a marvellous evolutionary achievement of converging all physical and mental resources in do or die situations. Activities of other internal organs that require energy are held in abeyance for maximizing the resources for fight or flight conditions. The body also has a suitable device to get back to normal activities after the highly demanding stress response is completed. The rollback mechanism is yet another proof of the design, whether we admit it or not.

When a sensory organ picks up a threat signal, it is transmitted directly by the thalamus to amygdala, the fear center of the brain. The amygdala releases the necessary neurotransmitters to the brain circuit to activate the hypothalamus, pituitary and adrenal glands. When the blood stream is flooded with cortisol and adrenaline, physical and mental responses converge to meet the challenge. The heart beats faster, the muscles become tense and the temperature and pulse are kept at higher than normal levels. The activities like digestion, immune functions and so on are kept on the back burner. The mind concentrates attention on the object of fear and evaluates the chances of success in a head on collision. If the enemy is formidable, it advises you to run away as fast as possible.

Once the threat perception is gone, the parasympathetic system releases enough chemicals to relax the body and mind.

The evolutionary objective of survival is ensured by the twin mechanism for developing stress and distress. False alarms are also sorted out by another system in the prefrontal cortex that appraises the threat perceptions. If the object of threat is proved harmless, a message goes to amygdala from the prefrontal cortex to take it easy. The quick responding amygdala is controlled by the more intelligent mechanism of prefrontal cortex. It is another amazing evolutionary achievement to avoid unwanted stress.

Chronic stress response in modern times is unnatural and unwanted. It leads to serious ailments of the body and mind like high blood pressure, heart and digestive problems. Mental faculties suffer from depression, insomnia, loss of memory and general fatigue. It all begins with false perceptions that give rise to anxieties, worries, and phobias. Unfounded fear of ghosts and possibility of terrorist attacks keep some people tense all the time. Chronic anxiety creates perpetual low-grade stress response that leads to the ailments mentioned above.

It is the paradox of evolutionary ascent. A reaction that is primarily designed for survival has now become the biggest killer of humanity. Millions are dying from coronary disorders and other ailments related to sustained stress response. We create anxieties out of nothing and invent imaginary objects of threat like dragons, monsters and UFO's. There is a recently developed system in the brain called 'bed nucleus of stria terminalis' that activates chronic anxiety. Amygdala has been spared for real emergency and anxieties and phobias are now assigned to a new folder. It is probably another evolutionary acquisition like neocortex.

Before we go deeper into the mind, we should have some clear ideas about consciousness. It would have been easier to understand this strange phenomenon if it originated from a specific location in the brain. There is a general tendency to equate the mind with consciousness. But it is erroneous as the mind arises only in a conscious person. It is also true that all conscious persons may not have the normal capacities of the mind. Animals also have different levels of awareness but they do not have our kind of mind.

In humans, consciousness, self-awareness, and the mind are the sequentially emerging qualities of an active brain. The mind has various advanced capacities like intelligence, freewill, compassion, and wisdom. In short, the mind is a comprehensive concept, which is the highest benchmark of evolutionary achievement. On the other hand, consciousness is a passive state, in which various capacities of the mind operate. This state of the brain is common to many forms of life. It only gives an opportunity without actively participating in subsequent developments.

Scientists like Antonio Damagio attribute consciousness to the electro-chemical interactions in the brain and upgradation of the awareness of the states of the body. Edelman suggests that consciousness is a physical function that arises from the reciprocal flow of information between groups or bunches of neurons performing selective functions. Dennet also confines consciousness to the functioning of neurons. He explains conscious perceptions in terms of a "multiple draft" theory, which states that the brain improves upon its own processes to produce the clearest image of reality. The mind according to him is an illusion created by vested interests seeking to place a ghost in the physical matter of the brain.

It is evident that scientific knowledge of the brain does not give us a credible explanation for the emergence of consciousness and the mind. An outstanding feature of our brain is the tremendous expansion in the prefrontal cortex area, which is not assigned to any specific task. It is much more evolved than any other cortical area, but still we have no definite clue about its processes that create thoughts and actions.

Clinical evidences show a very high degree of neural plasticity that enables some parts to take over the functions of damaged areas. MRI and PET scans reveal that several brain areas work together for performing a specific task. The neural connections in different anatomical areas do not converge in any central location to create consciousness. Even in the absence of consciousness, the brain works in an autonomous manner as we see in the case of blind sight. Consciousness is also related to some properties of objects when they are in our perceptual field.

To start with, we find that consciousness begins with a state of arousal. If the arousal is less, we fall asleep. A very high level of arousal makes us irrational and unstable. In a relaxed and conscious state, we find slow and regular alpha waves. While dreaming also, we find similar wave patterns. So we are sure that arousal has something to do with our awareness, which is accompanied by the emergence of the mind and its capabilities.

Our search for the roots of consciousness takes us first to the beginning of life. The fact is that we have no idea when we first begin to experience awareness. Some people say that a very low degree of awareness exists even in the foetal state. But many others see its emergence only after birth. Being a graded quality, we can take it as a developing capacity concomitant with the growth of the brain. Animals can also reach different levels of awareness. Some higher mammals like apes are even capable of becoming vaguely self-conscious like a human child.

Another key question is what exactly do we mean when we say we are aware or conscious? Does it mean that we feel the aggregate of all the activities of the neurons or a state of the brain created and maintained by their efforts? Are the neurons aware of what they are supposed to do? It seems that they do have some kind of awareness to find the ultimate location, a friendly neighborhood, and the discretion to send or suppress messages.

Even molecules seem to know what they are supposed to do in appropriate contexts. Yet another problem is the reconnections in the neural net by new experiences. Is it the individual neuron or the entire network that decides the kind of changes required in connectivity when we face a new challenge? Or is it the collective awareness of the neural network that decides such crucial structural alterations. We simply have no idea about any of these enigmas.

It is difficult to define consciousness or describe its emergence and functions accurately. But that should not detract our attempts to unravel its unknown features. In the conscious state, we are definitely awake and alert. Unlike in sleep, coma or dream, we are fully aware of everything around. We can spontaneously perform physical and mental tasks without getting into a state of readiness.

Animals also show the same kind of alertness in the conscious state. Anesthetic drugs and serious brain injuries can affect the quality of our awareness and animals also suffer the same consequences under similar circumstances. Our mental faculties become fully functional when we are conscious but the mechanism that creates this state seems to be very inadequate to conduct such gigantic tasks.

Cognitive studies show that the state of consciousness lasts only for a very short span of about fifteen seconds. We create an illusion of continuous state of awareness by adding up a series of short-term episodes. The spatial dimension of consciousness is also extremely poor to perform any great cerebral activities. A single conscious event can hold only about seven objects at a time. Maybe some people can hold one or two more items in their space of awareness. But the general rule shows that awareness is not a continuous capacity to perceive the external world at the same time. Not only that, a strong sensory signal can distract our short span of awareness of about fifteen seconds. How we achieve conscious capacities with a limited instrument is another intriguing question.

Our consciousness has the capacity to create continuity by cleverly concealing its shortcomings in temporal and spatial dimensions. It can assume, presume and edit information to give the impression that it is a coherent and endless identity. The editing job is also not done by any demon or ghost. The modern mind watchers attribute modifications to the unconscious mental processes. The problem is to reconcile with the unavoidable conclusion that the unconscious processes in the brain know all requirements of a conscious being. There is no indication about the source of the knowledge that enables the purely material systems of the brain to anticipate the future needs of an organism.

It means that complex neurological processes can take care of all intelligent decisions for our smooth existence. The conscious state is just an accidental outcome of neural activities. According to the modern high priests of reductionism, the raw brain knows the best. We are only a kind of autonomously conscious biological robots. Even our most private thoughts, desires and actions are already decided in the neural nets. It is like the electro-chemical intelligence of a conscious robot. How we accomplish such miracles is far beyond our present comprehension. And we have no idea how atoms and molecules acquire the intelligence to conduct affairs of life without any conscious intervention.

The latest scientific discoveries concede maximum concession to consciousness by assigning it the status of an internal mirror that reflects the external world. Incidentally, it can also reflect an image of the self as an additional advantage of the conscious capacities. But they do not tell us anything about the real viewer of the images projected in the conscious state. Some call it a 'perceptual center' sitting in a corner of the brain. It simply watches the drama of existence without participating actively in the performance. The real performers are the molecules that decide our destiny.

To get over logical inconsistencies, some others hold that the language has the central role of a reader. It tells us what the neurons think or do. Noam Chomsky suggests the idea of a modular mind in which consciousness acts like a CPU (Central Processing Unit). It has just enough computing capacity to access simultaneously the outcome of the processes in other modules. The other important function of the CPU is to integrate the sensory inputs without exercising any control over the proceedings in the modular mind.

In the electrical model proposed by Hebb, consciousness is attributed to the local activity in certain specific neural columns. Earlier, it was presumed that the general electrical activity in the brain gives rise to consciousness. In another model, Karl Pribram, suggested the possibility of slow chemical activities creating consciousness in the brain. In fact, slow and steady activities are required in the various microstructures to keep up the continuity of awareness. Another possibility is that its link with the high frequency gamma rays or 40 Hz electrical rhythm seen when an object is in the perpetual field, can be related to consciousness. But since the gamma rays disappear when the object is out of the visual field, they are probably more closely associated with perceptual binding rather than awareness.

The electrical activity of the brain and chemical reactions in the microstructures, do not indicate that consciousness arises at a particular phase of neural activity. When we try to trace the origin of consciousness by following the ionic disturbances created in the brain by the sensory signals, the electrical activities show close association with conscious processing, particularly in the temporal dimension. Similarly, the level of melatonin in the brain and the biological clock are also responsible for the onset of arousal, which makes us aware of the external world.

All these studies clearly establish the fact that the source of awareness is simultaneously spread over several brain areas. Our conscious experiences involve innumerable activities in different areas of the brain using the same resources. Every new experience opens up something like a new file, creating functional and structural modifications in the neural network. Our awareness cannot penetrate the brain processes that lead to conscious capacities and experiences. It shows our inability to understand the basic processes that lead to cognitive abilities.

Beyond the unknown brain processes and awareness, we are confronted by the more mysterious conscious capacities of the mind like freewill and several special cognitive abilities. The studies of brain processes have so far indicated that we cannot attribute personal experiences of emotions like pleasure or pain to any ghost like entity. They are created by trillions of atoms and molecules in the brain in a state of awareness.

But the basic question is whether ordinary matter is capable of receiving experiences or emotions for creating intelligence to function more effectively in an environment. Our scientific forays into the realm of consciousness did not answer the basic question as to what exactly is the experiencing entity in the brain. For convenience, we call it the mind.

Like consciousness, the mind also cannot be pinned down to any specific system or area of the brain. We have seen that awareness arises out of the simultaneous activities in different regions of the brain. Some scientists concede that the mind is a kind of perceptual ego center.

It has no physical location in the brain, but probably a locus of the bodily images imprinted in memory may be acting as the support for the conscious capacities of the mind. Some people assume that the ego center is located somewhere behind the eyes. As we are vision-dominated creatures, visual images are more prominent in our memory rather than any other sensory experience. For bats and whales, the images may be located elsewhere.

Science assigns the perceptual ego center, the central role of the mind as it can simultaneously access various regions of the brain. They claim that it can create a self-referential point even in animals when they are conscious. The grooming patterns of birds and animals clearly show that a physical image is well established in their brain. The image of the self that is deeply imprinted in long-term memory gets updated with new experiences. The mind is definitely utilizing various kinds of memory to create and extend conscious capacities.

Another way to look at the mind is to see what happens when it is totally or substantially absent. We find such unfortunate instances in serious mental disorders, brain damages and drug abuses. Even if awareness is more or less intact, they lose the coherence required for holding on to the physical image and motivation for purposive action. If the mind is absent, we are solely driven by the genetic algorithms, like animals. The acquired conscious capacities can no longer guide us to make the correct choices to live like humans.

It is true that without the mind, the brain can spontaneously perform most of the essential functions. The genetically evolved ego center in animals may not always guide them to make wise decisions, but it is sufficient to survive. Even if we are conscious, if the ego center does not function, we lose the self-referential point in time and space. But the self-referential point or the ego center or whatever we call it, has not yet been located in the vast network of biological matter in the brain. The brain is a physical tool comprising of cellular and molecular parts for conducting electrical and chemical activities. Simply stated, it is nothing more than a creative biomass.

The basic question is whether an intelligent mind can emerge from the multitude of micro level activities in the brain. Even if it is accepted that an ego-center exists in the brain, it requires a specific location for collecting all the processed information from other brain structures. That is probably the reason for assuming other qualities of matter like quantum coherence to explain conscious capacities. The systems and sub-systems of the brain dealing with memory, attention, and linguistic and other capabilities cannot create an integrated experience that the mind gives us. We have to identify a definite mechanism capable of creating the conscious capacities.

The perceptual center of the brain (if at all there is any) that scientists are now inclined to consider as the mind, should have the capacity to sort out and integrate trillions of sensory signals. The first step is to classify the vast multitude of signals that should go to different sensory organs like vision, audition and so on. After they are properly identified and processed with the help of the relevant memory date, they have to be bound into coherent images. As the perceptual field contains trillions of analogous sensory inputs, it is difficult even to imagine how the brain can conduct such gigantic tasks.

Perceptual binding is mostly done when we attend to certain specific features of the environment. In some lower forms of life there is automatic and unconscious binding of incoming signals. But even for such unconscious binding, attention has to be focused on that particular feature of the perceptual field. Some studies consider that the binding agent is the 40 Hz rhythms that appear when an object is in the perceptual field. It may probably contribute to the coherence necessary for identifying the object. There is no evidence to confirm this nor do we have any idea about the origin of such oscillations. Can we assume that the rhythm knew the correct level of coherence required for a perfect perception? An electrical wave cannot become conscious enough to carry out tasks involving evaluation of various alternatives.

Nancy Wolf proposed that the cholinergic forebrain system as the possible seat of the binding capacity of the brain. Since this system sends axons into every area in the cerebral cortex, it may be integrating the processes conducted by others. Moreover, it is also known to have an active role in creating mental images. When this area is stimulated by specific drugs, dreams emerge in a sleeping brain and in a conscious person it creates clear and colourful images that are not normally seen otherwise. Wolf suggests that this system creates images by initiating changes in the microtubules of neurons. A specific protein changes the structural configuration of a neuron and the coherent firings spread out the new imagery in the entire neural column.

Penrose also gives a prominent place to microtubules in his explanation of the mind. But the question is, can such microscopic activities in a corner of the brain create the binding capacity and other qualities of the mind? All that we can say now is that the mind has a much larger scope and space than what the aggregate of the activities of microtubules achieve in a small area of the brain.

When we look at the evolutionary processes involved in the binding of signals, we find that selective attention has placed a major part in its evolution. A primitive process of binding helps the lower level animals to survive in the environment by sorting out the innumerable signals that emanate from the environment. But in the case of highly evolved animals, simple binding alone will not help them to survive. The bound images have to be classified and kept in the brain to identify similar objects in future perceptions. The brain has the capacity to keep them in memory either in the short-term mode or in other long-term memory folders.

Having a perceptual center capable of binding the signals and the capacity to carry the images in memory may not give us the mind. It should also be able to control thoughts and actions. We have seen that the brain areas like thalamus, prefrontal and sensory cortexes are all important structures involved in the control process. They give selective attention to the chosen task and keep the focus constant at least for a short while. The most suitable brain structure for carrying out such manifold tasks is known as 'ERTAS'. The acronym stands for Extended Reticulo-Thalamic Activating System, which includes most of the neocortex areas. It is something like a blackboard where other brain systems can project processed images. The images become perceptible only when we are conscious. The continuity of the self-image and the symbolic representations of the physical world keep the blackboard capable of comprehending the messages projected by other structures of the brain.

'ERTAS' may be the brain structure supporting short term working memory and the capacity to extend perceptual binding and automatic skills. It may even be taken as the perceptual ego center, which can control action, thoughts and even emotions. Maybe we can treat it as the gateway to the conscious mind that experiences the world and understands it with the help of sensory inputs.

It may be capable of making correct choices to enhance sensations of pleasure and satisfaction. The perceptual ego center or ERTAS is capable of experiencing our existence as a composite entity. It can be the latest evolved conscious capacity of humans, as other animals do not have such highly specialized faculties. Scientists can finally heave a sigh of relief that something in the brain can be assigned the role of the surrogate mind.

This system is not fully activated in the early childhood. The child gets a separate identity card only after prolonged interaction with the world. It creates symbolic representations required for distancing itself from the environment. First comes the physical separation followed by emotional weaning from parental dependence. The ego center gets fully matured only in adolescence. The capability to make intelligent decisions is an acquired ability after the neural network establishes its synaptic connections of all kinds. Even after essential networking is completed, experiences go on enhancing the connectivity to meet new challenges that require a different kind of response.

Some people have the erroneous idea that the mind is an extended form of memory. There are different kinds of memory like short-term memory, long term memory, procedural memory, episodic memory and so on. Memory can be broadly sub-divided into individual processes and many combinations of the brain regions service each process. But the puzzle is how can we remember the events that happened several years ago even after all the molecules that created memory have already been turned over several times. Molecules can hardly last a few weeks, whereas the long-term memory remains stable throughout life. The mechanism that registers memory in the neural network is still unknown to us.

The current view is that it may be the strengthening of some synaptic connections by a process called 'long term potentation', involving certain type of target receptors and transmitters. In this process, sustained activity of incoming neurons is maintained to make the target cell more active to reinforce the synaptic connections. But even the molecules that increase the efficiency of the connectivity have a limited life span of a few weeks. Some activating genes within the neuron may be responsible for increasing the efficiency of the transmitter and other processes involved in memory storage and retrieval.

The effect of an experience is imprinted in the brain probably not by changing the internal structure of the neuron but by altering the connectivity between the neurons. Exposure to more experiences gives larger connectivity to the neural network. When we try to learn a new job with full attention, the neurons make some important proteins that help to strengthen the freshly laid connectivity. During the entire developmental period, the human brain creates new synaptic connections.

While adapting to a new environment, we change the neural connections to carry forward memories and their current perceptual impact. By associating with various aspects of the events, the entire memory folder can be readily retrieved. Another way to improve memory recall is to recreate the original episode in the mind and try to get at the missing details.

It is true that memory is a multi-faceted process involving several areas of the brain and has a major role in creating the mind. Some people even assume that it is like a hologram having enormous storage capacity. There is a kind of link between the perceptual center and the vast accumulation of memory that remain intact even in sleep and unconscious states. The mind and memory are two sides of the same coin and their mutual dependence is presently inscrutable.

It took about twenty million years for our mental software to evolve to its present level of perfection. We may be thinking, talking and feeling in the unconscious modules of the brain but it is the mind that receives all experiences. Benjamin Libet demonstrated that we become aware of sensory signals only after they are processed and sent to the cortex. It means that the unconscious modules in the brain take all our conscious decisions, which we are so proud of. We are simply cheating ourselves when we claim that they are all achievements of a conscious mind.

The fact that atoms and molecules are the intelligent backroom workers has so far been unknown. But the new tools like MRI & PET scans lay bare the utter falsity of our self-esteem. Admittedly, the molecules in the brain do the real work and all that we can say is that they do belong to us. But they are not our exclusive acquisitions; plenty of them are available for sale in the market.

Scientists have more or less achieved the target of keeping the mind within the physical domain of the neurons and their network. In spite of the assumption about perpetual ego center and ERTAS, they have not yet found their exact location. They hope to discover it eventually in the coherent firings or oscillations in the neural network.

Presently, science has no explanation for the process of 'binding' of trillions of inputs into cognizable images. Nor do they have any ideas about the non-local quality of the mind. The theory of complexity gives some explanations for the emergence of the mind, but they are not yet accepted by all. Complexity is definitely a strong contender for consideration along with many other candidates.

A complex structure like the neural network performs more and more additional· functions because of the emergence of higher capabilities. In such a system, addition of more units leads to sudden and unexpected turns capable of performing more difficult tasks. Consciousness and the mind are probably the outcome of higher levels of complexity in our neural networks.

It would probably explain the enhanced capabilities of humans as compared to mammals. Scientists are happy with such speculations that keep consciousness and the mind within the complexity of the neural network. But complexity cannot explain the binding problem and the distribution of the mind all over the brain. It is nevertheless an attractive proposition that deserves further exploration.

Another scientific explanation is the possibility of the emergence of quantum qualities in the neural network for creating congenial conditions for the mind to appear. Penrose attributes consciousness to the phenomenon of superposition of alternatives explicable in terms of quantum dynamics. The neurotransmitters and the action potential that controls them are likely to possess such quantum features. That can probably explain the binding process and the non-local nature of the mind. The argument that the mind is somewhere in the working memory or short term memory has very few takers. Memory cannot integrate trillions of inputs received by sensory organs. But it is essential for creating the mind.

An important conclusion that emerges from all these discussions is the actual role of the mind in our existence. Libet's experiments suggest that the mind only receives the outcome of the processes concluded by the brain. It means that the mindless molecules can take all decisions and act upon them. The mind can at best review the decisions taken by the brain if it strongly disapproves of them on some grounds.

The evolutional explanation for the passive role of the mind may be that natural selection does not require its intervention. It appears that the highly acclaimed human quality of freewill is yet another myth created by the mind to sustain its self-esteem. Maybe, it gives us a valid reason to continue existence even after the expiry of the active reproductive phase of life. You need something to think about in old age and memory adds enough spices to make life tastier.

We have seen that the neural network having considerable complexity can make all intelligent decisions. If that is so, we cannot claim any exclusive niche in the scheme of existence. Logically, a computer having the same level of complexity can replicate our thoughts and actions. That is exactly what artificial intelligence is striving to achieve! They have already created "deep blue", the computer that defeated the Grandmaster. But even if the computer could make excellent moves to match the choices of a highly intelligent human, it cannot have a mind to create the software to run the show. We will have to await the outcome of the experiments with "Lucy", the robot that is learning to acquire self-awareness and a mind.

All evidences from clinical studies and imaging devices fail to reveal what the mind is. It is still the most enigmatic gift of nature. Whether it is an illusion or reality, it is the sole recipient of the product of brain processes. Without the mind, we cannot experience emotions, and intelligent thoughts cannot emanate from it to initiate appropriate action And all that we get, even with the marvelous mind, is just like any other forms of life. It is a great mystery that makes us feel proud as well as uncomfortable that we do not know anything about it.

We feel helpless when it goes berserk, creates miseries and destroys cultural heritages and human values. It is probably an extension of the kind of energy that creates consciousness. The electro-chemical activities in the brain may be opening a window to reach out to external energy of universal consciousness. Both the mind and awareness are presently beyond the physical boundaries of our subjective reality.

Whatever it is, the mind is undoubtedly what makes existence an excellent experience. Without the mind, the questions asked in this book about its origin and qualities would never have come up. That gives us sufficient reason to feel proud of our precious possession. The magnificent magic show of life is performed by the mind, although we are yet to know the identity of the master magician.

GLOSSARY

ADAPTATION - It is a feature achieved by an organism in the process of evolution. It enhances the chances of survival and reproductive fitness.

ADI SANKARA - A renowned sage who belonged to the 8th century AD. He initiated the renaissance of Hinduism. His contribution to the Vedanta philosophy was the revival of the Upanishads. He also established the monastic tradition and institutions to propagate Vedanta.

AGNI - The Sanskrit name for the god of fire in the Vedic pantheon. He consumes the sacrificial offering made to gods and conveys them to the divine. Fire acts as a medium carrying messages.

ALGORITHM - It is named after the Persian mathematician Al-khuwarusmi. They are notations that give solutions to a mathematical problem. Computer programs are based on algorithms. Computer is in fact a physical device to implement instructions in the algorithms.

ALLELE - It is the alternative form of a gene. It differs from the gene by minor mutations in DNA sequences.

ANALOG - It is a continuous changing quantity as distinguished from the changes involving discrete steps. We find most of the natural phenomena occurring as analogs. In human brain, analog computing is involved in the creation and processing of memory.

ANTIPARTICLE - It is an integral form of every particle with an opposite charge but having the same mass. For e.g., Positron is the antiparticle of electron.

ARROW OF TIME - It is a great mystery of science that time moves only in forward direction. The assumption is that the arrow of time was created with the universe itself.

ARTIFICIAL INTELLIGENCE (AI) -It is the application of knowledge-based systems for creating tools and devices emulating human intelligence. Some such systems are created to imitate and perform intelligent activities more accurately without endangering human life.

ASANAS - They are postures for practising a holistic way of life in which the mind and the body function harmoniously. More than eighty postures are considered important in yoga and many of them imitate the postures of animals for a healthy and happy life.

ASHTAVAKRA - The story of Ashtavakra, one of the great Vedic thinkers, is mentioned in the Vanaparva of the Hindu epic called 'Mahabharat'. His main contribution was the logical insight that considered universal consciousness as the energy that created all kinds of existence. He belonged to the 6th century BC and followed the vision of the early Upanishads like Shevetasvatara, Mundaka and Mandukya. The advent of Buddhism, which does not subscribe to the concept of a God, is attributed to the vision of consciousness propounded by him.

ATMAN - It is the innermost soul in every being. Upanishads consider it as the reflection of the universal spirit called Brahma.

ATOM - There are ninety-two different natural atoms representing same number of chemical elements. It has a nucleus and negatively charged electrons orbiting it.

BELL'S THEOREM - It says that some predictions of quantum theory are not intelligible in terms of any other scientific theory enunciated earlier.

BHAGAWAD GITA - It is a part of the Hindu epic Mahabharata. Gita contains spiritual revelations in dialogue form between Arjuna, representation of the human character and Krishna, the incarnation of Brahman.

BIG BANG - According to this theory, the universe emerged out of infinite singularity with a tremendous explosion. "Red shift" and "background microware radiation" are the scientific evidences that establish the big bang theory.

BINDING MECHANISM - It is the process that integrates trillions of sensory signals to create identifiable image of an object. Nancy Wolf suggested that cholinergic forebrain system that can reach the entire cerebral cortex might be involved in the binding process. Axons from this system reach all cortical columns. It is also associated with mental imagery and when drugs stimulate it, a sleeping person starts dreaming. The binding mechanism is said to alter the geometry that aligns or attunes the neurons in a network to create coherence in the circuit.

BLACK HOLES - They are probably the outcome of the collapse of stars. Being extremely dense, no matter or even light can escape their gravitational pulls. Their presence was predicted using General Relativity and other theories of gravitation.

BLIND SIGHT - People with blind sight can locate objects in the blind spot even though they are not aware of seeing them. Blind spots are the outcome of some damage to cortical areas in the back of the brain. They feel blind but can actually see without being aware of it.

BODY CLOCK - It is a person's biological clock that keeps the body rhythm of waking, sleeping and various other functions.

BRAHMAN - It literally means 'grow' or 'expand'. In Hindu philosophy, it is assumed to be the entity underlying all kinds of existence. It is supposed to be the substrate that gives rise to the phenomenal world of matter and forces. According to Vedic thoughts, this entity is conceived as the original energy that existed even prior to creation. The essence of this energy, embedded in all kinds of beings, creates consciousness. It is the impersonal reality that is manifested in all forms of matter.

BRAHMIN - A member of the priestly caste entitled to conduct rituals and sacred rites. It also means the highest caste said to be proficient in spiritual knowledge. The Brahmins traditionally held advisory and priestly positions.

CASTE SYSTEM - This concept of a divided society originated in about 1500 BC among settlements of nomadic tribes. The system was originally conceived for regulating the position of each individual in the society according to his aptitude and abilities. It slowly deteriorated into a kind of vocational apartheid, which was initially not rigidly enforced. But in course of time, it created watertight compartments in society preventing any kind of inter-caste movements.

In later stages, the system further deteriorated to become the most inhuman tool to keep large sections of population in perpetual poverty and slavery. The lower castes always remained as the poorest segment of society. A clever coterie of upper classes exploited their ignorance by invoking religious sanctions.

CEREBRAL CORTEX - It is the outermost layer of the cerebral hemispheres that looks like a crumpled blanket. It is supposed to be the seat of conscious thoughts and intelligence.

CHAOS THEORY - It is a study of the emergence of patterns in complex systems like the weather. The quantity of randomness is considered to be relevant to the emergence of new products. It is not complete disorder but a kind of process based on the perception that there is no accurate level of order for long-term predictions. This theory is a useful concept for understanding non-linear processes like self-organization.

CHROMOSOME - It is a structure in the nucleus of a cell that carries DNA. There are 23 pairs of chromosomes in a human genome.

DARK MATTER - It is a kind of unknown matter that exists extensively throughout the universe. Motions of galaxies and formation of clusters of galaxies confirm the presence of dark matter. They interact weakly and do not emit any light; hence the name.

DARWINIAN EVOLUTION - It explains the cause of the appearance of a wide variety of life on earth in terms of random mutations of genetic instructions. In suitable contexts, the potential for creating new varieties of life already present in the gene pool, comes into existence through evolutionary changes. It ensures the survival of more successful organisms by improving their reproductive fitness and adaptation skills. In this explanation, the basic idea is that every organism has its origin in an earlier form of life and changes occur only through the mechanism of random mutation for natural selection.

DEEP BLUE - It is an IBM designed computer program that defeated Gary Kasparov in 1997. The fact that a mere machine could defeat a grandmaster established the superiority of mechanical intelligence over human intelligence. Proponents of Artificial Intelligence hail it as a victory for the materialistic approach to the mind.

DNA - It is the basic genetic material consisting of a double helix. It unwinds like a tape giving necessary instructions for producing specific proteins. When organized into genes, it gives instructions to create a particular type of protein out of chemical soup floating in the cell. The double-helix structure enables reproduction of the cell by division.

ELECTRO ENCEPHELOGRAM (EEG) - It is a device for amplification and recording of electric currents in the brain. It is a very useful tool for medical diagnosis and for studying the brain activities.

ENZYME - A Kind of protein that controls biological reactions and creates temporary structures by getting attached to a molecule. Enzymes act as chemical catalysts regulating metabolic processes.

FREE WILL - It is an assumed quality of the mind, which is expressed in purposeful behaviour and decision-making. Free will is not created by brain activities in any identified system or sub-system. There are no causal links in the choices of free will.

GALAXIES - They consist of large aggregates of gravitationally bound stars and lots of gas and dust. There are about 400 billion galaxies in the observable universe.

GAMMA WAVES - These 40 Hz oscillations are supposed to be instrumental in binding the products of several neural circuits that are active at the same time.

GENE - It is a stretch of DNA containing the code for making an amino acid. The code is transformed to make a messenger RNA, which creates the protein.

GENOME - It is the complete genetic material in a living cell. Human genome contains 3 billion units of DNA. The active genes contain chemical instructions for making proteins. One gene can make more than ten proteins.

GLIAL CELL - They are a kind of cells in the nervous system that perform supporting functions. They help the neurons to function efficiently and establish connectivity.

GUTs (Grand Unified Theories) - It is an ambitious theoretical attempt to unify the weak, electromagnetic, and strong forces into a single one. It can possibly happen at extremely short distances.

HIGGS FIELD - It is the theoretical field that gives mass to elementary particles.

HOLISM - It is a philosophical approach opposed to atomism. The holist considers the aggregate as more important, as it gives a better idea on a system, than the parts and their relationship.

HOLOGRAM - It is an interference pattern encoded by laser beams. The pattern can reconstruct a three dimensional image. An important property of the hologram is that information is distributed in every part of the hologram. Some scientists believe that memory is distributed in the brain in the form of holograms.

INDRA - The head of the Vedic pantheon of gods equivalent to Jupiter.

JANAKA - He was the legendary king of Videha mentioned in the Hindu epic Ramayana. He also figures in the epic Mahabharat and Brihadaranyaka Upanishad. The king was an avid learner and lavishly entertained many scholars in his court. He gave generous gifts to learned persons and contributed immensely to the codification of Vedic thoughts.

MAGNETIC RESONANCE IMAGING (MRI) - It is a non-invasive diagnostic method for producing computerized images of body tissues. It uses nuclear magnetic resonance of patterns within the body produced by radio waves. For creating such images, a special magnetic field of about 13000 times stronger than the normal magnetic field on earth is used. When the body is stimulated with radio waves, it responds with its own electro magnetic transmissions. The computer records the transmissions and creates a three dimensional image of internal features like blood vessels.

MAHABHARATA - It is a great Hindu epic about the conflict between two factions of the same family and their descendants. It also contains the Bhagavad Gita, which is the most sacred scripture of Hinduism.

MICROBE - A unicellular bacteria in which there is no well-defined nucleus and no complex chromosome structure.

MICROWAVE BACKGROUND RADIATION - It is the irrefutable scientific evidence of the creation of the universe in a big bang. After the big bang, the universe was filled with thermal radiations reacting with opaque matter. When the universe expanded and cooled to about 4000 K, space became transparent to radiation. It stretched the wavelength of the background radiation, which is uniform in all directions. Today we find a cold gas of photons everywhere, which has the wavelength falling in the microwave part of the spectrum.

MODULAR MIND - The concept that the mind comprises complex structures created by using repetitive modular parts. The modules are functionally autonomous, but combined with other modules they create harmoniously functioning entities.

OM - It is a holy word of Vedic origin representing

Brahman. The sound of the word is said to be audible in deep state of meditation.

PERCEPTION - It is a biological ability common to many forms of life. Human beings have five major perceptive senses in addition to about seven minor ones like sense of balance, sense of tension and relaxation of the muscles and the feeling of fullness or the emptiness of the stomach etc. Some animals have additional sensory equipments to detect ultra violet radiations and echolocation.

PHOTON - It is a particle that creates light and transmits electromagnetic force.

PRANA - It is a Sanskrit word, which means vital energy found in all forms of life.

PRANAYAMA - It means control over both inhalation and exhalation. While chanting Vedic hymns and doing asanas, yogis practice breath control. It is claimed that pranayama can give longevity and good health.

PROTEIN - It is a large family of versatile molecules constructed by compiling amino acids to form long chains, which is the molecular basis of life that performs almost all body functions. Proteonics is the study of proteins in an organism. There are about 500,000 to 1 million proteins like hemoglobin, insulin, Dopamine, etc. in the human body.

QUANTUM MECHANICS - The basis of quantum mechanics is Max Planck's discovery that energy is absorbed or radiated in discrete quantity called "quanta". Quantum is the unit of spin or angular momentum.

Quantum mechanics states that the exact position and momentum of an electron or other elementary particle cannot be known at the same time. They simultaneously exist as waves and particles. The duality is resolved only when conscious observation collapses the wave function, to create a particle of reality.

QUANTUM VACUUM - It is the concept of the lowest possible level of energy in the universe. It is devoid of any matter or force that can be perceived or measured. But it contains all potentialities for creating matter and forces. Waves and particles might materialize in different forms of the potentialities in the underlying vacuum just like waves appear and disappear in an ocean.

RED SHIFT - It is the reddening of light from a star moving away from our planet. Receding stars shift their spectra towards the red end of the spectrum.

REDUCTIONISM - The principle that states that the properties of any system made of component parts can be understood by knowing all about the parts and their relationships. In other words, a system does not have any property that is beyond the aggregation of the qualities of its components.

REM - The acronym stands for Rapid Eye Movement that occurs under the eyelids during dreams.

SELF-ORGANIZATION - It states that a complex and unpredictable substrate can develop simple but large-scale patterns. Examples of self-organization are crystallization, living organisms, Bose-Einstein condensations, and even whirlpools. They occur in open systems where matter or energy is allowed to pass through. An example of self-organization is the appearance of interesting patterns in computer simulations of the network of genes.

SEXUAL REPRODUCTION - It involves reduction of diploid cells to haploid cells to form sperm or egg by the process of meiosis. When the egg and sperm fuse, the diploid state is recreated. The mechanism of sexual reproduction started with some microbes about 2 billion years ago. It might have also introduced the death gene in an organism to terminate its life span.

SUPER STRINGS - A set of theories that suggest that fundamental particles like quarks and leptons exists as strings or closed loops and not as points. These theories claim that they can one day explain the ultimate questions of existence.

THEORY OF EVERYTHING (TOE) - It is a theory that will eventually explain the functional as well as causative details of everything in the universe. It will, according to proponents, one day achieve what is called "why understanding".

VEDA - In Hinduism it means revealed wisdom or the ultimate truth. The oldest Veda is the Rig Veda followed by Sama, Atharva and Yajur Vedas. They are inspired hymns directed to various gods of the Indo-Aryan pantheon.

VEDANTA - It signifies the end of Vedas and stands for the system of philosophy based on the Upanishads. Vedanta accepts only Brahman as the Supreme Being and does not approve the division of the society into classes and castes.

YOGA - It comprises of several disciplines for conditioning the body and mind for the ultimate realization of the supreme reality called Brahman. It is one of the six basic systems of Hindu philosophy.

ZYGOTE - It is a fertilized egg containing genetic instructions for the growth of an organism.

BIBLIOGRAPHY

Allport, G.W. 1966. *Becoming: Basic considerations for a psychology of personality.* New Haven: Yale University Press.

Andrei, Linde. *The self-reproducing inflationary universe.* Scientific American. Nov. 1944. pp 48-55).

Asimov, Isaac. 1986. *A Robot Dreams.* New York: Ace Books.

Ashworth, P.D. 1979. *Social Interaction and Consciousness.* New York: Wiley and Sons.

Baars, B. 1988. *A Cognitive Theory of Consciousness.* New York: Cambridge University Press.

_____. 1997. *In the Theater of Consciousness.* Oxford: Oxford University Press.

Baddeley, A. 1986. *Working Memory* Oxford: Clarendon Books.

Barkow, J.H., Cosmides, L. and Tooby. J. 1992. *The Adapted Mind.* New York : Oxford University Press.

Baron – Cohen, S. 1995. *Mindblindedness and the language of the Eyes.* Cambridge, Mass.: MIT Press.

Barrow, J.D. 1988. *The world within the world.* Oxford: Oxford University Press.

_____. 1983. *The left hand of creation.* New York : Basic Books.

_____. 1989. *Patterns of explanation in cosmology, in the Anthropic principle*, Eds., *Bertala & U. Curi*. Cambridge: Cambridge University Press.

Barthalomew, D.J. 1984. *God of Chance*. London: SCN.

Baskys, A and Remington, G. Eds. 1998. *Brain mechanisms and Psychotropics*. New York: WW Norton & Co.

Bates, E and Elman, J. 1996. *Learning the discovered science*, 274 (5294): 1849-1850.

Bateson Gregory. 1980. *Mind and Nature – A necessary unity* New York : Bantom Books.

_____. 1972. *Steps to an ecology of mind*. New York : Valentine Books.

Bateson, Patrick and Martin, Paul. 1999. *Design for a life: How Behaviour Develops*. Cape.

Becker, S and Hunton, G.E. 1992. *Self-organizing neural network that discovers surfaces in random-dot stereograms*. Nature. 355, 161-63.

Bickerton, Derek. 1995. *Language and Human Behaviour*. Seattle: University of Washington Press, Seattle.

Blakemore, C.B & S.A. Greenfield. 1987. *Mind Waves: Thoughts on Intelligence, Identity and Consciousness*. Oxford: Basil Blackwell. Block, N. 1997. *The nature of consciousness: Philosophical debates*. Cambridge, Mass.: MIT Press.

Bloom, F.E & A. Lazerson. 1988. *Brain, Mind and Behaviour*. New York : W.H. Freeman & Co.

Boden, M. 1977. *Artificial Intelligence and Natural Man* New York: Basic Books.

Bohr, Neils. 1958. *Atomic Physics and Human knowledge* New York: John Willey and Sons.

Brockma John. 1995. *The Third culture: Beyond the scientific revolution* New York : Simon & Schuster.

Brothers, L. 1993. *Friday's Foortprint.* New York : Oxford University Press.

Bruner, J.S. 1983. *Child's Talk: Learning to use language* New York: WW Norton.

Buss, David. 1994. *The Evolution of Desire* New York : Basic Books

Byrne, R.W. 1995. *The thinking ape: Evolutionary origins of intelligence* New York : Oxford University Press.

Caird, Rod. 1994. *Apeman – The story of human evolution, Ed:Robert Foley* New York : Simon & Schuster.

Calvin, William. 1996. *The cerebral cord* Cambridge, Mass.: MIT Press.

Calvin W.H. 1996. *How Brains think: Evolving Intelligence, then and now.* New York : Basic Books.

Capra, Fritjof. 1988. *Uncommon Wisdom.* New York: Simon & Schuster.

_____. 1983. *The Turning Point.* London: Flamingo.

_____. 1996. *The web of life.* New York: Anchor.

_____. 1991. *The Tao of Physics.* Boston: Shombhala.

Chalmers D.J. 1996. *The conscious mind: In search of a fundamental theory.* New York: Oxford University Press.

Chomsky, Noam. 1986. *Knowledge of language* New York: Praeger.

_____. 1988. *Language and Problems of knowledge.* Cambridge, Mass.: MIT Press.

_____. 1995. *Language and Thought* Wakefield, R.I.: Moyer Bell.

Churchland, P.M. 1996. *The Engine of Reason, the seat of the Soul.* Cambridge, Mass.: MIT Press.

_____. 1993. *Matter and consciousness.* Cambridge, Mass: MIT Press.

Churchland, P.S. 1986. *Neuro Philosophy: toward a unified science of the mind-brain.* Cambridge, Mass: MIT Press.

Churchland P.S & T.J. Sejnodski. 1992. *The computational brain.* Cambridge, Mass.: MIT Press.

Coen, Enrico. 1999. *The art of genes.* New York: Oxford University Press.

Clark, A. 1997. *Being there: Putting brain, body and world together again* Cambridge, Mass.: MIT Press.

Corsi, P. (Ed). 1991. *The enchanted loom.* Oxford: Oxford University Press.

Cohen, Jack and Ian Stewart. 1994. *The collapse of chaos: Discovery of simplicity in a complex world.* New York: Viking Penguin.

Cook- Deegan, Robert. 1994. *The Gene Wars: Science, Politics and the Human Genome.* New York: WW Norton.

Crick Francis. 1994. *The astonishing hypothesis: The scientific search for the soul.* New York: Macmillan Publishing Company.

Crick Francis and Christofor Koch. 1990. *Towards a neurological theory of consciousness.* Seminars in the Neuro Sciences, pp-263-275.

Corballis, M.C. 1991. *The lopsided Ape.* New York: Oxford University Press.

Corballis, M.C and Lea, Seg (Eds). 1999. *The descent of mind: psychological perspectives of hominid evolution.* New York: Oxford University Press.

Sagan, Carl. 1996. *A demon: Haunted world: Science as a candle in the dark* New York: Balentine.

_____. 1980. *Cosmos* New York: Random House.
Damisio, A.R. 1994. *Descartes' Error: Emotion, Reason and the Human brain.* New York: GP, Putna.

_____. 1999. *The feeling of what happens: Body and emotion in the making of consciousness.* New York: Harcourt Brace and Company.

Darwin, C. 1859. *On the origin of species by means of natural selection.* London: John Murray.

_____. 1871. *The descent of man.* London: John Murray.

Dawkins, R. 1987. *The blind watchmaker: Why the evidence of evolution reveals aUniverse without design.* New York: WW Norton.

_____. 1990. *The selfish gene.* New York: Oxford University Press.

Dennett D.C. 1991. *Consciousness explained* Boston: Little Brown.

_____. 1995. *Darwin's dangerous idea: Evolution and the meanings of life* New York: Simon & Schuster.

Donald M.W. 1981. *Origins of the modern mind: three stages in the evolution of culture and cognition* Cambridge, Mass: Harvard University Press.

_____. 2001. *A Mind so Rare.* New York: WW Norton & Co.

Davis, Paul. 1992. *The Mind of God.* New York: Simon & Schuster.

_____. 1984. *The last three minutes: Conjectures about the ultimate fate of the Universe.* New York: Basic Books.

Descartes, Rene. 1960. *Meditations.* New York: Bopps-Merill.

Dixon, Bernard. 1994. *Power Unseen: How Microbes rule the world.* New York: W.H. Freeman.

Easwaran, Eknath. 1996. *The Upanishads.* New Delhi: Penguin Books (India).

Eccles, J.C., Ito, M., & Szentagotchai, J. 1967. *The cerebellum as a neuronal machine.* Berlin: Springer-Verlag.

Edelman, G.M. 1992. *Bright air, Brilliant fire: On the matter of the mind.* New York: Basic Books.

Edelman G.M & Tononi, G. 2000. *A universe of consciousness: How matter becomes imagination.* New York: Basic Books.

Egan, K. 1997. *The educated mind: How cognitive tools shape our understanding* Chicago: University of Chicago Press.

Eldridge, N. 1985. *Timeframes: The rethinking of Darwinian Evolution & the theory of punctuated equilibria.* New York: Simon & Schuster.

Feynman, R.P. 1998. *The meaning of it all.* New York: Penguin.

Flanagan O. 1992. *Consciousness reconsidered* Cambridge, Mass: MIT Press.

_____. 1991. *The Science of the mind* Cambridge, Mass: MIT Press.

Freedman, David. 1994. *Brain Makers.* New York: Simon Schuster.

Fouts, R. and Mills, S.T. 1997. *Next of kin: What chimpanzees have taught me about who we are.* New York: William Morrow.

Freud Sigmund. 1965. *The interpretation of dreams.* New York: Avon Books.

Frisch, K. Von. 1967. *The dance, language and orientation of bees.* Cambridge, Mass: Harvard University Press.

Futiyoma, D. 1982. *Science on trial.* New York: Pantheon Books.

Fortey Richard. 1998. *Life: A natural history of the first four billion years of life on earth* Knopf.

Gallup, G.G. 1970. *Chimpenzee's: Self recognition.* Science 167, pp-86-87.

_____. 1982. *Self awareness and the emergence of mind in primates.* American Journal of primatalogy 2, pp-237-48.

Gamble, C. 1994. *Time Markets: The pre-history of global colonization.* Cambridge, Mass: Harvard University Press.

Garner, H.C. *The mind's new signs.* New York: Basic Books.

Gates, Bill. 1995. *The Road Ahead.* New York: Viking.

Gazzainga, M.S. 1988. *The Mind's Past*. Barkeley: University of California Press.

Gell-Mann, Murray. 1991. *The Quark and the Jaguar*. New York: WH Freeman.

Gregory, R.L. 1997. *Mirrors in Mind*. New York: Oxford University Press.

Gibson, W. 1975. *The Miracle Worker*. New York: Bantom Workbooks.

Gleick, J. 1992. *Genius*. New York: Pantheon.

Gold, I. 1999. *Does 40 Hz oscillations play a role in visual consciousness?* Consciousness and Cognition: VIII, pp-186-95.

Goldman-Rakic, P.S. Sep., 1992. *Working memory and the mind*. Scientific American, pp-112-17.

Gould, Stephen J. 1989. *Wonderful Life*. Hutchinson Radius.

_____. 1996. *The mis-measure of man*. New York: WW Norton.

_____. 1980. *The Panda's Thumb*. New York: Penguin.

Grey, Johns. 1992. *Men are from Mars; Women are from Venus*. London: Harper Collins.

Grof, S. 1992. *The Holotrophic Mind*. San Francisco: Harper.

Griffin, D.R. 1992. *Animal Minds*. Chicago: Chicago University Press.

Haldine, J.B.S. 1927. *Possible Worlds and other Essays*. London: Chatto and Winders.

Hull, D.L. & Ruse M. (Eds). 1988. *The Philosophy of Biology*. OUP, Oxford, 1988).

Harvey Andrew. 1996. *The Essential Mystics*. New Jersey: Castle Books.

Hauser, M. 1996. *The Evolution of Communication*. Cambridge, Mass: MIT Press.

_____. 2000. *Wild Minds*. New York: Henry Halt. .

Hawking, Stephen. 1988. *A Brief History of Time*. New York: Bantom Books.

Hebb, D.O. 1961. *Distinctive Features of Learning in Higher Animals* in Jambelamres Ed. *Brain Mechanisms and Learning*. Oxford: Blackwell.

Heilbron, J.L. 1999. *The Sun in the Church*. Cambridge, Mass: Harvard University Press.

Hillman, James. 1996. *The souls code*. New York: Random house.

Hobson, J.A. 1988. *The Dreamy Brain*. New York: Basic Books.

Horgan, John. 1996. *The end of science*. New York: Broadway Books.

_____. 1999. *The undiscovered mind*. New York: The Free Press.

Houston, Jean. 1998. *A passion for the possible*. London: Torsons.

Hoyle, Fred. 1994. *Home is where the wind blows*. Mill Valley, California: University science Books.

Humphrey, N. 1992. *A History of the mind*. New York: Simon and Schuster.

Hutchins, E. 1995. *Cognition in the Wild*. Cambridge, Mass: MIT Press.

Huxley, Aldous. 1990. *The doors of perception and Heaven & Hell*. New York: Harper and Rowe.

Huxley, J. 1953. *Evolution in Action*. New York: Harper & Bros.

Ingold, T. 1986. *Evolution and Social Life*. New York: Cambridge University Press.

Jamison, Kay. 1995. *An unquiet mind*. New York: Vintage Books.

Jaynes, J. 1976. *The origin of consciousness in the breakdown of the bicameral mind*. Boston: Boston, Houghton, Mifflin.

Johnson, G. 1995. *Fire in the Mind*. New York: Random House.

Jones, S. 1999. *Almost like a whale: The origin of species updated*. New York: Double Day.

Joseph, R. 1993. *The Naked Neuron*. New York: Plenum Press.

Julesz, B. 1995. *Dialogues on perception*. Cambridge, Mass: MIT Press.

Kagan, Jerome. *Three seductive ideas*. Cambridge, Mass: Harvard University Press.

Kaku, Michio. 1997. *Visions*. New York: Anchor Books.

Kawato, M. 1999. *Internal Models for Motor control and trajectory planning*. Current Opinion in neurobiology, pp-718-27.

Keller H.A. 1902. *The story of my life*. New York: Grossed and Dunlap.

Karmiloff–Smith. 1993. *Beyond Modularity*. Cambridge, Mass: MIT Press.

Kauffman Stuart. 1995. *At home in the universe*. New York: Oxford University Press.

_____. *The origins of order*. Oxford, England: Oxford University Press.

Kirk R. 1994. *Raw feeling: A philosophical account of the essence of consciousness*. New York: Oxford University Press.

Kimbrell, Andrew. 1993. *The human body shop: The engineering and marketing of life*. San Francisco: Harper Collins.

Kitener, Philip. 1996. *The levels to come: The Genetic Revolution and Human possibilities*. New York: Simon and Schuster.

Kuper, A. 1994. *The chosen primate: Human nature and cultural diversity*. Cambridge, Mass: Harvard University Press.

_____. 1999. *Culture: The Anthropologist's Account*. Cambridge, Mass: Harvard University Press.

Kuhn, T.H. 1970. *The structure of scientific revolutions*. Chicago: University of Chicago Press.

Kohn, Marek. 1999. *As we know it: Coming to terms with an evolved mind*. London: Granta.

LaBarge, D. 1995. *Attentional processing: The brain's art of mindfulness*. Cambridge, Mass: Harvard University Press.

Laing, R.D. 1990. *The divided self*. London: Penguin.

Leakey, R. 1993. *The Origin of Human Kind*. New York: Basic Books.

LeDoux, Joseph. 1996. *The Emotional Brain.* New York: Simon & Schuster.

Libet, B. 1993. *Neurophysiology of consciousness: Selected papers and new essays of Benjamin Libet.* Boston: Birk Hausar.

Lindsley, D.B. 1961. *The reticular activation system and perceptual indecoration.* in D.E.Sheer (Ed), *Electrical Stimulations of the brain* Austin: University of Texas Press.

Lindley, David. 1993. *The end of physics.* New York: Basic Books.

Lovelock, James. 1998. *Ages of Gaia.* New York: WW Norton.

Mandler, G. 1997. *Human Nature Explored: Psychology, Evolution, Society.* New York: Oxford University Press.

Margulis, Lynn and Dorion, Sagan. 195. *What is life?* New York: Peter Neuranmant Inc.

Maynard-Smith, J. 1978. *The Evolution of Sex.* Cambridge: Cambridge University Press.

Meginn, Colin. 1988. *The problem of consciousness.* Cambridge, Mass: Blackwell.

Milner, A.D. and Goudale, M.A. 1995. *The visual brain in action.* New York: Oxford University Press.

Mithen, S. 1996. *The pre history of the mind: A search for the origins of heart, religion and science.* London: Thames and Hudson.

Mukherjee, Radhakamal. 1971. *Ashtavakra Gita.* Delhi: Motilal Banarasi Das Publishers.

Nelson, K. 1996. *Language in cognitive development: Emergence of the mediated mind.* New York: Cambridge University Press.

Neher, A. 1990. *The psychology of transcendence.* New York: Dover.

Nikhilananda, S. 1964. *The Upanishads.* New York: Arthur & Row.

Norris, C. 1993. *The truth about most modernism.* Oxford: Basil Blackwell.

Noble, W. and Davidson. 1996. *Human Evolution: Language and Mind : A psychological and archaeological enquiry.* New York: Cambridge University Press.

Oliver, Richard. 1995. *Shadow of the stone heart: A search for manhood.* London: Pan Books.

Orustein, R. 1997. *The Right Mind.* New York: Harcourt Brace.

Passingham, Richard. E. 1979. *Brain size and intelligence in man.* Brain Behaviour and Evolution, XVI, pp-233-270.

_____. 1982. *The Human Primate.* New York: WH Freeman.

Penrose, Roger. 1989. *The Emperor's new mind.* New York: Oxford University Press.

_____. 1994. *Shadows of the mind.* New York : Oxford University Press.

Pillai, G. K. 2001. *Mystic Awareness for the Modern Mind.* New Delhi: Originals.

Pinker, S. 1994. *The language instinct.* New York: William Morrow.

_____. 1997. *How the mind works.* New York: WW Norton.

Polkinghorne, John.1994. *Quarks, Chaos and Christianity:* SPACA

Triangle Press.

Popper, K. R. and Eccles, J.C. 1977. *The self and its brain.* New York: Springer International.

Pribram, K.H. 1971. *Languages of the Brain Experimental Paradoxes and principles in neuro psychology.* New Jersey: Prendic Hall.

Przget. 1976. *The grasp of consciousness: Action and concept in the young child.* Cambridge, Mass: Harvard University Press.
Porter, Eliot and James, Glick. 1990. *Nature's chaos.* New York: Viking.

Priogogina. Ilya. 1980. *From Being to Becoming.* New York : Freeman.

Ramachandran, V.S. and Blakeslee, Sandra. 1988. *Phantoms in the brain* .London: Fourth Estate.

Raup, David .M. 1991. *Extinction: Bad Genes or Bad luck.* New York: Norton.

Rees, M. 1997. *Before the beginning.* Reading, Mass: Pergens Books.

_____.2000. *Just Six Numbers.* New York: Basic Books.

Rey, G. 1997. *Contemporary philosophy of mind : A contentiously classical approach.* Cambridge, Mass: Blackwell.

Restak, Richard. 1995. *Brainscapes.* New York: Hyperjon.

Richards, Robert. 1987. *Darwin and the emergence of evolutionary theories of mind and behaviour.* Chicago: Chicago University Press.

Sachs, O. 1990. *Seeing Voices.* New York: Harper Collins.

Schacter, D.L. 1996. *Searching for Memory.* New York: Basic Books.

Schaller. 1991. *A man without words.* New York: Summit Books.

Searle, J.R. 1997. *The mystery of consciousness.* London: Granta Books.

Searle John. 1994. *The rediscovery of the mind.* Cambridge, Mass: MIT Press.

Shaparo, R. 1986. *Origins: A skeptic's guide to the creation of life on earth.* New York: Summit Books.

Simon, Herbert. 1996. *The signs of the artificial.* Cambridge: MIT Press.

Singer, W. and Gray, C.M. 1985. *Visual feature integration and the temporal correlation hypothesis.* Annual review of neuroscience, XVIII, pp-555-586.

Smith, J.H. 1995. *Life at the edge of chaos.* New York Review, March 22nd, pp-28-30.

Smolin, L. 1997. *The life of the cosmos.* London: Phoenix.

Springer, S. and Deutsch. G. 1998. *Left Brain, Right Brain.* San Francisco: W.H. Freeman.

Steve, R. Grand. 1996. *DNA and destiny: Nature and nurture in human behaviour.* New York: Plenum Press.

Sulloway, Frank. 1996. *Born to rebel.* New York: Pantheon Books.

Symons, D. 1979. *The Evolution of Human Sexuality.* New York: Oxford University Press.

Tarnas, Richard. 1996. *The passion of the western mind.* London: Pimlico.

Tipler, Fraich. 1944. *The physics of immortality.* New York: Double Day.

Tomasello, M. 1999. *The cultural origins of human cognition.* Cambridge, Mass: Harvard University Press.

Toza, A.W. and Mazziath, J.C. *Brain Mapping: The Methods.* New York: The Academic Press.

Trefil, James. 1997. *Are we unique?* New York: John Wiley Sons Inc.

Turner, M. 1996. *The literary mind: the origins of thought and language.* New York: Oxford University Press.

Varela, F.A., Thompson, E. and Rosch, E. 1995. *The embodied mind.* Cambridge, Mass.: MIT Press.

Vygotsky, L.S. 1986. *Thought and Language.* Cambridge, Mass: MIT Press.

Waal, F.B.M. de. 1989. *Peace-making among primates.* Cambridge, Mass: Harvard University Press.

Walker, Allan. 1996. *The wisdom of bonds: In search of human origins.* New York: Alfred Knopf.

Webster, Richard. 1998. *Why Freud was wrong?* New York: Basic Books.

Weinberg, Steven. 1992. *Dreams of a final theory.* New York: Pantheon.

Weiskrantz, L. 1997. *Consciousness Lost and Regained.* New York: Oxford University Press.

_____. 1986. *Blindsight*. Oxford: Oxford University Press.

Wells, H.G. 1992. *The Invisible Man.* New York: Dower Publications.

Wilson, E.O. 1971. *The insect societies.* Cambridge, Mass: Harvard University Press.

_____. 1978. *On human nature.* Cambridge, Mass: Harvard University Press.

_____. 1992. *The diversity of life.* Cambridge, Mass: Harvard University Press.

Wilber, Ken. 1985. *Sex, Ecology and Spirituality.* Boston: Shambala.

_____.2000. *A Brief History of Everything.* Dublin: Gateway.

Wills, C. 1993. *The Runaway Brain: The evolution of human uniqueness.* New York: Basic Books.

Winson, J. 1986. *Brain and Psyche.* New York: Vintage Books, Random House.

Wolf, Fred Allan. 1995. *The Dreaming Universe.* New York: Simon & Schuster.

Wolf, N.J. 1997. *A possible role for cholinergic neurons of the basal forebrain and ponomesencephalon in consciousness.* Consciousness and cognitions, 8, 447-554.

Zeki, S.M. 1993. *A vision of the Brain.* Oxford: Oxford University Press.

Zoher, Dana and Marshall, I.N. 1990. *The quantum society.* London: Bloomsberry.

_____. 2000. *Spiritual Intelligence, the ultimate intelligence.* London: Bloomsberry.

Zukav, Gary. 1979. *The Dancing Wuly Masters.* New York: Bantom Books.

_____. 1990. *The seat of the soul.* New York: Simon & Schuster.

INDEX